Join the
FILMMAKING
Revolution

Today major technical advances, coupled with growing acceptance of film language, have turned millions the country over into enthusiastic filmmakers.

But there is more to this exciting creative activity than meets the eye—basic fundamentals and advanced techniques that make the vital difference in final quality.

How do you make your pick among the bewildering array of new cameras? Decide on your best film gauge? Clean a lens? Figure exposure time? Work up special effects? Employ a shooting script? Establish continuity? Shoot in daylight and after dark? Synchronize your sound? Cut and splice? Prepare the film for printing? Find the special equipment and services you may need at different stages of production?

These are but a few of the questions answered in full in
GUIDE TO FILMMAKING

Other MENTOR and SIGNET Books
of Special Interest

Guide to FILMMAKING

EDWARD PINCUS

Assisted by
JAIRUS LINCOLN

PHOTOGRAPHS: David N. Hancock
DRAWINGS: John E. Reid

A SIGNET BOOK from
NEW AMERICAN LIBRARY
TIMES MIRROR

Copyright © 1969, 1972 by Edward Pincus

Library of Congress Catalog Card Number: 78-92594

 SIGNET TRADEMARK REG. U.S. PAT. OFF. AND FOREIGN COUNTRIES
REGISTERED TRADEMARK—MARCA REGISTRADA
HECHO EN CHICAGO, U.S.A.

SIGNET, SIGNET CLASSICS, MENTOR, PLUME, MERIDIAN and NAL
BOOKS *are published by The New American Library, Inc., 1633
Broadway, New York, New York 10019*

FIRST PRINTING, OCTOBER, 1969

9   10   11   12   13   14   15   16   17

PRINTED IN THE UNITED STATES OF AMERICA

to jane

CONTENTS

Preface

This book is addressed both to filmmakers and to people who want to be filmmakers. By "filmmakers" we mean people who use motion picture film to achieve some conceptual whole. This can range from a well-done home movie to a full-length feature film. Films made for recording purposes, simple home movies, or data recording (as in missile photography) will not be discussed. Nor will we discuss full crew, Hollywood-style feature film shooting.

The book is intended to give a fairly precise idea of how much it costs to do various types of films and the way to go about making these films. It is a production manual, including all the information the serious filmmaker will need about the technical side of making movies.

A whole breed of filmmakers and potential filmmakers is appearing for whom 16mm is *the* professional film and super 8mm a serious amateur gauge which someday may be a professional gauge. Much of the information for one gauge is relevant to the other. This book discusses them both, emphasizing 16mm, pointing out the differences in the narrower film.

"The medium is the message." The width (gauge) of motion picture film chosen by the filmmaker largely commits him at the outset to its content (message). This is due both to the quality inherent in a chosen gauge and to the economic realities of making a film. A very expensive super 8mm film may cost $100, whereas a very inexpensive 70mm film may cost $1,000,000. But actual costs of the film raw stock and processing are a very high percentage of the total cost of an average super 8mm film (as high as 100 percent), whereas they account for 15 percent at most of the cost of a 70mm film. To offset this enormous production cost the 70mm film must reach an audience large enough to ensure some considerable financial return. When costs are much lower, one does not usually have to make one's investment back. Even if one does, it can be done by reaching a much smaller audience. The audience one attempts to reach will affect the content of the film.

The choices open to a filmmaker are determined by the technical state of the industry. For example, thirty years ago you could not make an inexpensive sound film. Today you can. Thirty years ago making a film required either a sponsor or else it was an investment with a good chance of profit. The concept of filmmaking has changed in great part because of recent technical advances. Some talk about the advent of super 8mm film as being comparable to the paperback revolution in book publishing. The hope is held out that someday it will be technically as easy to make a film as it is today to write. Then, perhaps, filmmaking will be free from an industry that fetters the filmmaker. Someday, to paraphrase Brecht, what there is shall go to those who are good for it. Thus, film to the filmmakers that they may change the world.

This book could not have been done without a little help from my friends: S. A. SHUTTLE, JON DOLGER, NINA FINKELSTEIN, RHODEN STREETER, DAVID NEUMAN, WILMA DISKIN, SY CANE, SALLY HANCOCK, KIT LASCOUTS, JOHN TERRY, ANDY HAWLEY, DANA FULLER, IRÁ SCHNEIDER, and my students at MIT. I would especially like to thank the copy editor, whose name I do not even know.

Guide to
Filmmaking

Introduction

Since the first publication of this book, several significant advances in equipment have been made. The book has also had extensive use in introductory courses in filmmaking, revealing omissions in its original content. This Introduction and some changes in the body of the text are meant to partially overcome these deficiencies. If some of the concepts used in the Introduction are not clear to the reader, he should refer to the appropriate section of the text.

Many commercial feature films are now being filmed in 16mm rather than the theatrical standard of 35mm. Recent features filmed in 16mm include *Faces, Woodstock, Gimme Shelter*, and sections of *Easy Rider* and *Medium Cool*. The 16mm original is blown up to 35mm for release to theaters. Usually a special liquid gate printing process is used, which minimizes grain and scratches on the original.

Several different camera modifications can be performed in order that a greater portion of the 16mm frame can be used during original photography. These systems are often called *super 16*. (See *The American Cinematographer*, June and November, 1970.) The advantages of super 16 are only realized in the blow-up to 35mm, and not in any currently used release system in 16mm.

Besides cost, the primary appeal of 16mm filming to the feature filmmaker is the portability of 16mm equipment. The new Arriflex 35BL is the first self-blimped, portable 35mm camera. Synchronous sound, hand-held footage can now be shot in 35mm with much of the same ease of 16mm shooting. The camera, unfortunately, is not as silent as some 16mm cameras, does not shoot as much film time on a single load, and of course uses 35mm film, which is significantly more costly than 16mm film.

New cameras continue to appear on the super 8 market. Several new models are equipped with intervalometers—a device to control time intervals between exposures when taking single frames. Its primary use is in time-lapse photography, where we want to see some action significantly speeded up. We can set the camera on a tripod and time the intervals so we can, for instance, study traffic patterns or film the blooming of a flower so that the motion is revealed to the eye when projected later. Several new models allow limited length dissolves with super 8 cartridges. Automatic fading devices allow for significantly smoother fades than can be achieved manually.

The Canon Zoom DS-8, the Pathé DS8 BTL, and the Elmo C-300 Double Super-8 all use 100-foot loads of double super 8 film. Instead of using 50-foot cartridges which simply slip into the camera body, these cameras use daylight loads of double super 8, which is loaded in the cameras semi-automatically. The film is similar to 16mm except that it has super 8 perforations. The film is shot through the camera, turned over, reloaded, and shot again. After processing, the film is slit down the middle and 200 feet of exposed super 8 is returned. Like single 8 and regular 8, these cameras have a pressure plate built into them. In general, this seems to lead to more consistent results. When using super 8 cartridges, results tend to vary cartridge to cartridge—some scratch the film, some have poorer registration. Unfortunately there is no simple way to test the quality of a cartridge before filming.

A really good sound system for shooting and editing super 8 sync sound is not yet available. The most versatile system currently available is Optasound (116 John Street, New York, N.Y. 10038), also available for 16mm. The system is fairly inexpensive (about $150 for camera modification and tape recorder module) and can be adapted to almost any camera and tape recorder. A cable is needed between camera and tape recorder for sync. Unless the camera is further modified, it will be too noisy for filming sync in most interiors.

Richard Leacock at the Massachusetts Institute of Technology has developed a super 8 sync-sound system to prototype stage. The system includes a self-blimped camera, cordless sync, transfer equipment, double system projector, and a horizontal editing table. When marketed, the system should cost less than one-fifth the cost of comparable 16mm equipment.

More and more labs are handling super 8 original. As demand grows, more possibilities will open to the super 8 filmmaker. As of now there are serious limitations on the range of lab services available. There are no latent edge-numbers on super 8 original and no machine edge-numbering is available. This means that if a workprint is made, the original must be conformed by eye, an extremely laborious process. The most serious limitation is print quality when duplicating super 8—contrast increases, definition suffers, and grain increases. Usually, higher quality duplicates can be obtained by making a 16mm blow-up and then an 8mm reduction print than by simply making a super 8 contact print.

Some labs will push super 8 EF one or two stops (increasing exposure from the normal ASA 125 to ASA 250 or 500), making it possible to shoot super 8 color under low-light situations. There is a marked decrease in quality.

Focusing most super 8 cameras is difficult. Cameras with a split image in the viewfinder are focused by lining up a divided circle in the center of the viewfinder. It is easiest to focus on a straight line in the subject which intersects the dividing line of the circle at an angle. The longer the focal length used, the more critical the focus, and the less accurate this system. Subjects without straight lines, and moving subjects, are extremely difficult to focus with a split image. Many super 8 cameras (and the 16mm Canon Scoopic) have *micro prism* focusing in their reflex system. In the center of the viewfinder is a micro prism focusing disc. When the subject is out of focus it is not blurred as on a ground glass, but rather it seems to fall apart in the micro prism. Micro prism focusing works best when designed for a particular focal length, and is not ideal for a zoom lens. The diopter adjustment is extremely critical with micro prism focusing. You do *not* use the method for adjusting the diopter with a ground glass (p. 21). Instead, you put the distance scale at infinity and set the lens at the longest focal length available. Find a clear, well-defined object, like a building at least one-half mile away. While looking through the viewfinder and focusing your eye on the object on the micro prism, move the diopter adjustment back and forth until the object appears as sharp as possible. If you make an improper diopter adjustment with a micro prism, your subject will be out of focus when filmed. An improper diopter adjustment on a ground glass only makes proper focus more difficult.

Camera manufacturers have been incorporating many of the advanced features found on super 8 cameras in their 16mm cameras. More and more 16mm cameras come with automatic exposure or the option of installing an automatic exposure module.

New motors available for such expensive cameras as the Eclair NPR and the Arriflex BL offer cordless crystal sync with the possibility of other filming speeds with the same motor. Some of these motors always leave the mirror shutter in the proper position for viewing when the camera is stopped, thus eliminating one of the annoying features of a mirror shutter camera.

The Bolex Pro 16 offers the maximum in automation of the expensive 16mm sync sound cameras. It features automatic threading, power zoom and focus, and the option of automatic infrared focusing. The camera rests nicely on the cameraman's shoulder. The camera is very expensive (about $10,000 equipped).

The new Eclair ACL looks as though it will prove to be the

most desirable portable synchronous sound camera. If it proves rugged in the field, it may make currently available sync sound cameras virtually obsolete for hand-held documentary filming. The camera with 200-foot magazine (400-foot magazines are supposedly being developed), lens, and motor weighs under 10 pounds (about half the weight of comparable cameras). The weight rests on the cameraman's shoulder, making it perhaps the easiest 16mm camera to hold steady without a brace. No longer is muscle power required for hand-held synchronous sound filming. ACL magazines can be changed in five seconds but are expensive (about $1,000 each). The camera is supplied with a crystal sync motor for cordless sync. The camera costs around $7,000 with lens and two magazines, putting it below the price range of the Eclair NPR and the Arriflex BL.

Early cordless sync systems used a tuning fork instead of a crystal. Tuning forks sometimes make an audible high-frequency noise. High quality crystals offer the accuracy of tuning forks without the bothersome noise. Many cordless systems are as accurate as cable sync. The chief advantage of cable sync is the possibility of a simple system of automatic slating. Cordless systems add weight, bulk, and cost to cameras not specifically designed for it. However, the advantages of cordless sync are overwhelming for documentary filming, and crystal syn is necessary for multiple camera sync sound filming. With cordless sync, cameraman and soundman are freed from an umbilical connection which seriously cuts down their mobility. Generally, the soundman wants to be as close to the action as possible, while the cameraman wants to roam around. This becomes simple when there is no connecting cable.

The least expensive professional self-blimped synchronous sound cameras are the Auricon Cine-Voice conversions done by several different camera stores. Equipped for 400-foot Mitchell magazines, an Angénieux 12-120mm zoom with shortened viewfinder, they generally cost under $4,000. Crystal sync motors are available for cordless sync. Several small manufacturers only use the Auricon movement and package the camera in a magnesium housing, resulting in a camera that weighs about 10 pounds. Camera Development Co. goes one step further, making the camera reflex so you are not limited to zoom lenses with auxiliary finders.

Several new zoom lenses have appeared on the market. The Canon 12-120mm f/2.2 Macro Zoom lens with Fluorite coating weighs the same as the Angénieux 12-120mm zoom, but is more compact. Whereas the Angénieux focuses down to five feet, the Canon focuses down to ⅜ of an inch of the front element. Canon claims that the new design eliminates some aberrations, making it an extremely sharp lens. It lists for around $1,500, whereas the Angénieux 12-120mm lists for around $1,000, and the Angénieux 9.5-95mm for around $1,250. Smaller, lighter, less expensive zoom lenses of very high quality are available in the 6X zoom range, such as the Agénieux 12.5-75mm listing at about $750. Smaller zoom lenses make sense for the smaller 16mm cameras such as the Beaulieu, Bolex Rex 4, and the Eclair ACL. The heavy 10X zoom lenses on these cameras put too much relative weight in front, making them top heavy and hard to hold steady. The new Angénieux 9.5-57mm f/1.6 zoom is light, good quality, and is more than one stop faster than most zoom lenses. This extra stop makes it an invaluable lens in low-light situations.

Arriflex cameras now come with an improved, heavy-duty stainless steel mount. Bolex cameras can be ordered with a heavy-duty mount for more accurate seating of zoom and very wide angle lenses. These improved mounts, in some cases, will obviate the need for a zoom lens support.

Adapters are available that allow some cameras to take lenses of different mounts. Arriflex lenses can be adapted to "C" mount, but not vice versa. Most lenses made for 35mm still cameras can be adapted to "C" mount. Only precision adapters should be used. Unless alignment of adapter, camera, and lens is performed by a specialist, the results will be risky. An improperly mounted lens, especially a zoom lens or a wide-angle lens, will not yield a sharp image.

Sylvania makes a light, portable SG-77 Sun Gun unit weighing 3 pounds and costing under $120, while larger units weigh over 17 pounds and cost over $400. With a 150W bulb, the smaller unit will only run 10 minutes but the batteries can be charged in an hour.

The Nagra IV tape recorder offers several advantages over the old industry standard of the Nagra III—e.g., one additional microphone input, plug-in modules for condenser microphones, bass roll-off filter, crystal sync module, higher quality automatic record, and improved sound quality. On the other hand, it is a bit more complicated to use, more expensive, a little less rugged, and it is not clear that the gain in sound quality of the original recording is preserved when the sound is optically reproduced from the release print. If the Nagra IV does not offer any particular advantages for your use, it may be worthwhile to purchase a used Nagra III.

The Stellavox Sp7 weighs less than the Nagra (8 pounds vs. 13 pounds) and is considerably more compact. It costs about the same, is less rugged, and has the option of a plug-in stereo module.

The Tandberg 11-1-P costs half the price of the Nagra, but is considerably less rugged. It is designed for use with dynamic microphones. The Arrivox Tandberg is a more versatile version of the Tandberg 11-1-P, accepting both dynamic and condenser microphones. It costs $1,100 while the Tandberg costs around $700.

The new Nagra SN fits into a jacket pocket, weighs 1.3 pounds, and can record broadcast-quality sound. It is a reel-to-reel machine capable of recording 27 minutes of sound at 3¾ ips (or 54 minutes at 1⅞ ips with a sacrifice in sound quality). It can be used instead of a wireless microphone directly on the subject or performer. Accessories soon to be available include crystal sync and radio-controlled operation so the camera can turn the recorder on and off. The SN costs a little over $1,000 with miniature microphone and without crystal sync. This recorder makes it possible to have a self-blimped, cordless sync sound rig which weighs just over 10 pounds ready to shoot.

In the past few years high quality reliable editing tables have been introduced in this country by Steenbeck and KEM. In contrast to the Moviola Series 20, which is an upright double system editing machine, the film lies horizontally on these machines. The advantages of horizontal editing tables over the standard Moviola are so great that editors will often wait days to work on one even though a Moviola is available. They are much faster and are significantly gentler on film. Steenbeck offers a comparatively compact table for one picture and one sound track for around $4,000. Six-plate models (usually two sound tracks and one picture) are larger, more versatile, and cost over $7,000. Steenbeck, and now Moviola, offer tables in this format. The KEM eight-plate machine can use any combination of three picture heads and three sound heads for a total of four. The possibilities of multi-screen editing or even single-screen editing on this machine are endless. Unfortunately, the machine is very expensive and very heavy. Manufacturers of editing tables offer many models in different combinations of picture and sound heads as well as models which will accommodate super 8.

The one important advantage of an upright Moviola is the ease with which additional sound heads can be rented and added to the machine. Unless you have one of the more expensive tables, you will be limited to the one sound track on the machine. It is, of course, possible to use a synchronizer equipped with two or more sound heads for multi-track editing. It may be worthwhile to rent a Moviola with additional sound heads for the time you will need to edit more than one sound track, which is generally only the last few weeks of editing.

The Siemens double system interlock projector has unfortunately been discontinued. It may still be possible to purchase a used one, though it is not a particularly rugged projector. The Siemens was the best double system projector for under $2,000. The new Sonorex and Bauer double system projectors are considerably more expensive. Unless the portability and ease of operation of a double system projector is required, a better solution to double system projection is a sprocket dubber and projector with a synchronous motor.

Projectors are constantly being improved, although there is still no ideal projector. Projectors equipped with tungsten-halogen lamps or Xenon Arc yield a significantly brighter and more pleasing image than do projectors equipped with conventional tungsten lamps. I have seen super 8 original projected on a Xenon Arc projector to a width of sixteen feet with a perfectly acceptable image.

I. 8mm and 16mm

Persistence of vision

Movies are made up of a series of still photographs, each of which shows a slight change in motion; when projected, they give the illusion of a moving image. The eye amalgamates the many still images into a continuous moving image. This phenomenon is known as *persistence of vision*. Each of these still photographs is called a frame. (See Plate 1)

Various film sizes

Silent movies are exposed and projected at 16 or 18 frames per second (depending on whether the film is 16mm or 8mm), while sound film is normally exposed and projected at 24 frames per second (*fps*).

The *gauge* of motion picture film is the measurement of the width of the film. It is usually expressed in millimeters. The standard gauges in America are 8mm, 16mm, 35mm, 65mm, and 70mm. This book will concern itself only with 8mm (of which there are two types: regular 8 and super 8) and 16mm films. The decision as to which gauge film to use is perhaps the most important single technical decision facing a filmmaker. This decision affects the cost, the quality of both picture and sound, and, ultimately, the size of the audiences who see the film.

16mm film

16mm film was at one time a purely amateur film gauge. Advances made in film stock and cameras made it an acceptable gauge for professional film work in certain circumstances. Almost all projection outside of motion picture theaters (other than of home movies) is done in 16mm. Almost every school and church has an easily portable 16mm film projector. Newsreels, many television documentaries, industrial films, and most experimental films are shot in 16mm.

In 16mm the filmmaker is offered almost all the advantages that a professional industry has to offer. There are a vast number of different types of camera and printing films available. Optical effects, invisible-splice printing, and sophisticated filming and editing equipment are offered to the filmmaker working in 16mm but denied, at present, to the maker of 8mm films because of that film's amateur status.

16mm film compared with 8mm film

The filmmaker who works in 8mm should consider the advantages of his film and use them, while keeping in mind its disadvantages. Whereas duplicates of high quality can be made easily from 16mm films, 8mm duplicates are far inferior to the original, which is itself less sharp and grainier than the original of a 16mm film. Sound reproduction can never be as good in 8mm as it is in 16mm film, because 8mm travels at one-half the speed of 16mm. Thus, music and marginal sound (such as that obtained in field recordings) have to be used with care in 8mm. The 8mm picture cannot be projected to as great a size as the 16mm picture. Again, little sophisticated sound equipment is available in 8mm, further limiting the type of work that can be done. 8mm is not an acceptable standard for television, and thus an important professional outlet is denied the 8mm filmmaker.

On the other hand, 8mm cameras are simple to use, less bulky, more automated, and less expensive than 16mm cameras. (See Plate 3) The cost of 8mm film and processing is one-third to one-half that of 16mm. Ultimately, the choice between 8mm and 16mm is cost versus quality, and that usually leads to a wholly different type of film shot in each gauge. The filmmaker who shoots in 8mm can shoot more film because of lower costs. He can carry the camera around with him more easily. On the other hand, an 8mm image can at best be projected to a size of six feet across. Further 8mm duplicate prints lose more quality relatively than do 16mm duplicate prints. This means that good quality and satisfactory projection can only be achieved using the original. However, 8mm projection equipment, cameras, and film stock are improving at a rapid rate, so that in the near future films may be published (as books are today) and distributed in 8mm at a reasonable cost. This would open up the possibility of many more people making and distributing their own films. Still, films shot in 16mm and then reduced to 8mm in printing will yield better prints than films shot originally in 8mm. In the same way, shooting in 35mm and reducing to 16mm is better than shooting and releasing a 16mm film.

Super 8, single 8, and regular 8

The old amateur standard used to be regular 8mm (alternately called double 8, standard 8, and cine 8). A few years ago a great improvement was offered in 8mm. By using smaller perforations, a picture 50 percent larger than the regular 8 picture could be gained. Further, a larger area could be preserved for a sound track of higher quality than previously attainable on 8mm film. Although it is slowly becoming obsolete, regular 8 equipment and film are still available, and will be available for many years to come. The new format films are called super 8 and single 8. Both super 8 and single 8 have the same film format and are compatible in every way except for the cameras they require. Since they come in different cartridges, they cannot be used in the same cameras (with the exception of several models). Single 8 allows for some in-camera effects that cannot be made with most super 8 cameras—such as double-exposures and dissolves.

Fujica is the only manufacturer supplying cameras and film in the single 8 format, and this means that single 8 is limited in a way that super 8 is not. At present, Fujica supplies as many films in single 8 as Kodak does in super 8. The thinner design of Fujica cameras may be appealing to some people, and if the camera is satisfactory in other ways, you may want to use the single 8 rather than the super 8 system.

When we talk about 8mm in this book we will mean all three 8mm films unless a note of exception is made. When we speak of super 8, we will also mean single 8 unless an exception is made. Regular 8 has 80 frames per foot whereas super 8 and single 8 have 72. 16mm film has 40 frames per foot. Thus, to get the same amount of running time you must shoot twice as much 16mm film as 8mm film. (See Appendix A for comparison of running times.)

II. The Camera

General considerations

Manufacturers of movie cameras provide the filmmaker with bewilderingly varied equipment. Camera prices range from $30 to the several thousands, and the highest price-tag does not necessarily guarantee the highest quality. Cameras are frequently encumbered by unneeded accessories which raise their cost.

Lens mounts

Although lenses will be discussed in the next chapter,* a consideration of the lens-camera attaching mechanism, that is, the *lens mount,* is relevant here. Since not all lenses are adaptable to all cameras, it is important to know in choosing a camera just what lenses it is capable of accepting. Some cameras have permanently mounted lenses, meaning that the lens is not *interchangeable.* This is typical of 8mm cameras (though some of the more expensive 8mm cameras do allow for lens interchangeability). A permanently mounted lens obviously limits the adaptability of the camera (see Chapter III) but has the advantage that the lens can be attached to the camera with a greater degree of fitting accuracy (tolerance) than can interchangeable lenses whose mounts often get some rough handling.

Interchangeable lenses and turrets

If the lenses are interchangeable (as they are on every professional 16mm camera with the exception of the Canon Scoopic), the camera may be able to accommodate only one lens (see Plates 3, 5, 13) or as many as three lenses at once on a *turret.* (See Plates 4, 7, 8) The turret mount is rotated to change lenses, thus saving the cinematographer valuable time when he wishes to change lenses. (See Plate 11) Unfortunately, the turret is not as stable as a single lens mount.

On some expensive 16mm cameras (e.g., the Arriflex S) a divergent turret is offered. (See Plate 10) This feature allows

---

* Many of the concepts used in this chapter are explained in greater detail in subsequent chapters. If the reader has trouble with any of these concepts, he should refer to the relevant sections of the book.

a greater variety of *types* of lenses to be mounted on the camera at one time (without which a wide-angle lens might pick up the edge or reflection of a longer lens on the film).

Singly interchangeable lenses come in a variety of mountings. Generally a camera only accepts one type of mount. The two most used are screw and bayonet mounts. The most common screw mount for 16mm cameras is the "C" mount, and the greatest variety of lenses are offered in this mount. (See Plate 17) However, this mount is not the strongest or most accurate. Heavy zoom lenses (of the 10:1 variety) often need additional support when used with a "C" mount. (See Plate 22) Bayonet mounts are often quicker to mount on the camera, are more stable, and support greater weight than "C" mounts. The Arriflex bayonet mount is one of extremely high tolerance.

The need for many different lenses has decreased considerably since the advent of high-quality zoom lenses (see Chapter III).

Camera weight and balance

All 8mm cameras are light. They differ, however, in their balance in the cameraman's hands and consequently in the ease with which they can be held steady. Pistol grips are helpful for steadying a hand-held 8mm camera (and some of the lighter 16mm cameras). (See Plates 3, 12) Heavier cameras (over 10 pounds) usually need some sort of supporting brace or shoulder pod for steady hand-held shooting, unless they are built to rest on the cameraman's shoulder. (See Plates 14, 15) The camera should be capable of balancing well on a tripod.

Viewing systems

The cameraman must be able to see what the camera is filming through the *viewing system*. The best viewing system is a through-the-lens *reflex system*. The image transmitted through the camera lens is projected onto a *ground glass* and seen by the cameraman through his viewfinder. (See Fig. I)

In other systems an auxiliary viewfinder transmits the image, and consequently there is a slight difference between the image seen through the viewfinder and the image projected onto the film. This is called *parallax*. (See Fig. II) You can observe the effect of parallax simply by pointing your finger upward about eight inches in front of your nose and by looking at the finger first with your left eye closed and then with your right eye closed. Your finger will appear to change its relationship to the background as you change from one eye

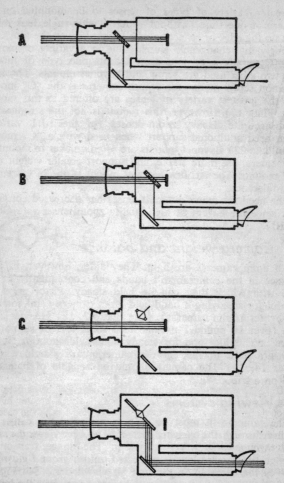

Fig. I. Three types of reflex viewing systems. In *A* and *B* the light passes through a partially silvered mirror to hit the film. Some of the light is deflected to a mirror and then to the viewfinder. In the case of *A* the viewfinder reflex system is an integral part of the lens. In the case of *B* the reflex system is part of the camera, and consequently many different lenses can be used. The reflex system illustrated in *C* involves a rotating mirror. While the film advances, all the light is deflected to the viewfinder for viewing, and while the film is stationary to be exposed, all the light is allowed to hit the film.

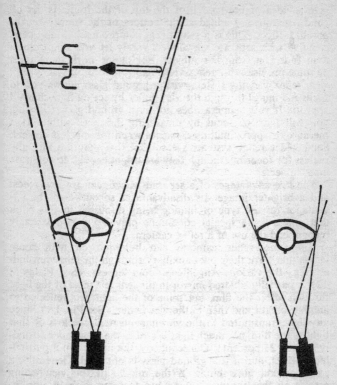

Fig. II. In the drawing on the left the viewfinder and the camera are seeing two different images. The difference is much greater in the case of the man, who is close to the camera, and less in the case of the bicycle, which is farther away. In the drawing on the right the viewfinder is adjusted for parallax and the viewfinder sees the same image as the camera.

to the other. Parallax becomes a serious problem only when you are shooting with lenses of a long focal length (see p. 33) or when the distance between camera and subject is short (less than five feet with a normal focal length lens).

If the camera is not a reflex camera, you will be very limited unless it has a built-in correction for parallax. You will find that footage which was properly composed when looking through your viewfinder has been recorded on the film with heads cut off and people half in the frame and half out. Some viewfinders have marks etched on the viewing glass which

give an idea of how much of the top of the frame is cut off
(and consequently added at the bottom of the frame) by the
parallax effect. This is a reasonable compromise. In any case,
cameras with separate viewfinders rarely let you shoot closer
than four feet from the subject. For closer work there must
be some provision for reflex viewing.

A reflex viewing system with a ground glass allows you to
focus the image through the viewfinder by seeing how sharp it
appears. If your camera does not have ground glass focusing,
you will have to focus by measuring distances with a tape
measure or approximating distances when focus is less critical.
Some older reflex systems are so dim that they are virtually
useless for focusing, though they are bright enough to compose
most subjects.

The two advantages of a separate viewfinder are lower cost
and a brighter image. Its disadvantages so outweigh the advantages for the type of filming being discussed in this book
that unless some special conditions prevail I would strongly
recommend the use of a reflex camera.

16mm non-reflex cameras can be equipped with zoom
lenses that have their own auxiliary through-the-lens viewfinder (e.g., the various Angénieux zoom lenses). (See Plates 5,
12) A partially silvered mirror in the lens lets most of the light
through to hit the film, but some of the light gets reflected to
another mirror and then to the viewfinder. (See Fig. IA) Since
any light transmitted to the viewfinder entails the loss of that
light to the film, not much light is sent to the viewfinder (usually around 25 percent). Consequently, the image is not particularly bright, and a full ground glass is not used. Generally, a
small ground glass circle in the middle of the viewfinding
area is all that the cameraman has to focus with. A non-focusing image (one that remains pretty much always in focus)
surrounds the ground glass circle.

Some 16mm cameras allow for reflex viewing or focusing
only when film is not being shot, via what is called a *rackover*
mechanism (e.g., some earlier Bolex models). The film is dis-
placed from the lens and is replaced by a ground glass on
which the cameraman frames and focuses his image. This type
of mechanism is helpful only when the camera is placed on a
tripod and the subject does not move out of the frame during
the shot.

The reflex system of viewing with a full ground glass
image is altogether preferable for most uses. In one such system a partially silvered mirror deflects the image to the
ground glass. (See Fig. IB) When the mirror is built into the
camera, it works with any lens (unlike the auxiliary viewfinder attached to zoom lenses). In another system, a rotating

mirror alternately deflects all the light to the film and then all the light to the viewfinder. (See Fig. IC) The latter system is far preferable, since much more light is available to the view-finder, making focusing considerably easier. Its main disad-vantage is that sometimes when the camera stops the mirror is in the wrong position (deflecting all the light to the film) and the cameraman must move a dial to reposition the mir-ror. Also, when the camera is running the image flickers; still, it is brighter than a reflex system employing a half-sil-vered mirror.

An advantage of some systems using a partially silvered mirror is that the mirror can be placed in front of the iris diaphragm (see p. 37). This means that as the lens is stopped down (see p. 38) there is no light loss to the viewfinder, and consequently the image is brighter and easier to focus, espe-cially when the camera is running. In super 8, several cameras have this feature, and in 16mm, the Canon Scoopic has it.

In comparing two cameras' reflex viewing systems you should compare their image magnification. Generally, the larger the image the easier it is to compose but the duller the image. You should also compare the ease of focusing on each of the cameras. The brightness of the image, the size of the image, and the coarseness (grain) of the ground glass are the three most important factors governing ease of focusing.

The eyepiece must be adjustable to the individual camera-man's eyesight (diopter adjustment). If you wear eyeglasses, you may find that you cannot sufficiently adjust the eyepiece so that you can focus without glasses. Some cameras can be supplied with custom eyepieces in such cases. It is important to focus the eyepiece for your eyesight before shooting. If shooting continues for some time, the eyepiece should be re-focused from time to time. To focus the eyepiece remove the camera lens, point the camera toward a bright surface (or the sky), and turn the eyepiece knob back and forth until the grain of the ground glass is sharp. If the eyepiece has a lock, it should be tightened at that point. If there is no time to remove the lens, the camera can be pointed to a smooth surface or the sky, the lens thrown out of focus, and the eyepiece focused on the grain of the ground glass.

Some care must be taken with a reflex camera so that light does not enter through the viewfinder and expose the film. When your eye is pressed against the viewfinder the light is blocked. But when the camera is mounted on a tripod, light behind the camera may enter when you are not looking through the viewfinder. Some more expensive cameras have a light trap to close off the viewfinder. If there is no light trap, you should place a card behind the viewfinder, especially if there is any illumination behind the camera. One disadvantage of wearing eyeglasses when filming is that light can enter the viewfinder since your eye is not pressed against it.

Automatic exposure and automatic diaphragm

Almost every 8mm camera and a very few 16mm cameras have a built-in exposure meter. (See Plates 3, 6) Built-in exposure meters often have the connotation of amateurism, yet a high-quality built-in meter, properly used, is a very important accessory. When the filmmaker is shooting carefully planned and controlled shots, he has no need for a built-in meter. When he shoots in changing lighting conditions, from room to room, or from shade to sun, a built-in meter can be of tremendous help. The best built-in meter is one that monitors behind the lens. This method guarantees that the area of light being measured is the same area that is being recorded on the film. Compensation is made for filters used, the particular transmission quality of the lens, and possible inaccuracies in f/stop settings. When the meter is separate from the lens, parallax problems similar to those encountered with the separate viewfinder must be dealt with. Further, a wide general area is being read by the meter, whereas the image being photographed may encompass only a small area since the meter makes no distinction as to focal length of lens being used. For example, the meter on the Canon Scoopic covers an area about the same as a 25mm lens, even though you may be filming at 75mm. The use and misuse of built-in exposure meters will be dicussed in Chapter IV.

Some 8mm cameras have no provisions for manually overriding the built-in exposure meter reading. The exposure cannot be set independently of the meter, and whatever the electric eye of the meter registers dictates the setting the filmmaker has to use. Since the exposure recorded is not always the one that should be used, this is a more undesirable feature.

The range of films that can be used employing the electric eye is indicated by a dial located on the camera. The dial is usually calibrated in ASA numbers. This number is a measure of the film's sensitivity to light (see p. 58). The greater the range of numbers, the greater the variety of films that can be used with the built-in exposure meter. Though there are relatively few different emulsion speeds available in super 8 at this time, this situation will surely change; and your electric eye might become obsolete for some films. In 16mm there are films presently available with ASA as low as 12 and as high as 1600. However, the ASA ratings of films that you will probably use most often are in the range of 16 to 400. For 16mm documentary work a maximum speed of 1200 or 1600 would often be convenient.

A further refinement in camera automation available on many super 8 cameras and some 16mm cameras is an *automatic diaphragm* which sets the (iris) diaphragm according to the amount of light reflected by the subject. As the meter perceives different light intensities, the diaphragm opens and closes automatically. The meter's sensitivity may be so great that a drastic and possibly unfortunate change of exposure can occur in the middle of a shot if, for example, the subject's reflectance changes momentarily. When there is a change of exposure, the diaphragm usually overshoots its mark and then comes back to the proper setting. This causes an unpleasant lightening and darkening of the subject in the shot.

If a camera has an electrically operated light meter, it should also have a battery check meter to test the battery's strength.

Some lens manufacturers offer zoom lenses with a built-in exposure meter and an automatic diaphragm. Kern Paillard offers this type of zoom lens for the 16mm Bolex. Angénieux offers several different models for some super 8 and 16mm cameras. (See Plate 21C)

Camera motors

Motors are either spring wound or operated by electric drive. A few models allow for spring and electric drive on the same camera. A few more expensive cameras allow for interchangeable electric motors of different types. The chief disadvantage of spring-wound motors is the limited amount of film that can be shot on any particular take (about 30 seconds). Electrically driven motors can take much longer shots and do not need the constant rewinding required of a spring-driven motor. They do, however, require a battery or some other source of electric power. In general, electrically driven motors are quieter, but they may not run in very cold weather, whereas spring-driven motors will operate at much lower temperatures. (Spring-driven cameras are usually used on Arctic expeditions.) Spring-wound motors generally allow speeds from 8-64 frames per second.

There are three types of electric motors: *wild motors, governor motors,* and *synchronous motors.* (The last will be discussed in the chapter dealing with synchronous sound.) Wild motors allow a selection of filming speeds: on some the fastest speed is 64 frames per second and the slowest, 2 frames per second.

If you film at a speed greater than normal, and then project the film at normal speed, motion will be slowed. If you film at a speed slower than normal, and then project the film at normal speed, motion will be speeded up. Slow motion is often used to analyze action or to call attention to motion itself. In Riefenstahl's *Olympiad*, a film of the 1936 Berlin Olympics, the movement of runners and divers is broken down and extended in time; slow motion, used in this way, gives us a greater understanding of motion and its beauty.

Speeded motion is used for comic effect reminiscent of the comedies of the silent-screen era. It can also be used to analyze growth or change, as in films showing the construction of a house or the growth of a flower, by condensing the development of the action into a very short time. Time-lapse photography of this sort requires a camera with a motor which is set to expose one frame at a time at regular intervals over a long period.

When film is shot at slower than normal speed, each frame is exposed for a greater length of time. Consequently, if the light level is too low for exposure at the normal speed and the subject does not move, the camera can be *under-cranked*, that is, run at a slower speed, to effect proper exposure.

Higher speeds can be used to lessen camera movements. When the camera is being hand-held, or when it is on a car, boat, or plane, camera movement and vibration can be minimized if we shoot the film at a higher than normal speed. When the film is projected at a normal speed, there will be greater spacing between uneven or jerky movements, and the picture will appear steadier. Of course, this cannot be done if people are moving in the picture, since their movements will appear unnaturally slow.

Another type of electric motor, the governor motor, usually runs at only one speed. In 16mm it is generally the speed of 24 frames per second, which is the normal 16mm camera speed when sound is to be used. In 8mm, it is usually 18 frames per second. Well-made governor motors run at their one speed more accurately than wild motors set at that speed. They are much less affected by a drop in battery power than are wild motors, which lose speed as battery power drops.

With most governor motors there is no possibility of changing from sound to silent speed. It is good practice to film all 16mm footage at sound speed (24 fps), even though no sound is being planned to go with the footage, just in case a commentary track or music track is added later. At 24 fps, 50 percent more film is used than at the 16mm silent speed of 16 fps, and this increases film costs by 50 percent. Super 8 cameras are generally supplied with a motor that runs at only one speed: 18 fps (the standard silent speed in 8mm). Super 8 may deny the filmmaker a chance to add as high a quality sound track as can be made at 24 fps.

A few 16mm motors can be run from house circuits, which is useful for some filming systems used when recording synchronous sound. It also prevents running out of battery power. However, camera mobility is limited.

If the camera is battery operated, the battery power should be checked from time to time. Some manufacturers put batteries into the pistol grip or elsewhere on the camera, which is a better method than wiring external batteries to the camera.

Camera film capacity

Super 8 is supplied in manufacturer-loaded *cartridges* or *magazines* (light-tight chambers holding the exposed and unexposed film) in 50-foot lengths. (See Plate 23) Regular 8 comes in magazines and in rolls as long as 100 feet of double perforated 16mm film (double 8) which is run through the camera twice. After processing, the film is split down the middle and 200 feet of exposed film is returned. Kodak has recently introduced films in the double super 8 format capable of being used in the new Canon camera. 16mm cameras usually have an internal loading compartment for 100 feet of film. More expensive 16mm cameras will accept different sized external magazines that hold 200, 400, 600, or 1200 feet. (See Plates 9, 13, 14) Their advantage is obvious: these magazines hold many times the three minutes of film which is the most possible from 100 feet at sound speed. However, rarely are shots longer than 100 feet needed unless sound synchronous with the picture is taken.

Single frame exposure

Some cameras allow for single frame exposure. Each time you release the shutter only one frame is exposed. The film then advances to the next frame. This can be used to speed up action or to produce a quick bombardment of images. The camera instruction book should be consulted to find the shutter speed when single frame exposures are taken.

Variable shutter

As the film is pulled through the camera, the film stops, then moves down. When it stops, a frame is exposed, and when the film advances, the *shutter* blocks the light so as to avoid exposing the moving film.

Some of the more expensive cameras are equipped with a *variable shutter*. This mechanism, entirely separate from the shutter basic to the camera, is a wheel set at an angle between the lens and the film plane, which has a pie-shaped hole cut out of it (some versions of which can be varied in area from a 320° angle to completely closed). Fully open the angle is most often 170° to 180°. This wheel is geared to the film-advancing mechanism and cuts down the light which reaches the film. Closing down the variable shutter has the effect of stopping motion more effectively than the standard shutter used by itself and of making each separate frame, though not necessarily the moving image, sharper.

Variable shutters can be shut down gradually, allowing less and less light to hit each successive frame, to effect an in-camera fade-out to black. The variable shutter allows us to use a very fast film outdoors by reducing the light which reaches it. Films with speeds about ASA 125 require small diaphragm openings in normal sunlight, and as most lenses only stop down to f/22, the variable shutter is useful in decreasing exposure, allowing us to use high-speed films outdoors. Since closing down the variable shutter means we have to open up the lens to a wider diaphragm opening, the variable shutter gives us some control over depth of field (see p. 36). As we close down the shutter, we open up the diaphragm, thereby decreasing depth of field. This is useful when we wish to separate our main subject from a confusing background. With less depth of field, we are able to throw the background out of focus.

A disadvantage of closing down the variable shutter is that it can increase the effect of what is called *skipping*. When the camera is moved across the subject (panning or tilting), there sometimes shows up in the projected image a stroboscopic effect where the movement is no longer smooth but appears to skip from one image to the next. This effect occurs when the camera moves too quickly in relation to the subject or vice versa and the motion is not fast enough to be a blur. It most often appears in improperly executed pans, when the subject moves horizontally across the frame, or in shots from moving vehicles when the vehicle is going fast and the camera is filming at right angles to the movement of the vehicle. The wider open the shutter, the greater the chance of avoiding skipping. The sharper each frame is, as happens when the shutter is closed down, the more likely skipping will show up. Cameras having wider shutter openings are to be preferred over cameras with narrower shutter openings. Although a

180° shutter is standard, there are many cameras whose shutter is only 130° wide.

Whenever the variable shutter is closed down, exposure compensation must be made (see p. 48). It is very important to check the position of the variable shutter before you go out to film. Many feet of film have been underexposed because the cameraman did not realize that the variable shutter was closed down.

Footage counter

Footage counters are helpful to let you know how much film is left as well as to measure how many feet have been shot on a particular take. Some counters are exact while others give only approximations. Some cameras, usually those that can make dissolves, have frame counters, too. This is only useful for in-camera effects, for some trick work, and for animation, where such a counter is often essential.

The camera start and stop button should be easily accessible when the camera is hand-held comfortably.

Cleaning the aperture and pressure plate

In most 8mm cameras and many 16mm cameras it is no easy matter to clean the *aperture plate*. The aperture is the rectangle in front of the film which masks light from the lens to form the frame. When dirt gets lodged in the aperture, its image is picked up on the edges of the projected image. The aperture should be cleaned after every roll of film is shot. On many cameras, access to the aperture and *pressure plate* (the plate on which film rests when it is being exposed) is difficult and this increases the possibility of having a dirty aperture and of causing scratches on the film from the buildup of emulsion on the pressure plate and aperture. The *emulsion*, the light-sensitive part of the film, is soft and is easily scratched off, which produces a buildup of material in the film path.

Q-tips (cotton swabs) are often useful for cleaning the aperture and pressure plates. Care must be taken that none of the cotton is left in the aperture as this too will show up in the film. A round-edged toothpick is often used for breaking up emulsion buildups. Acetone can be used when an emulsion buildup is hard to remove by other ways. However, acetone will often dissolve paint used in some camera interiors. In no case should any metal object ever be used on the aperture or pressure plate, for it can scratch them and thus indirectly scratch the film. Often a cameraman will rub his finger on his nose and rub the oil onto the pressure plate to prevent the film from sticking. Super 8 (but not single 8) has no pressure plate in the camera.

In-camera effects

Some cameras allow you to make film effects such as dissolves and fades in the camera. A fade-out is made by progressively cutting out the amount of light that hits the film as the camera runs by closing down the variable shutter. A fade-in is accomplished by progressively opening the completely closed variable shutter as the film is run until it is open for normal exposure. A fade-out cannot usually be accomplished by closing down the f/stop ring, since even at the smallest opening the image will not be completely black. A dissolve (lap-dissolve) is the melting of one shot into another. To effect this in the camera, it must have a way of winding the film in reverse. Since very few super 8 cameras (unlike single 8) allow for winding the film back, this effect is rarely found in super 8. A dissolve is made by combining a fade-out of the first shot with a superimposed fade-in of the second shot. If the film can be rewound, then double-exposures or superimpositions can be made.

In 16mm it is far preferable to make film effects when making prints of the film rather than in the camera. This gives you much greater control over where they are to be used. Most effects are much better done in the laboratory than in the camera. Unfortunately, it is very difficult to find a lab which will do effects using 8mm films. There are chemicals available at photographic stores which can be used for making fades (e.g., Craig Fotofade). The longer the film is immersed in the solution, the darker it gets. However, the results are usually disappointing.

Attaching filters

Some 8mm cameras have a built-in filter for using indoor color film outdoors. On 8mm cameras you will have to attach any other filters you use to the front of the lens. Certain 16mm cameras have provisions for putting a filter behind the lens. This cuts down the cost of filters quite considerably, since the less expensive gelatin filters may be used. Some 16mm cameras have provisions for a matte box which allows you to use gelatin filters in front of the lens. (See Plate 9)

Camera noise

Cameras differ greatly in the amount of noise they make when running. Some of the very expensive 16mm cameras especially made for filming when sound is being recorded are virtually noiseless. Most cameras, however, do make some noise, and it may be an important point in choosing a camera to decide whether the camera is too noisy for your particular uses. Camera noise is objectionable in at least two situations: when sound is being recorded, and when noise will disturb the subject being filmed, a situation that arises most commonly when you are shooting candid, when the subject is not aware that he is being filmed.

8mm cameras generally make less noise than 16mm cameras. 16mm cameras differ greatly in how much noise they make. The difference is not only from brand to brand, for cameras of the same brand will also differ. Usually, the longer a camera has been in use, the more noise that camera will make.

You cannot expect a camera to be *very* quiet unless you purchase one of the expensive cameras made to run quietly. Unless you have thousands of dollars to spend, you will be faced with having to settle for a relatively quiet camera if noise is one of your concerns. Noise, of course, is less of a problem outdoors. If you wish to compare various brands of cameras for noise level, load them before you test.

Camera quality

The most important consideration in choosing a camera is quality, and no checklist of accessories can give an insight into quality. Registration of the image (i.e., how much unsteadiness there is in the picture image from frame to frame) can only be checked by shooting film through the camera and checking it on a good projector. Ruggedness of the camera is usually a question of camera design. Some cameras (e.g., the Arriflex) have made their reputation in great part by their reliability.

Purchasing equipment

Usually equipment can be purchased used but in a like-new condition from one-third to two-thirds off list price. New equipment can usually be purchased in larger cities at a discount of 10-30 percent. Sometimes discounts can even be obtained on fair-traded items. Generally, equipment which is exclusively professional can be purchased at a discount of 10-20 percent off list price. Often dealers will let you test equipment, and it might be worth forgoing some discount to be able to test the equipment that you are contemplating purchasing. Consult the Yellow Pages of your local phone book for "Camera Stores" and "Professional Motion Picture Equipment" stores.

Testing equipment

If you test a piece of equipment, you need a projector to be able to evaluate your results. The projector should be of good quality and be in good running condition. Since the projector involves a system very much like that of the camera, it is important to be able to distinguish defects in the projector from those in the camera. If in doubt, you can try projecting the film on another projector to see whether the defect is still present.

One simple test to evaluate the camera's *registration*, that is, its steadiness of image, is to show the frame line during projection. The frame line is the area between consecutive frames, and it appears as a black line. Most projectors have a frame line adjustment so that you can make the frame line appear. If the frame line stays the same thickness, the camera has excellent registration. The more the line "breathes" the worse the registration. This test is independent of projector steadiness.

Light-leaks in the camera can be easily recognized. Flashes of light or streaks of light that appear on the film are signals of a light-leak in the camera *or* the improper loading of the film exposing it to light. On color film, light-leaks sometimes show up as a bluish or orange change in color, often accompanied by lighter frames.

If part of the image is blurred in projection, the camera shutter may be out of synchronization with the pull-down claw, a defect which must be repaired by an expert.

If frames alternately go in and out of focus, and the film was properly focused, then the film is "breathing," and there is most likely some problem with the pressure plate in the camera or projector.

You should test the camera's focus system. An easy test is to set up the camera at about a 45° angle to a wall on which there is a newspaper. Draw a heavy line down the newspaper vertically. Carefully focus the camera on the line. When the film is projected, the newsprint should be sharpest on either side of the heavy line. If not, then the camera's focusing apparatus is defective. This test is also independent of projector quality, although the sharper the projector's image, the easier it is to evaluate the results.

When more than one camera is used for the same film, it is essential to check that they both photograph individual frames in the same relation to the sprocket holes. If they do not, when footage from one camera is cut next to footage from the other camera, the frame line will jump when the film is projected. In 16mm, the perforation should be precisely opposite the frame line. (See Plate 1)

Renting equipment

High-quality 16mm motion picture film equipment can be very expensive to buy. On the other hand, if production time is not very long, it may well be to your advantage to consider the renting of equipment. If the type of film that you are interested in demands continual shooting every so often over a long period of time, then it will be less expensive to buy equipment. However, if a particular film will only take a few days to shoot, then you should consider rental. If any special equipment is needed for short periods of time (e.g., a sync-sound rig, a special lens, an editing machine), you can rent that also.

Professional camera stores and some smaller stores whose main business is the amateur market rent equipment. At professional camera stores the selection and availability will in general be greater. However, small camera stores will sometimes charge considerably less.

If you have not established credit at the place where you are renting, you may have to leave a deposit. To be sure of having the equipment you want, it is advisable to reserve it in advance. Some rental houses do not charge rental for the time the equipment is in transit if you are working out of town, but it will be shipped via air freight, for which you pay. Other places give an allowance of one day of travel, in which case it can be shipped in any way at your expense. Usually no warranty of performance is given on rented material, though you should not pay for defective equipment. Equipment to be rented for the subsequent day can generally be picked up around closing time (usually 5:00 or 6:00 P.M.), and must be returned before 10:00 A.M. the day following rental to avoid an additional day's rental charge. However, details such as these must be checked with the particular store you patronize.

All the large rental agencies have catalogs. You can often get a better price than the one quoted in the catalog if you ask. If you are renting more than one item, you may get a discount. Some rental agencies charge three or four times the daily rate for weekly rentals. If you are renting for more than a week, you may get an even greater discount.

The agency may not charge at all for weekends. That means that if you rent equipment on Friday, you very likely can use it for three full days while only paying for one. This is a common practice for low-budget productions.

You are responsible for all the equipment you rent and for damage other than normal wear. Theft is also your responsibility. This means that you must insure the equipment against damage and theft while you are renting it. Some rental agencies offer this insurance at an additional fee. Otherwise, almost any insurance agent can arrange to insure you promptly.

Before you use any rented equipment, you should test it. No matter what the rental house may claim as to previous tests or equipment reliability, you should be wary. In particular watch out for camera scratches and light leaks. Run a small amount of film through the camera and each of the magazines. Examine the undeveloped film for any scratches. Shine a strong light on the loaded camera and magazines from several positions and develop the film to see if there are any light leaks. There are one-solution film developers available, and no great quality controls need be exercised. Microphones and tape recorders should be checked for sound quality and the presence of any unusual noises. Remember, the footage you are shooting is often irreplaceable.

III. The Lens

The lens is the heart of any camera. If the lens on your camera is not interchangeable, you will be limited to its capabilities.

Some cameras with interchangeable lenses must be purchased with at least one lens on the body. Arriflex requires you to buy one lens for each lens *socket* unless you buy a zoom lens. Some camera manufacturers select lenses for their cameras and choose the best, thus enabling them to guarantee quality.

Focal length

Lenses are identified by their *focal lengths* (or in the case of zoom lenses, by the range of focal lengths), which are usually expressed in millimeters (or more rarely, inches: one inch equals approximately 25mm). (See Plates 18, 19) The focal length of the lens indicates the area of the subject the lens can photograph from a given subject-to-camera distance. (See Plates 41A-41G) The longer the focal length (the higher the number), the smaller the area the lens will photograph, and consequently the larger any particular detail will appear on the film.

For 8mm work a lens of approximately 12mm is considered a lens of normal focal length, whereas a 25mm lens is considered normal in 16mm filming.

In still photography, a lens is usually considered to be "normal" when its focal length is equal to the diagonal of the film format. It is by this standard that a 50mm lens is considered normal for 35mm still photography. By this standard a lens around 15mm would be normal for 16mm cameras, and a 7mm for 8mm cameras. The standards for a normal lens are different, however, for motion picture use. "Normal" means that under most conditions the lens yields an image of natural perspective. *Perspective* expresses relative sizes of objects at different distances. A normal perspective would be one that would appear on the screen in such a way that the size of objects diminish at what appears to be an expected rate as their distance from the camera becomes greater. It is important to understand perspective in the photographic image, for it is one of the chief controls a cameraman has in determining how objects in his frame relate to each other.

Perspective

Perspective is controlled by only one thing in photography—the distance between the subject and the camera. Most people tend to think of perspective as being controlled by the focal length of the taking lens, but this is only indirectly true. Any lens which has a focal length shorter than the normal lens is known as a *wide-angle* lens (e.g., a lens of focal length less than 20mm for 16mm film and less than 10mm for 8mm film). Any lens with a focal length longer than normal is known as a *long lens,** which means that the lens takes in a narrower angle of the scene.

In order to keep the subject the same size as you move the camera closer or farther from the subject you will have to change the focal length of the lens. As you move farther from the subject with any fixed focal length lens, you photograph more of the scene and consequently the subject becomes smaller. If you use a longer lens, you can keep the original subject size, but because you have changed the camera-to-subject distance, you will have changed the perspective. As you move farther away, perspective becomes flatter, objects farther from and closer to the camera do not appear to have the same distance between them as in fact they do. Objects which are farther away do not appear to be as small as they should. There is a compression of depth. (See Plates 42, 44C) This effect can be seen when a horserace is filmed head-on with a long lens. The distance between the front runner and the other horses does not appear to be as great as it really is. The horses seem to be running hard, but not moving very quickly. This effect occurs because of the great subject-to-camera distance and the consequent compression of depth. In recent films this foreshortening (or flattening) has been used quite a bit. For example, in *The Graduate* the hero is running in an attempt to interrupt a wedding ceremony. In one shot, taken head-on with a long lens, he runs very hard but appears to stay in the same place.

With wide-angle lenses, the opposite happens. We encounter an exaggeration of perspective. The distance between foreground and background seems greater than it is in life. (See

* Sometimes these lenses are incorrectly called "telephoto" lenses. A *telephoto* lens is actually a long lens which, because of sophisticated lens design, is more compact than a long lens that takes in the same area. Sometimes telephoto lenses are called *true telephoto* lenses.

Plates 43, 44A) Objects far away from the camera seem too small in relation to objects close to the camera. The wide-angle lens can be used to good effect when you wish to make a room seem larger. However, when people walk toward the camera, they will appear to walk too quickly and their steps seem too long.

In order to get a close-up of the head of a subject you have to be fairly close to the subject, and, consequently, you may encounter an exaggeration of perspective in the face. The nose seems too large, while the ears are too small and too far from the front of the face. Obviously, such close-ups are very unflattering. (See Plates 44A, 44B) In one recent television advertisement there was a good illustration of the extremes of perspective exaggeration. A dentist looking down into the lens (an extreme wide-angle lens of about 5.6mm in a 16mm format) moves his head even closer to the lens. Because the subject-to-camera distance is so small, the perspective is exaggerated and the dentist's nose grows at a very fast rate, giving the impression that it is shooting off his face into the lens.

It should be understood that the normal lens will only yield a natural perspective at intermediate filming distances. When distances are shorter, a slightly longer focal length lens is needed to achieve normal perspective. To film an extreme close-up of a face, a lens of about 50 percent greater focal length than normal is necessary for a natural perspective. Normal lenses have to be brought too close to the subject for a pleasing perspective. In general, for close-ups of people's faces it is better to err on the side of a flatter perspective (use a longer focal length lens with the camera farther away from the subject). However, when the perspective is too flat, a feeling of intimacy is lost from the close-up and the film viewer feels himself farther from the action. (See Plate 44C) The use of very flat or greatly exaggerated perspective often has a documentary style to it, just because the documentary cameraman often has no choice of subject-camera distance but must use the focal length which will properly cover his subject. When he is far away (as in nature photography), his perspective is flat (See Plate 42); when he is close (as in a crowd), his perspective is exaggerated. Wide-angle lenses also can be used to exaggerate heights from the top of a building to the ground, or from below a person. (See Plate 43)

Even though perspective will vary every time subject-camera distance changes, unless the changes are great they will not be particularly noticeable to the audience. There is an enormous amount of tolerance built into audience reaction to perspective change.

Perspective to the viewer is also controlled by where he sits in relation to the screen. When we say that a 25mm lens yields natural perspective in 16mm (at average working distances), we are assuming that the viewer is sitting at an average distance from the screen. When he sits very close, perspective is foreshortened, and when he views from a great distance, perspective is exaggerated.

Depth of field

Almost every lens has a provision for focusing on the subject. A point in the subject is considered to be in focus when it is registered as a point on the film by the lens. This is known as *critical focus;* all the points that are in critical focus make up what is called the plane of critical focus.* Any point outside the plane of critical focus will be registered as a circle (known as the *circle of confusion*). When the circle is small enough or far enough from the viewer, it will appear as a point to the eye. Consequently, there will be a region on either side of the plane of critical focus where points will be registered as circles so small they will appear as points to the eye, and will hence appear to be in sharp focus. This region, expressed in terms of the near distance and far distance where objects appear to be in sharp focus, is known as the *depth of field* (*not* the depth of focus, which is another matter). The smaller a subject is recorded on the film, the greater the depth of field. Consequently, the greater the subject-camera distance, the greater the depth of field. If you keep the subject-camera distance constant and use a wider angle lens (thereby also making the subject appear smaller on the film), you also increase depth of field.

Some inexpensive cameras have lenses which do not focus (they have what is sometimes called "universal focus"). They rely essentially on depth of field to produce acceptably sharp pictures. They usually have wide-angle lenses which do not allow you to get very close to the subject. The image is not really very sharp throughout the range of depth of field. The greater the size of the projected image, the less depth of field. Images shot with fixed-focus cameras cannot be projected to a large size with acceptable sharpness. With them, the cameraman cannot use *selective focus,* cannot choose what is to be focused and what blurred for a desired effect, such as throwing a confusing background out of focus.

---

* A lens which is properly corrected for aberrations, in particular curvature of field, will have a plane of critical focus. A lens which suffers from curvature of field will have a curved surface as its field of critical focus.

Lens aperture or diaphragm

There is one other variable which controls depth of field, and that is the lens aperture. Inside nearly every lens there is a device known as the *iris diaphragm*. (See Fig. III) This is a

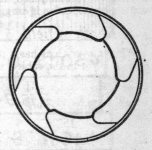

Fig. III. *The iris diaphragm:* The iris diaphragm can be adjusted to allow different amounts of light to pass through the lens. Overlapping blades can be opened and closed to form circles of different diameter.

mechanical device which can be set to form a large or small aperture in front of the center of the lens to alter the amount of light passing through the lens. The brighter the subject, the less light need fall on the film, so the smaller the iris diaphragm setting. Conversely, with a dim subject we open up the diaphragm to allow more light to hit the film.

F/stops

The amount of light that the lens lets pass (the *effective aperture*) is expressed in terms of f/numbers (f/stops). The f/stop is a ratio between the focal length of the lens and the diameter of the diaphragm opening ($f\# = \frac{F}{D}$ where F is the focal length of the lens and D is the diameter of the diaphragm opening). The iris diaphragm works in much the same way as the iris in the eye, which opens up in dim light and closes down in bright light.

When the iris diaphragm is all the way open, the lens can pass the maximum amount of light. The f/stop calculated with the diaphragm all the way open (where the diameter is the diameter of the front element of the lens) is known as the speed of the lens. This, along with the focal length of the lens, is usually engraved on the rim of the front of the lens.

The most common series of f/stops is 1, 1.4, 2, 2.8, 4, 5.6, 8, 11, 16, 22, 32. (See Fig. IV) The distance between consecu-

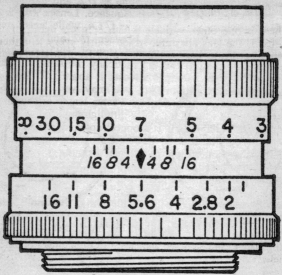

Fig. IV. A "C" mount lens showing barrel. The bottom scale has the lens' f/stops engraved: f/2, 2.8, 4, 5.6, 8, 11, 16. The top scale gives the camera-to-subject distance. The middle scale is a device for computing the approximate depth of field at a given f/stop. You find the two places the selected f/stop appears on the scale and look at the subject-to-camera distance above. This will give you the depth of field. For example, the illustrated lens is focused at 7'. If we were exposing the film at f/16 we would be in focus from about 5' to 12'.

tive numbers is called one *stop*. A stop represents the halving (or doubling) of the amount of light that the diaphragm allows to pass through the lens. The wider open the diaphragm, the more light enters the camera and the lower the f/number. Opening up one stop allows twice the amount of light to hit the film; this is achieved by turning the f/stop ring, for example, from f/5.6 to f/4 in the sequence of stops. Similarly, "closing down one stop" ("stopping down") is achieved by turning the ring to the next consecutive higher number (f/5.6 to f/8).

Your lens may not have *all* the numbers in the f/stop sequence engraved on it. The first number, representing the widest aperture, the speed of the lens, will often not be a number in the series given here; the next number and those which follow will be. Many lenses have a speed of f/1.9. For all practical purposes that is the same as f/2, and the next number will be f/2.8 in the f/stop sequence. Lenses with a speed of f/1.5 are basically the same as f/1.4, while lenses marked f/2.2 have maximum speed between f/2 and f/2.8. Some lenses are very fast and have an f/stop of f/.95 (e.g., the Angénieux 25mm lens); this is practically the same as f/1. The speed of most normal cinema lenses is about f/2. If a lens is considerably slower than that, you may well find it limiting for natural-light indoor filming. Faster lenses are used when it is necessary to shoot with very dim lighting.

As the iris diaphragm is stopped down depth of field increases. (See Plates 45A, 45B) The smaller the diaphragm opening, the greater the area where the image is sufficiently in focus. Therefore, the brighter the scene, the more depth of field we are capable of achieving. This is one reason that Hollywood sets are lit so brightly. Similarly, the more sensitive to light the film (the faster the film), the smaller the required diaphragm opening and the greater the depth of field.

Unlike the still photographer, the filmmaker does not have a great selection of shutter speeds, and he therefore cannot use a slower shutter speed in order to stop down his lens. He, for the most part, has to control his depth of field by controlling the lighting and/or his selection of film.

If the cameraman wants less depth of field, he can use a neutral density filter (see Chapter X) or he can close down his variable shutter (see p. 26) if his camera is so equipped. By using a smaller shutter opening, he allows less light to hit the film, and he must compensate for this by opening up his lens, thereby lessening his available depth of field.

In Appendix C depth of field charts are given. Some lenses have depth of field charts engraved on the lens barrel. (See Fig. IV) For critical work it is best to consult the charts in the Appendix. When two objects are in different planes and you wish to render each as sharp as possible, you should not focus at the midpoint between them but rather one-third closer to the near object. If one object is 10 feet away and the other 16 feet, to render them equally sharp, you would focus at 12 feet.

It is not true that the sharpest pictures are obtained with the smallest diaphragm openings. It is true that the smaller the opening, the greater the depth of field, but most lenses give their best results, are sharpest in the plane of critical focus, when closed down two or three stops from their maximum aperture. When the lens is closed all the way down an optical phenomenon (called "diffraction") sometimes occurs which reduces the overall sharpness of the image. Usually the highest number f/stop (smallest opening) engraved on the ring

yields an image considerably less sharp than wider open
f/stops. If the smallest opening is f/22, you will generally get
much better results at f/16.

Lenses come in a wide variety of focal lengths. For example, 16mm lenses are available in focal lengths from the extremely wide-angle 1.9mm to the extreme telephoto of
1000mm and more. Lenses differ greatly in how sharply they
can render an image. The greatest differences in lenses are
found from one manufacturer to another. But even within
the same model lens by the same manufacturer there are
often noticeable differences. If you have the opportunity, test
lenses against each other before purchasing one.

Bolex reflex cameras should be equipped with special
lenses suggested by the manufacturer when the focal length
of the lens is 50mm or less. Though any "C" mount lens will
physically fit Bolex reflex cameras, unless they are of a special type (marked RX) they will most likely deliver an inferior image.

Most lenses of normal focal length focus down to within a
few feet of the subject. Longer focal length lenses generally
do not focus so closely. Some lenses, called macro lenses, will
focus extremely close to the subject. They are often capable
of focusing so close to the subject that even a small subject is
registered on the film the same size it actually is. This means
that you can fill the screen with an object the size of a child's
tooth.

Lens quality

Lenses have to be corrected for various aberrations. The
better corrected the lens, the more expensive it is, and the
faster and sharper the lens, the more you have to pay.

Lenses made for 8mm cameras will not usually cover a
great enough area to be used with 16mm cameras. It is not a
good idea to use lenses made for 35mm cameras on 16mm
cameras or to use 16mm lenses on 8mm cameras since they
will not produce as good an image. High-quality 8mm lenses
are sharper for the field they cover than are 16mm lenses,
and, similarly, 16mm lenses are sharper than 35mm lenses.

Longer focal length lenses can be obtained in a telephoto
design which cuts down the length and weight of the lens but
increases its price. Cadiotropic, or mirror optics lenses, are of
a very long focal length (500mm to 1000mm), but they are
extremely compact, under 12 inches in length.

The normal set of three lenses for 16mm studio shooting
are the 16mm, 25mm, and 50mm lenses. Useful additional
lenses would be 12mm and 75mm lenses. For documentary

work a 9mm lens is often extremely useful either when space is tight or when a panoramic view is needed. A normal set of lenses for documentary work might be 10mm, 25mm, and 75mm lenses. Longer lenses of 100mm and up are needed for nature photography and when the subject is far from the camera. When filming from a car, a wide-angle lens is helpful for minimizing camera and car movement. Using an extremely wide-angle lens like a 9mm or even a 5.6mm from a moving vehicle can give a monumental feeling of movement and sweep.

Unless very fast, extreme wide-angle, or very long focal length lenses are needed, most filmmaking in 16mm and almost all in 8mm involve the use of a zoom lens.

Zoom lenses

The *zoom lens* offers the advantage of being able to embody various focal lengths in one lens. (See Plates 20, 21A-C) Focal length can be changed during a shot (zooming) or between shots. (See Plates 41A-41G) (This latter method has the same effect as replacing a lens.) On the other hand, zoom lenses are larger, heavier, more delicate, and of a lower quality than fixed focal length lenses, though the more expensive zoom lenses approach fixed focal length lenses in quality. Because their mounting is so critical, there are advantages in permanent mounting. This is customary on super 8 cameras but rare on 16mm cameras. Large 16mm zoom lenses, such as the 12-120mm and 9.5-95mm zoom lenses when attached by a "C" mount, should have a zoom lens support. (See Plate 22)

All the various focal lengths in the zoom range are what is called *color-matched*. Since different lenses have different transmission qualities, they often show slightly different results when used with color films. Therefore, a set of fixed focal length lenses should preferably be made by the same manufacturer and be color-matched to each other to give the same color rendition. Otherwise, there may be a slight color change within a scene if you change from one fixed focal length lens to another.

Zoom lenses also offer the advantage of having an infinite number of focal lengths within the zoom range since any of the intermediary focal lengths in the zoom range can be chosen. This is of great advantage when working from a tripod, since slightly altering coverage with a fixed focal length lens means moving the tripod, whereas with a zoom lens all one need do is move a ring on the lens to change focal length. Focal length can be changed virtually instantaneously with a zoom lens, whereas to bring a fixed lens into position takes more time, even when the lens is mounted on a turret.

If a zoom lens is used for zooming as opposed to merely changing focal lengths, some means must be used to zoom smoothly. Many 8mm cameras have motor-driven zooms. A motor limits you to preselected zooming speeds. External zoom motors which weigh a few ounces are available for 16mm zoom lenses. Mechanical zooming is achieved with a zoom lever or a crank. A zoom lever is a rod that extends from the zoom ring around the lens. The longer it is, the less any uneven hand movement shows, and hence the smoother the zoom. Cranks have a handle which when turned causes the lens to zoom. Smoother zooms can be achieved with a crank on a tripod. However, it is somewhat more difficult to crank the lens hand-held than it is to use a zoom lever. Zooming can also be done more quickly with a lever than a crank. Uneven zooming is often not noticed when filming, but will show up on the screen. Practice is required to execute a smooth zoom by hand.

There are zoom *data rings* available for 16mm zoom lenses. When placed on the lens they give the focal length, the distance, and the f/stop at which the lens is set. This is especially useful for hand-held shooting since the cameraman need not take the camera out of shooting position to look at the lens dials. The f/stop scale on the zoom data ring is perhaps the most useful, for this information is essential while shooting. If your camera does not have a built-in exposure meter and you have to change the f/stop because of changing light conditions, the only way to do it without a data ring is to remove the camera from shooting position and change the f/stop dial. Some older lenses have click-stops. The f/stop can be changed on these by turning by feel the f/stop ring one click for every stop.

If you place an object in the center of the frame with the zoom in the wide-angle position and then zoom the lens to a longer focal length, the object will no longer be exactly in the center of the frame. Almost every zoom lens exhibits this *side-drift* defect to some extent. To compensate for it you must pan the camera slightly to keep the object in the center of the frame.

When a zoom lens is working properly it must hold the same point of critical focus over the zoom range. If an object is in focus at the longest focal length, it should be in focus when the camera zooms to any wider focal length. If it is not, it is either a very inferior lens or should be repaired.

Focusing a zoom lens

Since when zooming over the zoom range the lens holds the same point of critical focus, and since at the longer focal lengths we have less depth of field, the proper way to focus a zoom lens with a reflex camera is to extend the lens to the longest focal length, focus, and then zoom back to the selected focal length. In this way the best point of focus will have been chosen, and any further change of focal length will keep the subject, assuming it hasn't moved, in focus. If focusing is done at a wider angle focal length and then the lens is zoomed to a longer focal length, it is unlikely that focus will be held, since at the wider focal length there is greater depth of field and the lens is less likely to be in exact focus.

Similarly, since there is less depth of field when the lens is widest open, it is easiest to focus wide open, and then stop the lens down to the selected f/stop.

Close-ups with zoom lenses

Zoom lenses do not generally focus as close to the subject as do fixed focal length lenses. Whereas many fixed focal length lenses focus down to around two feet from the subject, zoom lenses seldom focus closer than four feet. Close-up lenses (called *plus diopters*) can be screwed onto the front of the lens and allow you to film very close while still using the zoom effect. Plus diopters come in designations of +1 and higher; the higher the number, the closer you can focus to the subject, and consequently, the larger any particular object can be rendered.

Additional lenses

Even if you have a zoom lens, this does not mean that you will have no occasion to use fixed focal length lenses. You may need a lens with a wider angle of coverage than your zoom lens has or you may need a lens with a longer focal length than the maximum focal length of your zoom lens. Zoom lenses are generally no faster than f/2, and in dim lighting you may want to use a faster lens, possibly a fixed focal length lens rated at f/1.4 or even f/.95.

Changing the zoom range

Some zoom lenses can be fitted with a retro-focus wide-angle attachment (a *retro-zoom*) which allows for a zoom range of shorter focal lengths. For example, the 17-68mm Angénieux zoom lens can be fitted with a retro-zoom attachment that converts it to a 12-50mm zoom lens. No noticeable light loss occurs with retro-zoom attachments. On the other hand, *telephoto-extenders* which allow for a zoom range of longer focal lengths do require an exposure compensation. Besides, telephoto-extenders do not produce as good a photographic image as the unaided zoom.

Choice of zoom ranges

Zoom lenses come in many different ranges, usually from wide-angle to very long focal lengths. Most zoom lenses have less of the wide-angle and more of the long focal length. In particular, 8mm zoom lenses are often deficient on the wide-angle side. The zoom range is expressed by giving the shortest and the longest focal lengths. It is also often expressed as a ratio of the longest to the shortest focal length. Probably the highest ratio that you will encounter is 10:1, as in the Angénieux 12-120mm for 16mm or the Schneider Variogon 7-68mm lens for the 8mm. Angénieux also makes a 20:1, 12-240mm zoom lens for 16mm cameras. The higher the zoom ratio, the more you will have to pay for the lens. Many 8mm cameras come with zoom lenses of very limited range, as low as 2:1 or 3:1. You may well be faced with having to choose between saving money (as much as a few hundred dollars) and increasing the versatility of your camera. In general, the less you can set up your shots and the more unpredictable your subject matter is, the greater zoom range you will need. As important as the length of zoom range is the widest angle the zoom lens has. It may well be worth sacrificing focal length on the long side to be able to get a wider-angle coverage on the short focal length side (see p. 153).

Perhaps the greatest disadvantage of the zoom lens is its misuse. The novice cameraman tends to be "zoom-happy," using the zoom whenever he can. The zoom should be used sparingly. In a later section we will discuss why many filmmakers find the zoom effect unpleasant (see p. 70).

Care of the lens

The lens is the most delicate part of your camera and should be treated with great care to avoid shocks and prolonged vibrations. Extremes of temperature should also be avoided when possible, since extreme heat can loosen the elements (the several pieces of glass in the lens), and extreme cold can crack an element. Zoom lenses are particularly fragile. If a zoom lens can be removed from the camera, it should be removed whenever it is to be shipped anywhere and packed in a foam-lined case.

Whenever a lens is not in use it should be covered by a front lens cap to protect the front element from dust and fingerprints. When the lens is removed from the camera body, a rear element lens cap should be used. The mount of the lens as well as the lens socket on the camera should be kept clean and free from grit. When the lens is removed from the camera body for a time, the lens socket on the camera should also be covered with a cap.

When the lens is used at the beach or any place where it may be subjected to spray, sand, or winds, a clean optical glass or UV filter should be used over the front element. With these no unwanted filter effects (see Chapter X) can result. Many cameramen leave a filter permanently in place on the lens for protection.

You will find that no matter how careful you are, you will have to clean your lens occasionally. A dirty lens will cause a deterioration of picture quality. Most dust can be removed with a rubber ear syringe. These can be bought at any drugstore. When you squeeze the bulb on the syringe, a jet of air shoots out. If the lens is tipped down the dust will usually dislodge and fall off the lens. This is the safest way to remove dust because nothing touches the delicate front element. Some people use their breath to the same effect, blowing off the dust. However, saliva will fall on the lens unless you are careful, and it is easier to remove dust than saliva. Compressed air can be used, but some compressed air contains tiny drops of oil. Oil-free compressed air can be purchased at most photography stores.

If blown air does not get all the dust off the lens, a *clean* camel's hair brush, *reserved for the sole purpose of lens cleaning*, can be used to sweep the dust off the lens. Blow the brush gently to clear it of dust, but do not touch it with your fingers as any oil from them will stay on the hair. An alternate method is to fold photographic lens-cleaning paper over itself several times, and then tear off an edge, using the torn edge to brush the lens lightly. Never rub the element with lens paper, for you will simply grind the dirt into the glass.

Fingerprints and oil on a lens are more difficult to remove. They also interfere more with photographic quality. They should be removed as soon as possible, since they often are more difficult to remove the longer they are on the lens and, being acidic, may even cause permanent damage. To remove fingerprints and oil you should use photographic lens-cleaning paper. *Never* use eyeglass-cleaning paper or any silicon-coated lens tissue, since they can permanently damage the lens. Before using the tissue all the dust should be removed by the methods already described. Never apply the lens-cleaning tissue to a dry lens. Lens-cleaning solution can be used but the solution should not touch where the element is attached to the lens barrel since it may loosen the adhesive bond. As an alternative to lens-cleaning solution, you may breathe on the lens causing condensation on the front element. The tissue should be rubbed on the dampened element as gently as possible, using a circular motion combined with a rolling motion to lift any dust and grit present off the lens. Continually use a clean portion of the tissue so any grit picked up by the tissue is not rubbed into the delicate coating on the surface of the lens. The lens element should never be rubbed without moisture on it.

Lens shades

Every time a lens is used it should have a *lens shade* (*sunshade*) to prevent stray light from hitting the lens and causing picture quality to deteriorate. (See Plates 4, 5, 6) Whenever the light illuminating the subject is not behind the camera, there is some danger of light hitting the front element of the lens, bouncing around in the lens, and causing an overall fog on the film which results in the picture's losing its crispness and contrast. This is called *flare*. Some lens shades clip onto the lens, while others are screwed into the lens and often need an accessory holder. It is important that the lens shade be wide enough not to cut off any part of the picture. You should check this at close focusing distances. With a zoom lens it is important to check that the lens shade does not cut off any of the picture when the lens is used at its widest angle.

The longer the focal length, the narrower the width the lens shade need be and the more efficiently it cuts out stray light. With wide-angle lenses or zooms that contain a wide-angle focal length, the lens shade must be wider. With wide-angle lenses, especially, the shade should be as deep as possible to cut down the results of flare.

Often the lens shade cannot cut out the direct rays of light because of the angle at which they are hitting the lens. This frequently occurs when the subject is backlit (when the source of light is behind the subject). Flare usually shows up as a bright area in part of the image, and can often be observed on the ground glass with reflex cameras. In extreme cases, you see a bright shaft of light with multiple polygons, which are actually reflections of the iris diaphragm. Sometimes you can place a card in the proper position to block direct rays of light from hitting the front element of the lens. This cannot be done, of course, when the light source itself appears in the picture.

Filters can usually be used in conjunction with the lens shade. The most common way to attach a filter to the lens is with the aid of an accessory ring. Most lenses will take an accessory ring of a standard size, and then filters of the same size (series) can be used with it. (See Chapter X).

The matte box

Many professional 16mm cameras can accept *matte boxes*. (See Plate 9) Matte boxes usually have provisions for the use of gelatin filters. They offer the advantage of being able to accept less expensive filters. The same filter can be used for all lenses no matter what their size (with the exception of extremely wide-angle or extremely long focal length lenses). Matte boxes also act as very efficient lens shades.

IV. Exposure

Underexposure and overexposure

The most common photographic defect that makes footage unusable is improper exposure. The cameraman must learn how to determine properly the amount of exposure his film needs to yield a proper image. *Overexposure,* an excess of light hitting the film, results in a washed-out image. There are no blacks in the dark areas and no differentiation in tones in the lighter areas (the highlights). (See Plate 46C) *Underexposure,* an insufficient amount of light hitting the film, results in loss of detail in shadow areas, which become a uniform black, and an overall darkening of highlights. (See Plate 46B)

Automatic exposure

Many cameras, especially 8mm, offer built-in exposure meters (*electric eyes*). Although they offer several advantages, they must be used with care so that the subject does not "fool" the electric eye (see below). A built-in exposure meter is basically similar to a separate reflected-light exposure meter.

Setting for the proper exposure

To arrive at the correct exposure is to set the lens at the proper f/stop. Since different cameras have different shutter openings, you must find out the shutter opening for your particular camera. It usually is about 180° which gives an exposure of 1/50th of a second when the camera is run at 24 fps and of 1/30th of a second at 16 fps. At 18 fps, 8mm silent speed, the exposure is about 1/35.* You should check your camera instruction book to see what the shutter speed for your camera is at various camera running speeds. The light meter scale will tell you the proper f/stop to use, given the amount of light on the subject, the sensitivity of the film, and

* Shutter speed $= \dfrac{\text{Shutter opening}}{\text{Frames per second} \times 360}$. At 24 fps and a 180° shutter opening, we get a shutter speed of $\dfrac{180}{24 \times 360} = \dfrac{1}{48}$, or approximately $\dfrac{1}{50}$th of a second.

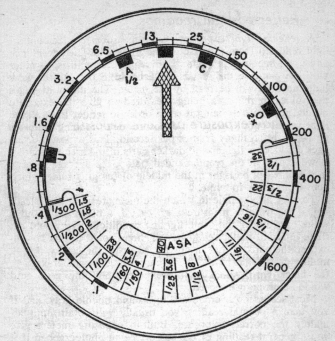

Fig. V. *The light meter scale:* We set the ASA speed for the particular film we are using. We get a meter reading and point the dial toward the proper number. We then look at the proper shutter speed, which will depend on the particular make of camera and the rate at which we are filming. At 24 fps, many cameras have an exposure of 1/50 of a second. We look opposite 1/50 to find the proper f/stop at which to set the lens. In the case of the illustrated meter this would give us a reading of f/4.

the shutter speed. (See Fig. V) The shutter speed will, of course, change if the camera motor speed is increased (for slow motion) or decreased (for speeded-up action). Some light meters have scales for cine speeds, that is, the number of frames per second at which the camera is running. The various markings assume that the camera has approximately a 180° shutter. If your camera is not so equipped, you will be better off using the scale that marks speeds in fractions of a second. None of this applies if you are relying solely on a built-in exposure meter, since your meter is calibrated already for your camera.

Reflected-light readings

A *reflected-light exposure meter* measures the amount of light reflected from a surface. (See Plate 24) The acceptance angle of a meter (the angle of coverage) determines, together with the distance the meter is placed from the subject, how large an area will be read by the meter. The meter averages the values in the area being measured to give the exposure needed for the film being used in order to render the average light values middle gray. An exposure meter reading indicates an f/stop at so many frames per second. This exposure averages the various lighter and darker parts of the area measured. If we expose at the recommended f/stop, the average tonality in the film will be right in the middle of the gray scale, which goes from black to white.

To take an example in which the meter reading is misleading, if we were to measure a gray card, a black card, and a white card under the same lighting conditions, we would get three different meter readings. All three would tell us how to expose the card so that in our filmed result the card will look middle gray. That is, the white card would be underexposed, the black card would be overexposed, and the gray card would be properly exposed.

Most scenes do average out to around middle gray, and if you take a general reading you usually will obtain approximately the correct exposure. Built-in exposure meters give you a general reading of the subject being photographed if it is a through-the-lens system, but otherwise usually read a larger area. General readings in unusual lighting situations or scenes with very dark or very light backgrounds can give very wrong readings. For example, if a person is against a black background, the most important area from the point of view of exposure is the person's flesh tones. A general reading will measure the unimportant background and the exposure will be wrong. When the main source of light comes from the area behind the subject being filmed, when it is backlit, a general reading will measure the light instead of the subject, which, consequently, will be rendered too dark.

It is important to avoid including too much sky area in your readings, since the sky is relatively bright in relation to most subjects, and your reading will very likely lead to underexposure. Care must be taken that no light source is read by the meter, since this too will lead to underexposure. You must often shade the meter when taking a reading so that stray light does not hit the cell, being careful to keep your hand out of the area being read by the meter.

When taking general readings or when using an electric-eye camera, you have to be very careful of high-contrast situations, when there is a great difference in the amount of light on different parts of the scene.

To generalize: when taking a close-up in sunlight with the sun hitting the person's face from the side (sidelighting), you should open the lens aperture one-half to one stop wider from the exposure given for a general landscape reading. If you are taking a close-up with the sun behind the person, you should open the lens up one and one-half to two stops. This procedure only applies if the background is of average brightness.

Snow and sand often fool an electric eye. Flesh tones will usually be underexposed if you rely on the electric eye in these situations. For close-ups, you will have to open up the iris diaphragm to get a proper exposure.

Stray light hitting the meter will give a wrong exposure, since the meter reads as though there is more light on the scene than there really is. When using a single light to illuminate a scene, a meter will often take the dark background into its reading, leading to overexposure of the foreground. When shooting at night beware of general readings.

There are several ways of determining exposure more accurately than by the general reading. For instance, Caucasian skin tones are usually properly rendered by giving one stop more exposure than indicated by the meter reading. If we were to take a reading of the face, the meter might tell us to expose at f/11. Since we wish to render the face lighter than middle gray, we would open the lens to f/8. In a scene with sunlight and shade, to get good shadow detail in black and white photography we should have the shadow area no more than two stops away from the exposure given. When shooting an outdoor, contrasty scene in black and white, if we were to take a general reading of the shaded portion of the picture (where we want good shadow detail) and the meter indicated exposure at f/4, we would not be able to expose the film at less than f/8 and still get good shadow rendition. As the cameraman gains experience he is able to evaluate how he wants various objects rendered on the film and, consequently, how he should expose to achieve the desired result.

Another standard method of arriving at an exposure reading is through the use of a gray card of 18 percent reflectancy which can be purchased at most photographic stores (the Kodak Neutral Test Card is one). This gray is equivalent to the reflectancy of the average subject. The card should be placed in the same light that is falling on the subject, and faced halfway between the subject and the main light source (the key light). A reflected-light meter reading is then taken of the card.

In situations where two values are to be rendered in a particular manner and they do not fall properly on the scale, the various solutions are changing the contrast of the film by altering the development time (this is very rarely done in motion picture work unless one has a highly controlled studio situation), compromising on rendition (the usual documentary solution), or changing the lighting.

Taking a reflected-light reading

The meter should be placed in such a way that you are reading the light in the direction in which it will hit the camera. Getting as close as possible to the area to be read, keeping the meter monitoring device pointed in the same axis as the lens, we take our reading. It is very important to make sure that the shadows of the meter and/or your hand do not fall on the area to be read. The danger of the meter's shadow being read is greater when the subject being read is fairly small and you are reading close to it. If the cameraman takes a reading of his hand (which in the case of average Caucasian skin, as already noted, will be one stop brighter than the average scene), or some other particular area, he must be sure that his meter is reading *only* that area.

Photoelectric or selenium meters give fairly quick readings. However, cadmium sulfide (CdS) meters sometimes take several seconds for the meter needle to come entirely to rest. (See Plates 27, 29) It is very important to wait until the needle stops moving to obtain the correct exposure.

Spot meters

Spot meters read the reflected light from a very small area of the subject. (See Plate 28) A device incorporated into the meter enables you to see exactly what the meter is reading. Spot meters can often help extricate you from difficult situations, especially when the subject is very small or far away. They also guarantee that you read a small area precisely.

Their acceptance angle varies from 1/2° to 7°.

Incident light readings

The *incident light* is the light *falling on* (rather than *reflected by*) a subject. To read incident light accurately, the meter is equipped with a hemisphere, sometimes called a *photosphere*. (See Plates 25, 26) The larger the hemisphere, the more accurate the reading. The hemisphere simulates a three-dimensional subject. We place the meter in the subject's position and point the hemisphere toward the lens of the camera. The hemispheric reading accounts for all the light hitting the subject—key, fill, back, whatever—and averages them. In the previous example of the black, gray, and white cards, had we taken an *incident* reading, all three readings would have been the same, since the amount of incident light hitting all three was the same. When the subject is excessively bright or dark, an incident reading may be misleading. For example, if we take an incident reading of a beach scene, our reading will result in overexposure.

Exposure meters

If any extensive amount of camera work is to be done, a separate exposure meter should be purchased even if your camera has a built-in exposure meter. In general, built-in exposure meters are not of as high quality as separate exposure meters. If your built-in exposure meter breaks, you will be without a camera while it is being repaired. If you have a separate meter, you can wait until the camera is not being used to have the meter repaired.

Usually, a meter either works or it does not. If no exposure is indicated, it is obviously broken. If it reads, it will probably read accurately, assuming it is of good quality. It is easy to test one meter against another to be sure they give the same results. For these reasons, it is fairly safe to purchase a used meter. A used Weston meter (one of the most commonly used) may cost as little as $10.

There are many variables when determining exposure: the transmission quality of your lens, variations in film, lab development, and exposure meter inaccuracy. When these variables cancel themselves out there is no need for worry, but when they are cumulative you may get an incorrect exposure. If your results are consistently slight overexposure, the film's ASA rating should be increased on the exposure meter's scale. If your results lead to consistent underexposure, decrease the ASA rating. (See p. 58 for discussion of ASA rating.)

Many *cine lenses,* that is, lenses made for motion picture use, are engraved with a series of T/stops in addition to the series of f/stops. T/stops are defined as the same number f/stop of a lens of 100 percent transmission. In other words, a lens is rated as T/2 if it lets through the same amount of light as a lens rated at f/2 which allows all the light to pass through. All lenses absorb some light, so T/stops will always be higher than f/stops. With most lenses the difference is inconsequential, being less than one-fourth of a stop. However, with zoom lenses, there is often as much as two-thirds of a stop difference between the rated f/stop and the actual T/stop. T/stops change with the life of the lens, and when the T/stop evaulation is heavily relied on, as in professional studio work, it should be recalibrated every year or so. ASA numbers are usually calculated for f/stops of fixed focal length lenses (that is, an assumption is made that a small amount of light is absorbed by the lens), and the use of T/stops will not necessarily lead to more accurate exposures. You should decide whether to use the f/stop or T/stop scale and change the rated ASA speed depending on the accuracy of your results.

The most common use for T/stops is in setting several different lenses to yield the same exposures. If you are using two or more lenses at the same location, you will want to make sure that their exposures are consistent. Setting the lenses to the same f/stop will not guarantee consistent exposures, since different lenses will absorb different amounts of light. Since the T/stop takes this into account, consistent exposures can be achieved by setting the lenses to the same T/stop.

In purchasing an exposure meter, you must decide whether you want an incident or reflected-light meter. Although many meters allow both types of reading by means of changing a component on the meter, the meter is primarily an incident or reflected-light meter and does not give as good results when used in the other mode. The best professional incident light meter is the Spectra, which gives direct readings in f/stops by the use of slides representing different ASA ratings. A series of slides is supplied with the meter. Each slide represents one ASA number. When the slide is placed in the meter and a reading taken, the meter needle will read the proper f/stop directly. Unfortunately, the Spectra is expensive (models are priced from $79).

Cadmium-sulfide (CdS) meters have the advantage of being able to take readings in extremely dim light. They have the disadvantage that the indicator needle often takes several seconds to come to rest. Since it is very rare to shoot motion picture film in dim light with long exposures (as in still photography), the advantage of low-light meter readings is a dubious one. CdS meters often have a narrower acceptance angle than other meters and are generally very accurate.

The power source for a CdS meter is one or two small batteries which must be checked from time to time. Any meter should be adjustable to set the zero calibration. With no light, the meter should give no reading. The calculator scale should be easy to use and should have an adequate range. The f/scale should go at least from f/1-f/32 and the ASA scale from 10 to 2500. It should also have a needle lock to hold the needle in the position of the last exposure reading. Some meters which have a fairly narrow acceptance angle have a viewing device to let you know approximately what area you are reading, which is helpful. The viewing device on a spot meter must be precise if error is to be avoided.

With practice the cameraman will get an idea of what lighting situations demand what f/stop for a given film. It is easy to learn the standard outdoor light situations and what exposure they require.

The question of how precise exposure should be often arises. It is difficult to say, for the answer depends in part on what type of film is used and in part on the nature of the subject. In general, exposure must be more precise for color film than black and white film, and more precise with reversal film than with negative film. With color film the exposure latitude (the variable amount) is as little as one-half a stop. On the other hand, with black and white negative film, you can often vary exposure as much as two stops and get acceptable results. Optimum results will be achieved when exposure is as accurate as possible. A few exposure errors can be corrected when making prints (see p. 95).

V. Film Raw Stock

The unexposed film that is to be shot in the camera is called *raw stock*. The selection of the proper raw stock for your work is extremely important, and it is important to understand the limitations and potentialities of the many types of raw stock offered by film manufacturers.

Composition of raw stock

Raw stock consists of at least three layers of material. The top layer is called the *emulsion,* in which are suspended the light-sensitive particles of the film. Then there is a binding material, which makes the emulsion adhere to the base, or support, material. (See illustration in Appendix B) Built into the emulsion of the film are the inherent contrast, graininess, sensitivity to light, and sharpness of the film. All of these factors may be modified to some degree when the film is developed (and through laboratory handling in general).

Negative film

Some film when developed yields a *negative image* (negative film). (See Plate 47A) All the tonalities of the subject are reproduced on the film opposite to what they were in the subject. Thus, light objects in the scene are rendered dark on the film, and vice versa. In order to see the film with tonalities correctly produced a *positive* print must be made from the original negative.

Reversal film

Films are also made which when developed (using a process different from *negative* development) yield a positive image. These are known as *reversal films.* The only films available at this time in super 8 are reversal films. In 16mm the choise is open to the filmmaker.

Comparative costs

As will be discussed in the chapter on editing, a workprint or copy print of the camera original should be made for editing purposes. If, however, in order to save money no work-print is made, reversal will cost less. If the filming is being done for practice, reversal should definitely be used, since the reversal print can be projected directly, whereas a print must be made from a negative in order to be able to project a positive picture. If a workprint is made, the negative system costs about one to three cents less per foot as compared with the reversal system. This is due to the higher cost of a reversal workprint. However, if not all the original film is to be work-printed, if you want to print only certain sections, the reversal process may end up costing less.

Comparative handling

It is very difficult to see what you have on film by looking at the negative image, since all the tonalities are reversed. On reversal film we have a positive image and can decide what is usable footage without having to make a *workprint* (an editing copy). The main reason for workprinting the original is to protect it from dirt and scratches. Reversal film (with the exception of Ektachrome Commercial) is much less susceptible to scratches since it is made for projection. Dust shows as black on reversal film and white on negative, and white sparkle (dust spots) is much more noticeable than black dust spots. We can search our camera original if reversal with much less danger of damaging it than we can when the original is negative. Since we are eventually going to cut up the original to conform to the edited workprint (see Chapter XII), reversal film's scratch-resistance and the relative minor importance of dust constitute important advantages.

Comparative quality

Reversal film has more contrast, less grain, and greater sharpness than negative films. Reversal original far surpasses a positive print from negative film in photographic quality. However, it is rare that an original is projected, so reversal quality should be compared from a copy print. Since printing usually increases contrast in the print, reversal film often yields a print which has too much contrast (i.e., an insufficient range of gray tones). To avoid this an intermediate stage of printing is often used, and a dupe (duplicate) negative is made (see p. 100). Negative film is less contrasty, and consequently allows a greater degree of tolerance for over- and underexposure (exposure latitude). This is a great advantage when lighting conditions are uncontrollable, as in documentary work.

ASA ratings

Reversal films are usually a little less sensitive to light than are negative films. They generally need about a half-stop more exposure than do comparable negative films.

The usual method (in the United States) of rating the sensitivity of film to light is the ASA number. The higher the number, the greater the film's sensitivity to light. A film rated at ASA 125 is exactly one-half as sensitive to light as one rated at ASA 250. The film manufacturer lists a recommended ASA speed. Laboratories often recommend an ASA speed for their "normal" processing which may differ from what the manufacturer suggests. You should use your laboratory's recommended speed in the absence of other information (such as results of tests done with the same raw stock at the same laboratory). Most laboratories will process your film at a different ASA value if so requested. They may charge extra for this service.

Changing the value from the recommended ASA causes changes in the film's graininess (which increases), its sharpness (which decreases), and its contrast (which becomes greater if the ASA is changed to higher, less if lower). ASA values are changed a) to increase film speed or to lower it, b) to change the contrast of a scene, c) to simulate a "documentary" look by increasing the amount of grain, and d) to compensate for a mistake in the shooting of the footage. In this last case, the mistake may be determined by a test of a portion of the footage. If a mistake was made in the type of raw stock used and it was discovered before processing but after shooting, the film might be saved in the lab by changing its ASA rating.

Forced processing

When film is *pushed* or *force-developed* to a higher ASA, it is left in a developer for a longer than normal period of time. This procedure increases the density of the film emulsion and proper exposure is achieved with less light.

Actually, not all the densities are increased by the same amount. The more exposed portions of the film increase in density at a greater rate than the less exposed portions when the film is pushed. This means that there will be a greater density difference between dark and light areas than if the film had not been pushed; the contrast has increased.

Contrary to a popular misconception, reversal films usually push better than negative films. Most reversal films can be pushed to double their normal sensitivity (one f/stop) with virtually no loss in quality and as much as two stops with what to some will be an acceptable loss in quality. Negative film, on the other hand, can rarely be pushed two stops and still be considered acceptable.

Color versus black and white

The other main choice that faces the filmmaker is color versus black and white. Sometimes the subject matter of the film dictates the answer to this question. A lyrical film about nature may demand color, whereas a documentary about coal miners may call for black and white. The other main consideration is cost. Color will double all the 16mm laboratory costs over those for black and white. This is not true of 8mm, where the costs are approximately the same.

If photography need be done under very low-light conditions, then black and white film may be necessary. The fastest color film in 16mm may be processed at ASA 500 (some labs will push it to ASA 750 and 1000, but quality suffers and the chance of getting back usable footage is very low). It is possible to get acceptable black and white footage at ASA 1200 or 1600.

In 8mm there are more serious limitations. The best color films are very slow (for example, Kodachrome II has an indoor speed of ASA 40).

With the increase in emulsion speeds and improved color rendition in currently available films, color film is much more practicable to use than ever before. The chief photographic limitation in the use of color film is its inherent contrastiness. It is much less able than even black and white reversal film to render satisfactorily a scene with great variation in subject brightness (for example, a scene that is part in sunlight and part in deep shade).

General comparisons of films and 8mm films

Although there is a color negative film available in 16mm, most people feel that it is too grainy. Furthermore, it is not easy to find laboratories that will process it for you. Recently, however, a new printing material has become available which will in all probability make 16mm negative color popular.

Kodachrome II is the most popular film for 8mm work. It is the sharpest and finest grain camera film (film made for the camera original) produced by Kodak. It has one great drawback (and hence its amateur status in 8mm and 16mm): it does not reproduce well. Kodachrome II is fairly contrasty, and when a print is made from it, there is a substantial increase in contrast, which results in a loss of detail in the highlights (a washing out of the light areas) and shadow (shadow detail in the original may reproduce as black in the print). There are often color shifts in the print. If you are planning to project your original and make no prints, Kodachrome II is the perfect color film in both 8mm and 16mm. However, if you are planning to make prints, you will have to cope with the loss of quality in printing Kodachrome II or look for another film. If you must make prints from Kodachrome II, you should avoid shooting in contrasty situations. By keeping the contrast in the subject down, the ultimate increase in contrast in the printed film will not be as troublesome.

In selecting a film, certain general rules should be remembered. The faster the film (the more sensitive it is to light), the grainier it is and the less sharp it is. The faster the film, usually the less contrast and more exposure latitude it has built into the emulsion. When the highest photographic quality is desired, the slowest film capable of photographing the scene at the desired f/stop should be chosen. For example, in super 8 Kodak offers two black and white reversal films: Plus-X Reversal and Tri-X Reversal. Plus-X, the slower of the two (ASA 50 in daylight), should be used when there is sufficient light. Of course, if for some special purpose you want to get more grain in the image or more depth of field, then you should use a faster film.

Kodak offers a high-speed color reversal film in super 8 cartridges, Kodak Ektachrome EF (Tungsten) SO-105. The film is rated at ASA 125 Tungsten (one and one-half stops faster than Kodachrome II). The film is much grainier and less sharp than Kodachrome II. It is similar to Kodak Ektachrome EF 7242 in 16mm. For a discussion of the characteristics of the film, read the sections about Ektachrome EF 7242 in 16mm below.

Since many super 8 cameras were made before Kodak announced the EF film, you may find that your camera will not take the new film, or else the automatic exposure system cannot handle the higher-speed film. The camera manufacturer should be consulted. He may offer a modification of the camera so that it can be used with EF at ASA 125.

16mm films

In 16mm black and white, when there is sufficient light and negative film is being shot, Eastman XT negative (Type 7220) with an ASA rating of 25 (now discontinued) or Eastman Plus-X Negative (Type 7231) at ASA 80 can be used. Double-X (Type 7222) is by far the best negative film for low-light conditions. Kodak rates the film at ASA 250, though it is not unusual to find labs which normally process Double-X at ASA 500. Eastman 4-X (Type 7224), ASA 500, is very grainy, and unlike Double-X, does not respond well to forced processing. I would rather push Double-X than have to shoot 4-X. Of course, all these considerations depend to a great extent on the lab you are using, and it would be a good idea to consult with them.

The slowest and finest grain Kodak 16mm reversal film is Kodak Plus-X Reversal (Type 7276) at ASA 50. The recently introduced Kodak 4-X Reversal (Type 7277) has an ASA of 400. The film is of very high quality for its high speed, and responds well to forced processing. Kodak TRI-X Reversal (Type 7278) has an ASA rating of 200. It is a very good film, since it is of fairly high speed, yet has an excellent gray scale and very little grain. Dupont offers several black and white films which are comparable to the Kodak films of the same film speed. Laboratories often use different developers, and results can differ greatly using the same raw stock at different laboratories.

The best 16mm color reversal film to use when prints are to be made and there is sufficient light is Eastman Ektachrome Commercial Film (Type 7252), which is sometimes called "ECO." The original is of low contrast and does not look good. However, prints made from it on suitable printing stock are of very high quality. The color is much less garish than that of Kodachrome, and I personally find it more pleasing. ECO original is not intended for projection. The emulsion is soft, and the original will scratch easily. The chief disadvantage of ECO is its slow speed (ASA 16 outdoors and ASA 25 at 3200°K). The new ECO, Type 7252 (replacing Type 7255), can be pushed one stop without a serious loss in quality.

Kodak Ektachrome MS, Type 7256, is a daylight balanced film that is faster than ECO with an ASA 64 in daylight. The film is of no higher quality than Ektachrome EF, which is even faster than MS. Kodak Ektachrome EF (which replaces the older ER film) comes in two forms: Type 7241 is balanced for daylight and has a speed of ASA 160. Type 7242 is balanced for 3200°K at ASA 125. Outdoors with a #85 filter, it is rated at ASA 80 (see Chapter IX). Both EF films are intended for direct projection. They have acceptable projection contrast and strong emulsions. These films also reproduce fairly well. Kodak is offering several acceptable companion printing stocks for them. EF films respond well to forced processing, and may be pushed two stops and still yield sufficient quality for many uses. When pushed three stops (to ASA 1000), the image may be acceptable for some uses but the results are much less dependable. A nighttime scene has a lot of black areas and so the deteriorated image may be acceptable. However, when reversal film is pushed a good deal, the blacks tend to become poor and muddy.

When you are shooting under artificial illumination, EF 7242 (tungsten) should be used. Though daylight film with a Kodak Wratten filter 80A can be used with 3200°K lamps, the filter cuts down the light by two f/stops and produces some loss in color quality. The tungsten film with a #85 filter is of equal quality to the daylight film used outdoors. EF tungsten is one stop slower than EF daylight outdoors, but you do not generally need the speed outdoors. A UV or skylight filter should be used with daylight film since the film is very sensitive to ultraviolet light, of which there is usually a lot outdoors. A #85 filter has a UV filter already built into it and so there is no need to use another one with tungsten film shot outdoors. Because EF tungsten is more adaptable, it should be used in preference to EF daylight, unless some use can be made of the additional stop that the daylight film affords outdoors.

It is not good practice to mix two different types of film originals in one scene unless some special effect is desired. No two films will reproduce a scene in the same way, and there will be a noticeable change of picture quality when you cut from one type of film to another. This change may well look as though the location has changed or there has been a time gap. When different scenes have been shot on different raw stock, the change is not as serious since the change is to be expected. Reversal film cannot be intercut with negative film unless one of them is reprinted to match the other in emulsion position (see p. 97).

In manufacturing raw stock there are differences between batches. (Kodak has the reputation for the greatest amount of consistency from batch to batch.) In black and white the differences are usually very slight. However, in color there are often easily noticeable differences from one batch to another. If one shot from a scene comes from a roll from one batch and a different shot in the same scene comes from another batch, the two shots may not match very well in quality. To avoid this it is a good idea to make sure that every scene is shot with film from the same batch or, even better, shoot the whole film from the same batch. On every roll of film there is an emulsion number which indicates the batch it is from.

Care of film

All photographic materials change in time. Color dyes, which fade, are the least stable. Kept under proper storage conditions, they can last a very long time. Raw stock, too, changes with time. Usually, the older the film, the less sensitive to light it becomes. There is often an increase in graininess, and with color films there is a shift in the color reproduction. Raw stock should be as fresh as possible. When the film has been shot, it should be processed as soon as possible. Long delays, especially in hot and humid climates, can lead to a considerable deterioration of the latent image. Film that comes in 100-foot rolls usually has an expiration date on the side of the box. What this date represents is a time when, under average conditions, film quality will begin to show noticeable deterioration. Professional length raw stock (e.g., 400 feet) usually has no expiration date and therefore should be purchased from the manufacturer or a reliable professional store. Incidentally, most Kodak and Eastman 16mm films can be purchased directly from the Eastman Kodak Regional Marketing and Distribution centers at the same price that dealers purchase the film. The Eastman Kodak center usually has in stock almost any film in any length, and the film will be fresh.

The two great enemies of film emulsions, especially color, are heat and humidity. If raw stock is stored at low temperature, its shelf-life will increase. If you wrap raw stock in a plastic bag and freeze it, you increase its storage-life by at least one year.

You may encounter opportunities to buy raw stock from an individual. Unless you have reason to know that it has not been improperly handled (stored on a radiator, for instance), it is a good idea to pass it up. Most footage you will shoot is not easily replaced and it is not worth taking a chance to save a little money on raw stock. Out-of-date film can be purchased at a reduced price. If you do not care about the loss of picture quality (less serious in black and white) and the film is only recently out of date, you might test some of the film to decide if you will use it. If you have a camera that takes 400 feet of film, you may have the opportunity to buy *short ends*. A short end is a length of film which is shorter than the original roll. If you shoot 250 feet of a 400-foot roll, you break the roll in two at the end of the day, send the exposed film off to the lab, and pack the unexposed film in a can and a bag labeled for a 150-foot short end. Short ends should only be purchased when you are absolutely sure of the reliability of the seller or when you are in a position to take chances. It is good to remember that raw stock constitutes less than one-third of the total cost of the raw stock-development-workprint expense.

VI. Filming

Editing and filming

It is important to understand the relationship between editing and filming. The editor is not going to be able to construct a film successfully from the footage shot unless adequate footage is returned from shooting. The editor will not be able to vary camera angle, achieve continuity, or give the film an acceptable pace unless the footage is adequate to the task. When the film is shot, the filmmaker must have an idea of what goes into the editing process so that he can know what to shoot and how to shoot it. Of course, this is more important for a narrative film than for an abstract film-poem which may be made almost totally in the editing.

Shooting ratios

The unedited footage is called *rushes* or *dailies*. Almost invariably there is a considerably greater amount of rushes than there is of final film. The ratio of film shot to final footage is usually between 5:1 and 10:1. But the ratio varies tremendously depending on the type of film being made and the method of filming. Peter Emmanuel Goldman's underground classic *Echoes of Silence* was done using a ratio of less than 2:1 for an hour-long film. At the other end of the spectrum, documentary filmmakers who use no script often shoot ratios higher than 40:1, which means shooting over 90,000 feet to end with an hour's length of film. Often one of the most difficult tasks in writing up a budget for a film is to estimate the amount of footage that will be needed.

When there is a script for a film, a great deal of additional footage is shot to give the editor a selection of shots and to guarantee that there will not be any continuity gaps either within scenes or in the story line. It is not unusual, when two possibilities for a story line exist, for *both* to be filmed and the final choice delayed until the film is being edited. Often the same action is filmed several times in several "takes" to get different camera angles (positions) and to guarantee that the actors have performed their task well.

When no script is being used, either because actors are improvising or because action is being filmed directly from life, much footage is simply wasted because the cameraman is unable to predict what will happen, and, more often than not, nothing interesting does happen.

Film time and film space

Film time and film space are very different from actual space and time, and it is important to understand how. Film time and space are created in the editing room. One of the most difficult concepts for the novice filmmaker is the realization that the sequence of events as they happen in real life or as they are acted out is not necessarily the way those events will appear on film. Take the case of a film that is acted from a script. There is a tendency for the novice to shoot the events to be filmed in the order that they will be edited, but this may be unnecessarily inefficient. Scenes to be shot at the same locale and scenes using the same actors should be shot close to one another in time, though they may be far apart in the final film. Similarly in the space that a film creates, one person may appear to be looking at another, though the two people were not filmed in the same place or at the same time. (See Chapter XI)

People speak of "editing in the camera," by which they mean shooting scenes in the order that they will appear in the final film and shooting only one take of each action. The final film is the same as the rushes. This method eliminates the need for editing. Its drawbacks are so great, however, that the method is only adequate for home movies, or films which rely on a home-movie style. The filmmaker is giving up all the tremendous control he exercises in the editing room. Bad takes, continuity gaps, technically deficient footage, become part of the film. Many cameras may expose a frame or two (called *flash frames*) as the camera comes to a stop. These must be edited out to avoid an annoying flash between shots.

Continuity shooting

If the type of film you are making demands continuity of action within scenes, that is, the action is to look as though it occurred in a continuous time period, various precautions must be exercised in shooting to guarantee the editor footage adequate to the editing of such scenes. Whenever the editor has to make a cut within the scene, he has to have two shots which match, that give the illusion that no time has passed between them. When one take ends and the next begins with a different camera angle or a lens of different focal length, and the action involves the same actor, there must be what is called an overlap of action. That is, whatever action was performed toward the end of the first take must be repeated at the beginning of the next take. This will allow the editor a choice as to what point to cut. It guarantees that there will be no gap in the action, no discontinuity. For example, if in the first take the actor strikes a match and lights his cigarette and in the second shot we want a close-up of him puffing, we will take the first shot through his puff. The next take (using another cigarette) might start just before the puff and continue through it. The overlap of action gives the editor some freedom and guarantees continuity.

It should be obvious that details and continuity of actions must match from shot to shot to allow for continuity editing. Positions should be the same, cigarettes should not be longer in shots appearing later in a sequence, neckties should not change color in mid-scene, hand positions should not jump unexpectedly from one shot to its successor, and so forth. In Hollywood filming there is a script girl whose special function it is to make sure that such disconcerting changes do not occur within scenes.

When the rushes are not adequate to bring off some piece of continuity, the editor needs a *cut-away,* a shot not in the main action. A cut-away could be someone reacting to the main action or perhaps an important object. The rushes should contain enough cut-aways to get the editor over such humps, above all when the footage cannot be reshot.

In general, all the camera angles should stay on the same side of the action to avoid disconcerting changes of position (see p. 121). When camera angles or focal length are changed for successive shots, the changes should not be so radical as to be disorienting nor so minor as to be meaningless, unless you have some special motivation. Camera movements should have meaning, either to follow action, direct attention, or the like. Camera movements should not be used because you are bored with shooting in one position. Every camera movement primes the audience for additional information and this should be taken into account. Any improper camera movement, like an uneven pan or slight zoom made by error, should be reason enough to film the shot again.

Camera supports

The camera is either hand-held or it is placed on a support such as a tripod or clamped to something, like a car seat.

Hand-held shooting, no matter how steady, causes jiggles and bounces which show up noticeably on the screen and make the film much more difficult to look at. There are two reasons for not using some sort of camera support like a tripod to yield a steady picture. The first is that the situation may require a hand-held camera. This could be because quarters are too cramped for a camera support or, more commonly, the portability and speed of the hand-held camera is needed. When a tripod or other support is used, camera set-ups take time. Camera position cannot be changed quickly. The great need for the hand-held camera arises in documentary work where action is unpredictable and the cameraman must move quickly. His equipment must be easily portable so he can follow action.

Another reason to use a hand-held camera is to achieve a special effect. The hand-held camera can be used to heighten the sensation of action (as in close-ups of a fight scene), to simulate the point of view of the subject (as when the cameraman walks down a street while filming), or to approximate the documentary or newsreel style.

Hand-held shooting has become one of the mannerisms of the American underground filmmaker. Most of the underground footage shot could have been made using a tripod, but the advantage of a steady image is sacrificed to the ease of shooting, giving the filmmakers what they consider a greater chance to be spontaneous.

Unless some specific effect is desired, it is undesirable to intercut hand-held and tripod shooting in the same scene. The two types of shooting can be intercut when the viewpoint is supposed to change from objective to subjective.

When footage is shot hand-held with a heavy camera, a body brace may be used. (See Plate 11) The brace distributes the weight of the machine over the cameraman's body and helps to steady the camera. A heavy camera used with a brace often yields steadier footage than can be gotten from a light hand-held camera. Similarly, cameras that rest on the shoulder usually give steadier images than the lighter cameras which use pistol grips. (See Plates 15, 16) Body braces have the disadvantage of encumbering the cameraman's movements and making him more noticeable, which is of some concern in documentary work.

The wider the angle of the lens, the less hand movement shows. Consequently, if you wish to minimize camera jiggles and bounces caused by hand movement, you should shoot at the widest possible angle. It is better to move in closer and use a wider angle as far as camera steadiness is concerned.

Shots of stationary objects can be particularly annoying when shot hand-held since there is no motion in the subject to distract the eye from hand movement. Conversely, when there is a lot of subject motion, as in a crowd scene, the use of a hand-held camera is likely to be unnoticeable on the screen. When a subject is shot close-up and the background is completely out of focus, an effect easily achieved with a long lens, there are no stationary objects for hand motion to be compared with and camera movement will not be too obvious.

When filming a walking person with the camera hand-held, the cameraman should match his steps to the subject's to effect a smooth shot. The camera can be held in its normal position or cradled in his arms while he walks next to the subject, pointing the camera up at the subject and using an extremely wide-angle focal length to ensure that he stays within the frame.

If the cameraman can sit while hand-holding his camera as it rests against him, his results may be quite steady. There are several types of clamps available, made so that the camera can be clamped to poles, cars, door frames, or most any steady base. Clamps can be used as a means of steadying the camera without the use of a bulky tripod. They are often used when shooting in an automobile. If the camera is attached to any part of the automobile, the automobile shock absorbers will take most of the bumps and the pictures will be steady. If you are shooting people traveling in the car, the camera will move in relation to them and they will appear steady on the film, although the background will jump as the car moves along.

Monopods are single poles that go from the camera to the ground. They are useful for steadying footage that would otherwise have to be shot hand-held.

The most common camera support used in non-Hollywood productions is the tripod. (See Plate 30) With a tripod it is easier to achieve smooth zooms, pans, and tilts. The cameraman can compose and set up his shots easily. The tripod can be used almost anywhere except in the most cramped quarters or in cases when a moving camera is required.

A tripod, which is subjected to great wear and tear, should be well made to take punishment. It should have a pan-and-tilt head operated by a handle or crank. A *pan* is a horizontal movement of the camera across the subject and a *tilt* is the corresponding vertical movement. Tripods made for still-camera work usually have pan-and-tilt heads, but they do not allow you to perform these motions smoothly. Any uneven movement in a pan or tilt will show up markedly on the screen. Some friction-heads available for motion picture work can be panned smoothly with practice. Silicone-dampened heads are easier to pan smoothly but they are expensive (around $200). Tripod heads of the more professional brands can be purchased separately from the legs. In any case, it is important that the tripod be strong enough and sturdy enough to support the weight of your camera. Professional models are usually rated by the maximum weight of the camera they can support. With 8mm cameras and the smaller 16mm cameras there is no weight problem, but care should be taken to purchase a very sturdy tripod.

The longer the panning handle, the easier it is to execute smooth pans. A telescopic handle has the advantage of folding up compactly when used in cramped quarters. You should make sure the camera balances well on the tripod and has no tendency to fall over. The pan-and-tilt devices should have locks so that when a static shot is desired, the camera will stay in position.

The tripod should be steady when the legs are fully extended. Some tripods have a center pole for additional height. This may unsteady the camera a bit when extended. If the tripod head is detachable, a *baby tripod* with shorter legs can be used for lower angles. A *hi-hat* is a device that accepts a pan-and-tilt head so that the camera can be used a few inches off the ground. (See Plate 31)

The best type of head is a *floating head*. The whole head can be moved in any direction so that the camera can easily be leveled (placed on a horizontal). Spirit levels are an aid in making certain the camera is properly leveled and the horizon line will not be lopsided when filmed. If your tripod head is not the floating type, you will have to adjust its legs until the camera levels properly. With a floating head, you just rock the head until it is in the right position.

A *spider* is a gadget used for preventing tripod legs from slipping on smooth surfaces. Three pieces of metal radiate from a central point, with a place for the end of each of the three tripod legs to fit. (See Plate 30) The metal pieces are extendable in case you wish to spread the tripod legs farther. A *triangle* is a similar device, but here the three pieces are in a triangular shape with a socket for a tripod leg at each corner. The disadvantage of a triangle is that the spread of the legs is not adjustable. However, wheels can be placed under the triangle to facilitate shooting smoothly with a moving camera and to make it easier to move the tripod and camera between shots to other positions. The wheels should have a provision for locking them in position.

Pans and tilts

Panning and tilting must be executed with great care. It is better to think of an alternative to the pan unless you have the proper skill and equipment. Jerky pans and pans with stroboscopic movement (see p. 26) are visually annoying. Pans must be made very slowly to avoid stroboscopic movement, and because of this pans can destroy the pacing of a film. *Swish pans* are very rapid movements of the camera from one position to another: the camera is moved so quickly that the intermediary positions are blurred. Swish pans are easier to execute than normal pans, but are more limited in use. They can often be used to describe subjectively a person's looking from one object to another or to effect a sudden change of locale.

The moving camera

The moving camera, the use of which is closely associated with the German Expressionist directors of the 1920's, is one of the most expressive tools that the filmmaker has at his disposal. When the camera itself moves through the subject, depth and fluidity are imparted to the shot. The cameraman walking with his hand-held camera or shooting from a moving vehicle are common examples of the moving camera. Steady moving camera shots often require special equipment. Most Hollywood shooting is done using large "crab dollies" and cranes, equipment that is extremely expensive. Simple dollies can be improvised to give adequate results. A *dolly* is any vehicle upon which a camera can be mounted and wheeled about during a take. A small coaster wagon or a wheelchair can be used for dollying. Air-inflated rubber tires not quite full give the smoothest results whether on a car, under a triangle, or on a wheelchair. If the subject-to-camera distance changes as you dolly, you must refocus (*follow-focus*) as the take proceeds. Sometimes an additional assistant is required for this purpose.

Zooming

It is possible to achieve an effect similar to dollying with a zoom lens. As noted in the section on lenses, perspective changes as subject-to-camera distance changes. On dolly shots perspective will change as we move in or out from the subject. But as we zoom in or out from our subject, perspective is the same since we are not changing camera-to-subject distance. When we dolly in to the subject, objects pass by the camera, giving a feeling of depth. When we zoom, the sensation is two-dimensional, much like coming closer to a still photograph. This feeling can be relieved somewhat by panning while making a zoom. The chief aesthetic objection to the zoom is that it does not give a feeling of depth.

Because freedom of camera movement is restricted in many types of documentaries, the zoom becomes one of the few tools the documentary cameraman has at his disposal to change viewpoint and direct audience attention. Films acted from a script often use the zoom to simulate a documentary look. In Shirley Clarke's *The Cool World* and Cassavetes' *Faces*, both the hand-held camera and the zoom were used for this effect, while in the Canadian film *Nobody Waved Goodbye* the camera was often tripod-mounted, but the zoom was used to heighten the impression of documentary style.

Cutting from a camera movement

One of the standards of camera technique is beginning and ending all pan shots, dolly shots, and zooms with a static camera. Sometimes exception is made for tracking shots where the camera is moving across the subject in a line parallel to it. Sometimes a dissolve is used to join one movement to another. However, many editors prefer to have a pan start from a static shot and end on a static shot. Like all rules, it is sometimes desirable to violate this one.

Panning to simulate a moving camera

The illusion of a camera moving parallel to a subject in motion can often be achieved with the help of a very long lens. If a walking subject, for example, is shot with a long lens, the camera mounted on a tripod following the subject, the illusion is produced that the camera is moving parallel to the subject rather than just rotating at a point to follow it. If there is a background whose relation to the subject can be judged by the viewer, the effect is diminished. For example, if the person is walking by store windows, and we are shooting from the other side of the street, the illusion of a moving camera will only occur for the time that the lens is approximately perpendicular to the wall. The longer the focal length of the lens, the longer the illusion can be maintained. The effect can last from a second to much longer depending on the focal length. When there is a nonspecific background such as sky, the illusion can be kept up for a very great length of time.

Actual vehicle speed versus its appearance on film

When you shoot from a moving vehicle at right angles to the direction of the vehicle, the vehicle speed will appear to be about twice as fast on film as it is actually moving. When you shoot in the same direction the vehicle is moving, speed appears normal. At intermediate angles, the speed is somewhere between the two. As should be clear from the discussion of perspective, wide-angle lenses will make the vehicle movement seem faster than will longer lenses. Lens focal length, the angle of shooting from the moving vehicle, and the speed the vehicle is actually moving at must all be taken into account in determining how fast the vehicle will appear to move in the film itself.

Filming at higher than normal speeds will smooth the bumps in the vehicle's movement and will make the vehicle appear to travel at a proportionately slower speed. If we film at twice sound speed, 48 fps, the vehicle will appear to travel at one-half its normally filmed speed. If we film from a car head-on at 30 mph and 48 fps, the vehicle will appear to travel at 15 mph in the film. If we film at right angles to the car traveling 30 mph (which would normally appear to be 60 mph on the screen) and film at twice normal speed, the result will look like 30 mph on the screen. Of course you cannot change camera speed very much if there are people moving in the scene, for their movements will look unnaturally fast or slow.

When you are shooting from a fast-moving vehicle, it is important to avoid the stroboscopic effect known as skipping (already discussed in relation to pans and on p. 26). The effect is most noticeable when you film at right angles to the subject, especially when the subject has strong vertical lines such as are encountered in buildings. If you must film at a right angle from a fast-moving vehicle, you should attempt to drive the vehicle as slowly as possible, not much faster than a quick walking speed.

Focusing and framing

Make sure the diopter, or eyepiece, on the viewfinder is set for your eye if yours is a reflex camera and has a diopter adjustment (see p. 21).

In shooting close-ups of people, the practice is to focus on eyes. Normally the eyes should be in sharpest focus unless some special effect is desired.

When two objects are in different planes of focus, to achieve maximum sharpness using the available depth of field you should focus on a point between them, but *not* the midpoint. The point should be one-third the distance behind the closer object, and two-thirds the distance in front of the farther object. Consult the depth of field charts in Appendix C to be sure both objects are within your available depth of field, or both objects may be equally out of focus and your footage ruined.

With a reflex camera, you should always focus with the lens wide open, at its maximum aperture, and in the case of zoom lenses, at the longest focal length (see p. 43). After focusing, the lens should be stopped down to the selected f/stop and zoomed back to the selected focal length. With a reflex camera the image should be moved in and out of focus to find the sharpest focus. Moving the lens to a point where the subject appears sharp is not always sufficient. Though sharp on the ground glass, it may be fuzzy when projected. If you turn past the point of best focus and then back to it, your subject will more likely be in proper focus.

If the camera or the subject moves during the shot, the camera may have to be refocused during the take. The procedure is termed follow-focus. If possible, the shot should be mapped out beforehand with a rehearsal. It is best that an assistant make the varying focus adjustments at certain cued places—for instance when an actor reaches a point marked on the floor. The assistant can stand by the lens and change the focus ring to preselected points.

Great skill is required for impromptu follow-focusing. A safer alternative is to use a wider angle lens to obtain greater depth of field. Sometimes we can zoom back to a wider angle in the middle of a shot to ensure adequate depth of field.

Focusing is sometimes done with a tape measure. The distance between the film plane (where the film rests as it is exposed) and the subject is measured, and then the focus ring is set to that measurement. Some cameras have the exact position of the film plane marked on the camera body. It is important to measure from the film plane and not from the front of the lens. On close-ups the difference can be significant.

If the camera is not a reflex type, it is important to remember to correct for parallax when you are shooting close to the subject or using a long lens (see p. 19).

You should compose each shot carefully, keeping in mind what will be the adjacent shots in the final film. When camera angle is changed for successive shots, focal length should be changed so that when the two shots are cut an actor is not skipped from one part of the screen to another.

Composition should be natural in effect. If a man is walking and the camera following, there should be more space on the side of the frame in the direction he is moving. This is termed *leading* the action. Horizon lines should usually be photographed with their horizontal lines parallel to the horizontal frame line. A lopsided shot is said to be *canted*.

When the camera is shooting up or down at the subject, vertical lines in the subject will converge. This is particularly noticeable with architecture. If we shoot up at a tall building, the convergence of the parallel verticals will increase the sensation of height. If we shoot up at the building at a slight angle, convergence becomes very disturbing. The building will look as though it is tottering and about to fall. Unless you choose to film an establishing shot of a building at a radical angle, it is best to place the camera at such a height that it will not require tilting to frame the entire structure.

To enhance three-dimensionality and the perception of depth, as many sides of an object should be shown as possible. Head-on we see one side, from an angle we see two, and looking down we can see three sides. The more we see, the better we are convinced of depth and solidity.

Shots with unusual viewpoints, looking straight down on the subject, should be carefully justified according to the content and imagery of the film, not used arbitrarily.

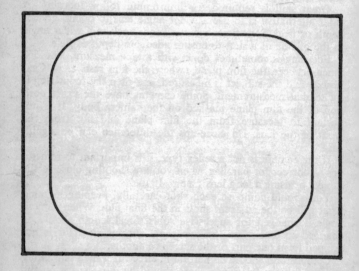

Fig. VI. *Television cutoff:* The inside line approximates the amount of picture received on the average home television set. This area is called the *safe action area.* If the film is to be shown on television, all composing of pictures should take into account that this is the image that will be seen by the home viewer. Titles should have an even greater safety margin (the *safe title area*).

It is fruitless to discuss the fine points of composition. In the end, the filmmaker's vision should be personal and ultimately developed through practice and not by an adherence to any set of rules or description of someone else's visual formulas. He will come to understand how he must use his camera to attain his end in visual terms.

When you are shooting for television, you must exercise special care in framing a shot. Although *nearly* all of the image is transmitted to the home television receiver, a small area along the outer edge of the frame is cut off from the television viewer. Professional cameras can be ordered with a viewing system that marks approximately the amount of cutoff you can expect when the film is viewed on television. (See Fig. VI) Important subject matter, therefore, cannot be framed to the edge of the picture, but must be placed a little bit farther into the frame.

Field work

It is important to keep all parts of the camera clean. Before doing any large amount of filming, you should test the camera to see that it does not scratch film, that it delivers a sharp and steady picture, has no light leaks, and is in good general working condition.

Rain should be wiped from the camera with a cloth, and water drops on the lens should be wiped off carefully with photographic lens tissue (see p. 45). Any points where emulsion from the film can build up should be checked as often as possible and cleaned when necessary. In particular, the aperture and pressure plate should be cleaned frequently. Any dirt in the film gate can cause scratches and cause dust to show up on the outside edge of the picture. The film gate should be checked after each roll is shot. Many professionals check the film gate after every take. With some cameras, special care must be taken not to damage the shutter, which must be moved out of the way.

No strange noises should emanate from the camera; they indicate malfunction. Perhaps the film is simply improperly loaded or, much more serious, the shutter is damaged. If the camera is not correctly loaded, the loops may not have been properly adjusted. All films that are not pre-loaded in the magazine by the manufacturer must have a loop at the point before the film enters the film gate and after it leaves the gate as well. (See Fig. VII) If the loops are not properly adjusted, you may get a fuzzy image, scratched film, jammed film, or the film may chatter, or any number of combinations of problems.

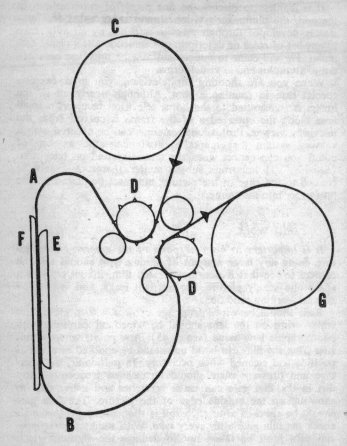

Fig. VII. *Typical threading diagram* (Arriflex S): If the camera is loaded spool to spool, care must be taken to make sure it is properly threaded and, in particular, that the loops are properly adjusted. The upper loop (*A*) and the lower loop (*B*) should be approximately the same size. When the film is run, the loops should not be so large that the film touches some nonmoving part of the camera, nor should they be so small that the film is strained when running. The film travels from the feed spool (*C*) over the sprocket wheel (*D*) into the film gate, which consists of the pressure plate (*E*) and the aperture plate (*F*). The film then goes through another sprocket wheel (*D*) and onto the take-up spool (*G*). Different cameras have different threading diagrams.

Avoid light leaks. All covers should be tight fitting. If you have doubts about the camera's light-tightness and you must shoot, you can tape the camera lid to keep light out. Daylight-loaded film should be loaded in subdued light. You must expect to lose a few feet of film at the head and the tail of the roll as the film fogs unless you load and unload the film in a changing bag.

A *changing bag* is a double-lined, double-zippered bag that has two tight-fitting sleeves for your arms. It is, in effect, a portable darkroom. (See Plate 32) Film and camera are put in one end, the bag zippered to keep out light, and your hands go through the sleeves. Any work in the field that requires total darkness can be done in the changing bag. It is worth buying a good-quality bag that is a bit larger than the minimum possible size for your equipment. It should be checked fairly often for light leaks and it should be kept free from lint inside since lint can stick to the film, get caught in the aperture, and show up on the developed image.

Excessive heat and moisture are very bad for film and equipment. Above all, keep your film and light meters outside of automobile glove compartments and trunks, for these become ovens under sunlight.

After the film is loaded, a few feet should be run off to see if it is running properly. If it is possible with your camera, leave the lid off to see if the film is taking up properly, if the take-up or feed spool is bent, and if the loop adjustments are proper. With 100-foot 16mm daylight loads there are punched numbers on several consecutive frames about six feet into the roll, and at least six feet of the film must be run through to avoid having perforations show up in the middle of a shot. The last few feet of film may be damaged by lab handling. To be safe these last few feet should be counted as unusable.

If the film is loaded in a cartridge or manufacturer-loaded magazine, the cartridge should fit into the camera easily without being forced.

If the camera *jams*, if the footage stops running because it is not being taken up on the spool properly, it should be repaired at once. In non-cartridge cameras, if the jamming occurs before footage has been shot, tear off the waste *leader* (the footage used for threading the camera) and start again. If it still jams, check to see if the loops are properly adjusted, the film path clean, none of the reels bent, and that the take-up reel is turning. If the film jams after footage has been shot, you can split the roll at that point, preferably in a changing bag so as not to lose more footage. When you split a daylight roll you need a spare take-up spool and can. With darkroom loads, you need an extra core and can with black bag. If you do not split the film and can get the camera running again, but with the possibility that the film is damaged, it is imperative that the lab be informed at approximately what point in the roll the camera jam occurred. Otherwise the film may jam or break in the developer and ruin not only the footage on that roll but on other rolls loaded in the developer after the defective roll.

When a super 8 movie cartridge jams, there is no way to repair it so that the rest of the film on the cartridge can be shot. If a cartridge jams, check the polarities of the camera batteries. Improperly installed batteries will cause some cameras to run in reverse, causing a cartridge jam. When a cartridge jams it is usually a case of camera malfunction rather than the result of a defective cartridge.

Especially with high-speed films used in cold weather, static electricity marks may show up on the film. The marks are light on positive and dark on negative film and vary in shape and pattern, most commonly appearing as jagged lines in a brush pattern. Antistatic solutions used in the film gate will cut down the likelihood of static electricity discharging on film. Another preventative measure is to ground the camera by running a wire from a point on the camera to a ground.

Before shooting, it is wise to make a checklist of all the equipment needed. As many spares as possible should be on hand. All equipment should be placed in a bag or case when doing field shooting. Delicate equipment should have sturdy casing to protect it adequately under field conditions.

Assistants

A Hollywood film often involves more than a hundred people on the production end. Many an underground film has but one person—the filmmaker. He must be jack-of-all-trades. He raises money for the filming (producer), he writes the script (scriptwriter), shoots the film (cameraman), directs the action (director), records the sound (soundman), carries the equipment (grip), lights the set (lighting technician), edits the film (editor)—to list only his major responsibilities. The question may arise: If or when does he need assistants?

In making dramatic or even improvised films, the filmmaker is at great advantage if he does not actually operate the camera. He can still set up and compose every shot, but leave the shooting to an assistant. If he must pay a great deal of attention to camera operation as well as concern himself with the directing of actors, he is severely hindered. If he must change film, set up lights, and carry equipment, his concentration will almost certainly be splintered and valuable time lost.

In documentary sound shooting, where speed is of the essence, an assistant to change film is especially useful. If sound is being recorded with the action, a soundman is simply essential. During impromptu shooting, the filmmaker should be involved directly as one of the shooting crew. In general, when the people filmed are not acting but just living out their lives, the camera crew must be as unobtrusive as possible. If it's feasible, only the cameraman and soundman should be present.

The film should be edited by the filmmaker, or at least editing should be supervised by him. The importance of editing varies according to the type of film being made. But even a film with a well-worked-out script requires intelligent editing.

When creative decisions are spread among too many people, the film's integrity of conception may be lost. An individual, or several collaborating, will work out a purer and stronger film when they control as many aspects of the film as possible. To the filmmaker it is worth making sacrifices in photographic quality, lighting, and other technical factors to achieve greater control over the film.

Image sharpness

Sharpness is the partly objective and partly subjective measurement of the film image's ability to render detail to the viewer. Resolution or resolving power is an objective measurement of the ability to separate fine details. Resolution charts when photographed give an idea of the resolving power of the lens and the film (i.e., how many lines are distinguishable in a millimeter with the equipment and film used). Such charts may be purchased from most camera dealers.

Image sharpness is controlled by many factors, and it is helpful to trace the film through its various stages to see how image sharpness is affected at each stage.

The film gauge affects sharpness. The larger the film format, the more detail can be recorded on a frame and, consequently, the sharper the image. Because super 8 has a larger area than regular 8, it is the sharper of the two.

Lens quality affects sharpness to a great degree. Lenses differ greatly in their ability to give a sharp image. Zoom lenses often render a sharper image at some focal lengths than at others. Lenses render an image sharper in the center than at the edges. Zoom lenses are generally not as sharp as lenses of fixed focal length. The sharpest results possible are obtained with fixed focal length lenses of very high quality.

There is an f/stop or range of f/stops at which any lens is sharpest. It is usually two or three stops from the maximum aperture. A lens is usually least sharp wide-open or stopped down to its smallest aperture. As noted earlier, though depth of field is greatest when the lens is stopped all the way down, sharpness is lost at the plane of critical focus. This effect is greater the wider the angle of the lens.

Sharpness is reduced if the lens is dirty. A lens should be black inside its barrel. If paint begins to flake inside the lens, it should be repaired at once by an expert. Flare inside the lens deteriorates image sharpness. The deepest available lens shade should be used to cut down flare. If the shade does not keep all stray light off the lens, a hand or card should be used to shade the lens. Backlighting will cause more flare than front or side lighting.

The lens must be properly mounted on the camera to obtain sharp images. Zoom lenses and wide-angle lenses have much less tolerance for improper mounting and must be watched carefully for signs of looseness or poor fit.

The camera must expose the film while the film is completely stopped and must hold the film flat during exposure to achieve a sharp image. If the film is not at rest during exposure, that is, if the pull-down mechanism and shutter are not properly synchronized, the image will be blurred. If the pressure plate is not working properly or if it is removed, the image will go in and out of focus. Some cameras are better designed than others and are capable of delivering a sharper image. Cameras with pilot-pin registration usually give sharper and steadier images.

The camera must be in focus to deliver a sharp image. Any parts of the subject outside the plane of critical focus will be less sharp. The smaller the f/stop or the wider the angle of the lens used the greater the depth of field will be and the sharper those parts of the subject outside the plane of critical focus will appear.

Hand-held shooting will return a less-sharp image than tripod shooting. Moreover, a sturdy tripod will deliver a sharper image than a shaky tripod.

The quality of the lighting affects sharpness. The sharper the shadows, the sharper the image appears. Sunlight yields a sharper image than overcast light.

Proper exposure leads to the sharpest image. Underexposure and overexposure lead to grainier and softer images. If the subject has a good contrast range going from a rich black to bright highlights, the image will appear to be sharper. Good color contrast also yields what appears to be a sharper image.

Film raw stock has a built-in resolution and graininess which affects sharpness. Generally, the faster the film, the less sharp it is. Other things being equal, it is better to use a slow film, and thereby gain the advantages of finer grain and increased sharpness, than a fast film.

Certain films rated at the same speed have different resolution and grain characteristics: for example, reversal film is inherently sharper than negative film of the same speed.

Copies are always less sharp than the original. Copies of copies are inevitably even less sharp.

Processing at the recommended speed yields the sharpest result. Forced processing (pushing the film to a higher ASA in the lab) will lower image sharpness and increase grain.

Laboratories vary. Some sacrifice image sharpness to increase film speed as a matter of course.

The projection system must be as good as the camera system to project an image as good as that which the camera has recorded. Most projectors are of considerably lower quality than the camera used to record the scene. A projector lens may cost only $15, yet it is called upon to project an image obtained with a lens costing several hundred dollars. Image sharpness suffers. The projected image will look sharper if the light being sent through the film is strong, the viewing room is dark, and the image being projected is small. The normal viewing range for projection is between two and six times the width of the screen.

In general:

When you are filming you should constantly check your footage to make sure no camera problems have arisen. Lenses must sometimes be recalibrated. If your footage is consistently out of focus, have the lens checked by an expert repairman. Dirt in the camera can cause scratches on the film and may appear on the edge of the projected image.

Cameras must eventually be overhauled. They should be sent to the factory or dealer for an overhaul every few years, depending on the manufacturer's suggestion. If they develop strange noises or break down often, they should be sent in for an overhaul.

It is a good idea to check your light meter once in a while. You can check it against another light meter of the same make.

It is essential that you load the camera properly, never using a bent spool. The loops must be properly set. If the loops are too small, the image will bounce and the camera may chatter. If the loops are too large, the film may rub against the camera body and get scratched. You should check the size of your loops by running the camera slowly with its lid removed. With cartridge-loading cameras you do not have to worry about properly adjusted loops. When using 100-foot loads, do not forget to run off enough footage to get past the punched numbers on the film. This guarantees that you will not be shooting with film that was fogged during loading.

Make sure that all footage is properly marked with a roll number, name of production, type of film, and what ASA speed it was exposed at.

If you are planning to use the film commercially, it is a good idea to obtain legal releases from all performers. A lawyer can draw up a release form for you. Releases are necessary for films used for advertising. On the other hand, as you move over toward public affairs or newsworthy events, the need for releases becomes less clear. When filming adults who know what you are doing, there may be a notion of tacit consent even if they have not specifically given you permission to film. In any case, the whole legal problem is unclear. If you feel you may be sued for any reason, or if there is a significant amount of cost involved in the production, it is worthwhile to consult a lawyer. You should realize that lawyers tend to be conservative in their opinions, and filmmakers often have to stray beyond current legal opinion to achieve what they are after.

VII. Lighting

Lighting is usually considered the responsibility of the cameraman. The amount and kind of light available decide what type of raw stock can be used and what the depth of field will be. As in still photography, the distribution of light and how it models the subject is the main pictorial element other than composition.

Key light

The *key light* is the main light illuminating the subject. It is usually placed close to the camera or to the side of the subject. This is the light which most often determines what f/stop is to be used. If the key light is placed high enough, people being filmed will not squint and shadows will be lower and not particularly bothersome. If the key light is a spotlight (a light with a concentrated beam) shadows will be distinct and the subject strongly modeled. If the key light is a flood, hence more diffuse, illumination will be flat, possibly unflatteringly so, but will produce a more documentary appearance.

The key light should remain consistent throughout a scene and should approximate the quality and direction of the light which seemingly illuminates the scene, be it a lamp, sunlight, window light, or a fire. Varying other lights when cutting from, say, a close-up to a long shot is much less noticeable than varying the key light.

Fill light

The *fill light* is a light generally placed near the camera, on the side opposite the key light, to lighten shadows cast by the key light, or to make them disappear. The fill is used to minimize skin texture and wrinkles.

Lighting ratio

Manufacturers usually recommend a lighting ratio for each of their raw stocks. The ratio represents the relative amount of light from fill light to key light. For example, Kodak recommends a lighting ratio (fill to key) of 1:2 or 1:3 for its color films, and instructs that it ought never exceed 1:4 unless special effects are desired. A 1:2 ratio indicates that the key light is one f/stop brighter on the subject than the fill light, a 1:3 ratio indicates a stop and a half difference, and with a 1:4 ratio there is a difference of two stops. The most accurate way to determine the lights' relative strengths is to measure each light alone. Outside you can measure separately the side of the subject reflecting the greatest amount of light and the shadow area. When sunlight is available it serves as the key light, and reflections from the sky and ground serve as fill.

The importance of the lighting ratio is that each film is able to accommodate only a certain range of subject brightness. Once the exposure has been determined, any object too bright for that exposure will show as white in the positive print, and any object too dark for that exposure will show as black in the positive print. The subject brightness range is basically the number of f/stops that represent the difference between the darkest object and the lightest object in the subject as determined by a reflected-light reading. If part of the subject is outside the brightness range that the particular film can accommodate, it will appear underexposed if it is darker, and overexposed if it is lighter.

The less the inherent contrast of a film, the greater the range of subject brightness it can accommodate. Since color film is contrastier than black and white, it can accommodate a smaller brightness range. For color films the brightness range should not exceed four stops. (If we measure the darkest object that is to show some detail and similarly the lightest object, there should be no more than four stops difference between them. If there is, the color film will not successfully reproduce the scene.) Black and white film can accommodate a range of five or six stops difference from the brightest to the darkest significant object in the scene. When the lighting ratio is within the manufacturer's recommendations, the film will accommodate the brightness range of average subjects in the scene with that illumination.

Back light

The *back light* is usually a very bright spotlight placed behind the subject which casts a rim of light outlining the subject. (See Fig. VIII) It is useful for creating a feeling of depth, since it helps to separate the subject from the background. Backlighting, especially when emphasized, gives a theatrical feel to the image. Unless its source is natural, it should be avoided if you wish a realistic feel to the image. In general, documentary-flavor lighting tends to be very flat (that is, a very low fill to key ratio).

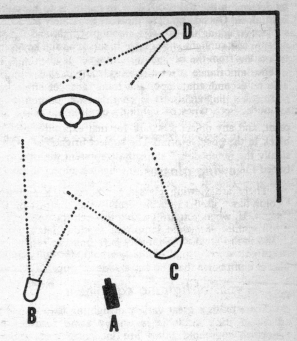

Fig. VIII. *Simple three-light setup:* A spotlight (*B*) which serves as the key light and a flood light (*C*) which serves as the fill light are set up near the camera (*A*). The back light (*D*), usually a spot, is used to separate the actor from the background and to give an edge light.

Types of lighting

There are often other kinds of lights—some to fill in un-wanted shadows, some to illuminate particular objects, some to burn out shadows, etc.

Light is identified by its relationship to the camera. *Front light* is any light from the camera position or from the front of the set to the subject. An extreme form of front lighting is front axial lighting. If the light is a spotlight and quite close to the lens, the camera will see precisely those areas which the light illuminates. The lighting will be very flat, but rounded objects will have a sharp shadow at the edge (termed a *contour shadow*). To emphasize the effect use a longer focal length lens so that the spot can get closer to the lens axis. *Side light* and *top light* come from the side and top of the subject respectively.

When most of the set is in shadow and just a few high-lights define the subject, the lighting is known as *low key*. Low-key lighting is characteristically used to heighten suspense and create a somber mood. *High-key* lighting has few shadows and the important tones are rendered in middle grays and highlights. It is characteristic of comic and light moods. Both types of lighting permit some black and some white areas. Every well-exposed and well-lighted image will possess tones going from black to white unless a special effect is desired.

Viewing glasses

There are viewing glasses for both black and white and color films, used to check visually the contrast of a lighting setup. If, when you are looking through the appropriate glass, you cannot see some important shadow detail, the lighting ratio is too great. One remedy is to increase brightness of the fill light or lower that of the key light. In the latter case, you would, of course, have to use a wider f/stop.

Types of lighting equipment

There exists a great variety of lighting fixtures and mounts. Basic lighting available is usually some form of tungsten. Normal household bulbs are inefficient and generally too weak to be of much use. If the situation demands using household fixtures, higher-wattage bulbs should be substituted for normal ones. Be careful not to overload the circuit. (Household incandescent bulbs will not yield the proper light for color filming. See Chapter IX.) Most household circuit fuses are rated between 15 and 30 amps.

It is easy to estimate the amount of amperage you require. All lights have their wattage marked on them. Household line voltage usually varies in the United States between 110 and 120 volts. The equation is:

$$\text{Amperage} = \frac{\text{Watts}}{\text{Voltage}}$$

To be on the safe side (and guarantee against changes from drops in line voltage), we can estimate the voltage to be 100. If we divide the wattage by 100, we will get a rough approximation of amperage. Thus a 500-watt bulb will draw 5 amps, a 750-watt bulb, 7.5 amps, and a 1000-watt bulb, 10 amps. If the fuse on the line is a 15-amp fuse, you can expect to be able to install 1500 watts of light. (On a 110-volt line without voltage drop it would be precisely 1650 watts.) If you need more wattage, you will have to use another circuit. By unscrewing each fuse in turn and noting which lights go out, you can find which outlets are on different circuits. Of course, other fixtures drawing current from the same circuit must be considered in your calculations. Be sure to have a number of spare fuses with you.

The three most popular types of lights in use for low-cost film production are photofloods, reflector, and quartz-iodine (or tungsten halogen) lights. (See Plates 33A, 33B) Each light has advantages and disadvantages. *Photofloods* are similar to regular household bulbs except they are overrun, that is, run at a higher voltage than bulbs which yield a long life. Overrun bulbs come in wattages from 250 to 1000. They rapidly become very hot, have a short life (from two to eight hours), and they dim and change their color characteristics with age. Their color temperature makes them easily convertible for indoor color films. (See Chapter IX) However, since their color characteristics change with age, they are not ideal for color filming. Photofloods have a very bright light output for their small size. Some photofloods have built-in reflectors, such as the RFL-2, and are good as a general source of illumination.

Reflector-type lights, such as the R-40, come in various wattages and color temperatures. They have built-in reflectors, and come in spot and flood (less concentrated beam) models. One of their attractions is that there is a set of fixtures which take R-40 bulbs that is light, inexpensive, and easy to assemble called Lowel-lites. For about $6 you can get a porcelain socket on a directional swivel and a bracket which makes it easy to attach the Lowel-lites to just about anything. Lowel also makes what is perhaps the best *gaffer's tape*. Gaffer's tape is a wide gray tape that will stick securely to surfaces but will not mar surfaces in good condition when removed. It is a useful tape to have since it will serve many purposes besides its main use: helping to attach lightweight lighting fixtures to walls. Lowel-lite "barndoors" are also available. A *barndoor* is a black flap to block the light from shining into the camera lens or wherever it is not wanted. (See Plate 33A) R-40 bulbs come in wattages from 150 to 500. The higher-wattage bulbs can be purchased with color temperatures suitable for color film.

The most versatile and efficient tungsten lights are the *quartz-iodine* (or *halogen*) lights. They are making the higher-wattage tungsten bulbs all but obsolete for motion picture work. Unlike regular tungsten bulbs, they do not blacken with age or grow dim. They keep a constant color temperature throughout bulb life, which is important in color filming. They can be packed in smaller units than conventional tungsten lamps and have made possible small, lightweight housing that can deliver a lot of light, yet be easily carried and mounted. Lighting housings weigh as little as three pounds and there are both focusing and non-focusing models. A focusing lamp allows you to change the light from a spot to a flood position.

Quartz lights offer a great variety of accessories: barndoors with two leaves or four leaves, *dichroic daylight conversion filters* to change the light to the same color temperature as daylight, *heat filters* for cutting down the heat generated by the lamp, *intensifier skirts* for increasing light output, *scrims* for reducing and diffusing the intensity of the light, and others.

Tripod-like lighting stands are available which will accommodate almost all lighting fixtures. *Polecats* are single poles that go from ceiling to floor or from one wall to the wall opposite. Almost all light fixtures can be mounted on them. Clamp-on brackets to hold lights can be attached to pipes, molding, and the like. Tape-on brackets can be mounted on surfaces with gaffer's tape. When attached with gaffer's tape they can only support the lighter-weight fixtures.

All lighting equipment, including mounting equipment, can be rented at a fairly low cost. Some rental houses charge you for the bulbs, which in the case of quartz bulbs can be fairly expensive. (They cost about $10 each.) Some rental agents rent the units with used bulbs without a guarantee as to remaining bulb life. If you want to take a chance that the light may go out during a filming session, it might be worth renting equipment with a used bulb. Quartz bulbs usually have a life of more than 500 hours.

In documentary filming a portable light is useful for night shooting, for people going from outdoors to indoors, and for fill light outside in sunlight. Small, battery-powered lighting units (sometimes called *sun guns*, Sylvania's brand name) are available. (See Plate 33C) Battery belts are made for the more powerful units, which will give light for about 30 minutes with a 250-watt bulb. The more powerful lights are also available with encased rechargeable batteries. These batteries deliver 30 volts and one model can be recharged in one hour, another in six hours. Lamp life is about 12 hours. A 350-watt bulb can be used, but this reduces the running time to about 20 minutes. Running time for a 150-watt bulb is approximately 50 minutes. Smaller units available, such as the discontinued Sylvania Sun Gun Model SG-70, are much less expensive and much lighter. Larger units weigh as much as 17 pounds for a complete unit, whereas the SG-70 weighs 3½ pounds. It accepts only a 100-watt bulb and has a running time of but 10 minutes. Sixteen hours are required to recharge its batteries. All these lights come in color temperatures acceptable for color filming indoors. For daylight work with color film they can be fitted with dichroic filters.

When the battery gets low, the light output is reduced and the color temperature lowers (which adversely affects color rendition). As soon as the light from a battery-operated light has noticeably lowered, you should recharge it.

Small portable lights that run off house current are also available. They have the advantage over battery-operated lights of greater light output and constant power. However, they are not as portable, since they are connected by a wire to a wall outlet. They come in models with one or more lights.

When a single light source illuminates the scene as is likely when these portable lights are used, it is a situation with a key light without a fill light. When the light source is away from the camera, we get very dark shadows which probably show no detail. If the light source is placed very close to the camera (or mounted on it), the lighting will be very flat (front axial). Faces will be washed out, showing almost no modeling of facial structure. When given the choice between these unpleasant alternatives, most cameramen opt for placing the light away from the camera (about 30°-45° off the camera-subject axis), achieving some modeling at the cost of heavy shadows.

If at all possible, a single light source should be bounced off a ceiling or wall. The light on the subject becomes diffuse and much more pleasant. However, a great deal of light is lost when bounced, and care should be taken to ensure that adequate light is still available for filming. White surfaces, of course, will bounce the greatest amount of light to the subject. When using color film, it is important not to bounce light off colored surfaces, for that will impart a color cast to the image.

White or aluminum reflectors are useful lighting accessories. They can be used to reflect the key light to fill in heavy shadows. Outdoors, they are primarily used in sunlight. Indoors, they are a useful surface for bounce light.

Problems with daylight filming

When you are filming in bright sunlight, shadows will be pronounced, and subject-brightness range may be greater than the film can satisfactorily record. Facial shadows will be very deep and lacking in detail. Some sort of light should be added to brighten the shadows when filming close-ups. White reflectors used for photographic work will direct light into the shadows and not change color rendition. Alternatively you can use a fill light. If the light is battery-operated, fit it with as high-wattage a bulb as possible to make it effective as a sunlight fill. In color filming, lights must be fitted with dichroic or other filters to balance them for daylight (see Chapter IX). Color casts will be especially noticeable on skin tones if unfiltered light or off-color reflectors are used.

Backlighting, shooting against a window (as in a car), requires some additional light on the subject so that the background and foreground are properly exposed. In filming someone in an automobile, there will often be several stops, difference between the proper exposure for the person in the car and the outside background. If you were to expose the person properly, the background would completely wash out. On the other hand, were you to expose for the background, the person might turn out black. This is an example of a situation in which the brightness range of the subject is too great for the film. In order to remedy this, the subject is usually lit to bring him closer to the brightness of the background. To film someone in a car, then, we could use a light to illuminate the person.

In backlit situations you usually want the background to remain brighter than the subject and therefore should not raise the light on the subject to equal that on the background. When you are shooting the subject against a window or in a car, the background should be about one to one and a half stops brighter than the foreground subject.

VIII. The Laboratory

Dealing with the film laboratory is possibly the most difficult and frustrating part of filmmaking. To avoid the usual lab problems, you must know what instructions to give the laboratory, what you can reasonably ask of the lab, and how to evaluate their work.

Much slipshod work and many errors are made by laboratories, but seldom do they equal the number of errors made by the filmmaker. Filmmakers tend to blame all technical photographic faults on the laboratory, and it is a rare laboratory that will admit that *it* has made the error.

Choosing a lab

You probably will not have much difficulty with the processing of the 8mm film. The usual practice is to purchase the film with a mailer which includes the charge for development. All the necessary information is marked on the mailer, which, after the film is exposed, is sent to the laboratory (often a licensee of the film manufacturer). The lab develops and returns the processed film. Mailers are available for some 16mm films—in particular, Kodachrome II, which can be sent to Kodak for processing. If you are going to have little use for a laboratory (either because you are working in 8mm or because you do not plan to ask for copy prints or special processing), it may be worthwhile to use mailers. (You can purchase mailers for requesting copy prints from your 8mm color films.) If you plan to have special work in 8mm you must find a lab.

Many professional filmmakers spend their whole lives changing labs. For any single lab you will find someone who will tell you it is the best and someone else who will tell you it is totally incompetent. You are forced, therefore, to experiment to find the lab best suited to your needs.

A lab is a business, and a good one will observe good business practices. Labs have been known to overcharge, promise impossible delivery times, and indulge in other bad practices.

Labs vary greatly and offer diverse services. They will develop your film, make a workprint, edge-number your film, conform your negative, make a freeze, and so on. Here I will deal only with photographic services offered by labs. A single lab may also offer services such as sound recording and editing, which are dealt with in other sections.

If you live in a large city you will have a choice of several laboratories. Some cities have only one and smaller towns, none. If you use a lab in the city where you work, the service is comparatively faster since there is no need to ship film, shipping costs are saved, and face-to-face encounters may make things go more smoothly with the lab. Nevertheless, many filmmakers (other than TV newsmen, to whom speed is essential) ship their work to another city where they feel they can get superior work done. New York and Hollywood (Los Angeles) are the two centers for laboratories. Washington, Chicago, and Kansas City also have excellent labs.

Should you use a large lab or small lab? If you are not shooting much footage, it is a good idea to avoid the large labs in the major film centers. Your patronage is not usually appreciated there and your service will suffer. If your work needs a lot of special handling and you wish to consult your lab often, asking technical advice, you will usually find better service at a smaller lab. There is no reason why you should not simply ask how you will be treated. If you give the lab an idea of the sort of film(s) you will be making, approximately how much footage you will shoot, how much forced processing you'll need, how many prints you will want, how quickly you will need your prints (rushes, answer print, etc.), and tell the lab how experienced you are, the lab should be able to give you a fair idea of the service you can expect. There are a few labs which specialize in handling the problems of young or inexperienced filmmakers.

Costs differ from one lab to another. The lab may charge you less for frequent or large jobs than the stated catalog price. But you must discuss this before you send them your work. The lab may make no charge or grant you a discount for some special service, such as forced development, if you are willing to accept slower delivery.

Comparative shopping is worthwhile. For example, in one city a certain laboratory charges over ten cents a foot for negative development and workprint and another charges just over six cents for the same service. You may find it worthwhile to pay a little extra if the lab does better work or is more cooperative with you.

To deal efficiently with a lab you should find out which person or persons to contact when problems arise. In the larger labs different people are in charge of credit, scheduling, and technical advice. In a smaller lab these may all be handled by one or two people.

Raw stock can usually be purchased from a laboratory at a slightly higher cost than from the manufacturer.

Information to be sent to the lab

After your film is exposed and sealed in its can, label it clearly with the following information:

1. Type of film (e.g., Plus-X Reversal) and the approximate footage.
2. Manner in which it was exposed (usually expressed by the ASA speed at which you shot it).
3. Your name and address.
4. Title of the production.
5. Camera roll number.
6. Shipping instructions as to how the material is to be returned (e.g., rush return, hold for pickup, special delivery, air freight) and to whom it is to be shipped. Note if the original is to be held at the lab until further instructions, and only the workprint returned.
7. Whether a workprint is to be struck immediately or not. There may be decisions to be made as to the type of raw stock to use for the workprint. In ordering the workprint you should always request that the latent edge-numbers be printed through. You should specify whether you want the workprint on single- or on double-perforated stock. (See p. 96.)
8. Your preference as to whether your footage be returned on cores or reels.
9. Whether your rolls of original (and/or workprint) are to be marked with your camera roll number, and if you wish the various rolls to be spliced together to make longer rolls. If so, how long.
10. Special printing instructions for the workprint. For example, you may want your workprint to be lighter or darker than usual or always printed at the same printer light.
11. Special handling of any nature.
12. Your purchase order number. If none, say "none."
13. If test footage is included, this should be clearly noted (see below). If there has been a camera jam, it is essential that you explain as clearly as possible where on the roll it occurred. If you do not, you may ruin your subsequent footage and possibly someone else's as well.

All these instructions need not be attached to every roll of film (1 to 5 should be, however). The lab should be forewarned that your footage is coming, especially if you are not known to the lab or your work requires special handling.

Exposure tests

Whenever you begin a film it is a good idea for you to make a test exposure. The lab may process your preliminary tests at no charge or for a nominal charge. You may use exposure test cards with a gray scale or you can film a standard situation that you will encounter in the film. Place a card in the scene showing a written description of what you are doing. To help evaluate your results bracket your exposures by shooting the same scene at one-half, one, and two stops under and over normal exposure. Each separate shot should include a card identifying the exposure used. Each exposure requires no more than a foot or so of film. Leave a bit of footage on either end of the test shots for leader. Your lab should be happy to help you evaluate the results.

In a situation where the cameraman must guess at exposure, or where, in an important take, he is for some reason unsure of his exposure, if the whole roll has been exposed in this same condition the cameraman can make a test at the head or the tail (preferably the tail) of the roll and ask the lab to cut off that section and develop it at the ASA that the cameraman thinks is most likely correct. Then he can decide what the best development time for the exposure is. Such a test strip should be 10 or more feet in length since the lab will have to cut off an approximate amount and you want to be sure they don't cut into non-test footage. On the can you must clearly mark the test (e.g., EXPOSURE TEST TAIL 10 FEET). You must also inform the lab if you want to see the test footage or if you will leave the choice of development to them. If the scene is straightforward, a competent lab can be trusted to decide whether it is properly exposed. However, if the scene is unusually lit, abstract, or was shot at night, it might be best for you to have a look at the test shot before the rest of the roll is developed.

Your lab should be willing to supply at no charge extra film cans, black bags, and cores.

When the film is returned to you, you should view it on a good projector. The source of any picture problems should be discovered immediately. If defects such as scratches, mottle, edge fog, bad registration, or blurred image appear on the film, check to see if these defects appear on the original. If they do not and they are not serious, the lab probably will *not* reprint the film free of charge. They assume that a workprint, since it is only used for editing purposes, need not be of release-print quality. But if the defect is serious, the lab ought to reprint without charge.

Timing

A workprint is usually "untimed" (and if in color, it is also uncorrected). A slight amount of overexposure and underexposure can be corrected when making prints from the original material by varying the amount of light used in printing each scene. The selection of the proper amount of light for each scene is termed *timing* (or *grading*), and a print so made is called "timed." This operation involves considerable labor and consequently the lab charges extra for the service. Since your workprint is generally used for editing purposes only, you can usually ask for the less expensive "one-lite" workprint. This way the whole roll is printed with the same printing light; no scene-to-scene light changes are made. Some labs print all their one-lite workprints at the normal light (that is, for average exposure) unless requested to use more or less light when doing the printing. Other labs look at some of the roll to determine which is the best average light for your exposures. You should discuss this point with your lab.

Storing the original

It is usually best to store the camera original at the lab, where it can be kept in a vault at optimum storage conditions. You should ask whether your lab has such a vault and if they will keep your work in it. Usually no charge is made for storage of films in production.

Film cans

Unless requested to do otherwise, a lab will return 16mm film in lengths of over 200 feet on cores and 8mm film on reels. Shipping by cores saves weight. If you wish your rolls mounted on reels larger than 100 feet you may be charged for the reels plus a small labor charge for the mounting. You should specify the size of reel that you prefer. Reels come in sizes of 50, 100, 200, 400, 600, 800, 1000, 1200 feet, and larger. If you want the reel placed in a film can the lab will probably supply the can for you. Cans are very useful for keeping dust off film in storage and for protection when the film is being shipped. Usually labs will supply raw stock cans to you at no charge. Cans made particularly for reel storage are charged for. They are made of a heavier-gauge steel and are the right size to accommodate reels. In my own work, I generally store film for editing purposes on 800-foot reels in cans made for 1200 feet of raw stock. These cans accommodate two 800-foot reels of 16mm film.

Edge-numbers

Most 16mm films have an edge-number photographically printed on the edge of the film every 20 frames (every half foot). (See Fig. IX) When the film is developed, this edge-number (termed *latent edge-number*) is also developed. If this number is printed through to the workprint, you have means by which to locate the section of original corresponding to any shot from the workprint. Edge-numbers are an aid to conforming the camera original to the edited workprint when we are ready to make our release prints. An alternate method is to use *machine edge-numbers,* the only presently available choice in 8mm. Machine edge-numbers are printed on both original and workprint so that the same number appears at corresponding points. There are two disadvantages to this method of numbering frames. The ink sometimes spreads onto the picture area (though this occurs rarely, the less the original is handled, the safer it will be). The other disadvantage is that there is no guarantee that the original and workprint were properly lined up and, consequently, there may be some error in matching the two. Machine edge-numbers are far easier to read than the other variety.

Fig. IX. Most 16mm films that are used professionally have a latent edge-number every foot or half foot on the edge of the film.

Single- and double-perforated workprints

With 16mm you have a choice between a single- and double-perforated workprint (as with the 16mm raw stock original). If sound is to be magnetically applied to the film, by all means order your workprint made on single-perforated stock. Though magnetic sound stripping can be applied to double-perforated stock, it is markedly inferior (see p. 141). Whatever your choice, the entire workprint should have the same number of perforations so as to avoid ripping incorrectly loaded film. Some types of splicing are a little easier with double-perforated film. Double-perforated film can be flipped, but single cannot. However, the image will go slightly out of focus when the film's emulsion position isn't the same from shot to shot. Using single-perforated film guarantees that when the film is loaded into a viewing mechanism the viewer's orientation will be right, but its use means sacrificing ease in some editing operations where orientation is not important.

8mm and the lab

Most 8mm color films cannot be pushed to a higher ASA. You may be able to find a laboratory that will force-process 8mm black and white films or Ektachrome EF. 16mm blow-ups can be made from 8mm (i.e., the 8mm original is enlarged to fit onto 16mm film). Obviously the quality will be inferior to film shot originally on 16mm. The blown-up film can be projected to a larger size for showings, and all sorts of 16mm lab services become available if you wish to make additional 16mm prints. The blowup costs about 30 cents an 8mm foot.

It is also possible to make an 8mm reduction print from a 16mm original. You might reduce the film either because you wish to release it in 8mm or because you wish to cut some footage shot in 16mm into an 8mm film. If the latter, you must be sure that the emulsion position of the reduction print will be the same as the other 8mm footage, that is, that they are of the same wind (see below).

Emulsion positions and winds

The whole business of "winds" is fairly confusing, and it is worth taking the time to understand it. The term "wind" has its primary application to 16mm raw stock perforated on one edge. Basically, all cameras take "B" wind film. When the film is wound so the emulsion faces in and the end of the film leaves the roll at the top, "B" wind will have the perforations to the right of the observer, while "A" wind film will have the perforations to the left. It is unlikely that you will come into contact with "A" wind raw stock, and so this distinction is unimportant except when you order film and are given a choice.

The more important concept of wind for the filmmaker concerns emulsion position. Camera original is said to be "B" wind (or camera wind). Anytime a contact print is made of the original, the image is reversed and the resulting print is an "A" wind (or print wind).

"B" wind emulsion position means that the picture reads correctly through the film's celluloid base. As a mnemonic device we can remember "B" wind from the *b* in base. A scene is said to *read correctly* if, when placed heads up (front end up), a title or scene appears correctly, not mirror-reversed. When the scene reads correctly through the emulsion we have an "A" wind print.

When an "A" wind print is loaded in the projector, the emulsion must face away from the lens for the image to project properly. On most projectors this means the print must be loaded base side out. Since most prints are "A" wind, film wound base out is sometimes referred to as *projector wind*. "B" wind prints are projected properly when the emulsion faces the lens. On most projectors the film must be wound emulsion out on the reel to get "B" wind prints to project properly.

Other lab services

Whenever you have a contact print made, the image is reversed and the wind changed. To print a film properly all the individual shots must be of the same wind, having the emulsion on one side or the other throughout. If there are two shots of different winds spliced together, one will print flipped from left to right. The laboratory can reprint film for you to change the wind. It is fairly expensive to do this and, as always, quality is lost in the reprinting.

While editing you can ask your lab to edge-number the synchronous sound track (if you have one). If parts of the workprint have been damaged, blank leader may be inserted, or you can reorder replacement footage from the lab. The amount of footage to be replaced may be very little, and if you do not wish to reprint the whole roll or cut the original, for an additional price the lab will do what is called *clip-to-clip* (*cord-to-cord*, *tab-to-tab*) printing. Some mark or thread is placed at the head and tail of each shot to be reprinted. Only those sections are then printed. This method is also sometimes used when making master positives and internegatives (see p. 100).

Color correction on workprints can also be done scene-to-scene, but this is rarely worth the additional cost. Scene-to-scene balancing is usually done at the release print stage.

To save money you can order a black and white workprint from a color original. (There is a saving of about three or four cents a foot.) The disadvantage is that you have no idea of your colors and the workprint is considerably more grainy than a color workprint would be.

You may need an editing copy in addition to the cut up, spliced workprint. For example, when doing the sound mix (see Chapter XVI) you should have a print that will go through the projector without tearing. A reversal dupe of low quality (often called a *slop print*) can be ordered from the lab. This usually costs the same as a reversal workprint.

Color workprints and release prints

With a 16mm color original you will have a choice of workprint stock. In general, you should have the workprint done on the same stock as your final prints to give you a better idea of how the final print will look. The choice is not always easy. If your original has been shot on Ektachrome Commercial, your final print should be done on 7387 (Eastman Reversal Color Print Film). Most labs must send this film to Kodak for processing. There is a companion stock to Ektachrome Commercial that many labs can process (7386: Eastman Ektachrome Reversal Print Film). This film does not take as good a sound track as 7387 and cost a bit more, but it takes less time to process.

If your original has been shot on Ektachrome EF, either 7241 or 7242, the best companion printing stock from the point of view of color rendition and contrast is 7389 (Eastman Ektachrome R Print Film). This film can be processed in many labs and a workprint obtained quickly. Few labs can apply a good optical sound track on 7389. In general, higher quality optical sound can be gotten on 7387. You may be forced to choose between better sound with an increase in picture contrast (7387) and inferior sound with virtually no increase in contrast (7389). It usually takes a bit longer (perhaps one day) to get a 7387 workprint, but it is less expensive.

Scene-to-scene color correction and effects

When editing you must know what printing techniques your lab is capable of. With color film you will want to know if the lab can make scene-to-scene color correction. If it can, more footage will be salvageable in printing than otherwise and you will be able to exaggerate off-color effects if you wish to. It is important to know if the lab can print effects such as fades and dissolves on the same printer roll of different lengths and specifically what length these effects can be. (Some labs make all such effects 48 frames long, while others allow for a great deal of variation.) Similarly you will want to know what is the shortest shot that the lab will separately time and balance. Some labs will make corrections on shots a couple of frames in length, while others demand that the shot be at least a foot long.

Master positives and duplicate negatives

You may have occasion to make a *master positive* (some-times called simply a *master*) or a *dupe negative*. If you want to use the same shot in two films or twice in the same film, you will need a copy of the shot to be cut into the final printing rolls. The copy must be of high quality, as close to the original in quality as possible. If the original is negative you will want a dupe negative. To keep contrast down, there is an intermediate step: a fine-grain master posi-tive. If the original is reversal, you can often go in one step to a reversal master. However, if the contrast will be too great you might have to make an intermediate dupe negative (*an internegative*). If a master is made in one step, you have the choice of keeping the same emulsion position as the origi-nal or flipping it. The latter method is less expensive but can-not be used if the master is to be cut in with the original foot-age for it will be of a different wind. Not all labs can make a master in one step, preserving emulsion position.

If finances permit, a master or dupe should be made of an entire scene, not just of one shot, to ensure the image quality will be consistent. Otherwise, no matter how careful the lab is, the master or dupe will be of noticeably different quality.

The optical house

You will probably have to go to a special laboratory to get your optical effects made. Optical effects involve changes made in the actual image or in the sequence of frames within a shot. Some effects can be made in the camera (fades, dis-solves, split screens, superimposed titles), some can be made in A&B roll printing * (fades, dissolves, and superimposed ti-tles and scenes), and some can be done only at an optical house (wipes, bi-pack multiple exposure, freezes, etc.).

Optical effects

Some optical effects used for transitions between scenes are:

The fade: The shot gradually disappears into black (fade-out) or appears out of black (fade-in). This effect should usually be done in final printing unless your lab cannot do it

---

* A&B printing is discussed in detail on pp. 106–8. It is a method of printing in which the shots of the film to be printed are divided into two rolls. This method of printing has the advantage of allowing cer-tain effects to be made during printing and in making splices between shots invisible.

because, for example, the fade is exceptionally long or short, or because you have several fades very close to each other.

The dissolve (lap-dissolve): Two shots are superimposed, in which the second shot gradually appears out of the first shot. The same remarks that apply to the fade apply to the dissolve except that some labs can do fades on reversal film when printing from a single strand, though dissolves and fades on negative printing always require A&B roll printing (see pp. 106–7).

The wipe: Two shots in which the second shot pushes the first off the screen. The varieties of wipes are endless. Some optical houses offer over a hundred different varieties. A *flipover wipe* is one in which the image turns over revealing the second on what appears to be its other side. Most optical houses will supply cards showing examples of the variety of wipes available.

Some optical effects are used to change composition or camera movement:

Change of image size: Part of the image can be enlarged to change composition, to crop unwanted elements from the picture, or to enlarge an element. The image can also be repositioned to adjust an off-angle horizon line. Some shaky hand-held shooting can often be steadied through special optical printing.

Change of emulsion position: The shot can be printed so it will project as its mirror image, or a copy can be made which will preserve emulsion position.

Optical zoom: An area of the image can be progressively enlarged in successive frames to approximate a zoom-in. However, as the successive frames are enlarged grain size increases and image resolution decreases.

The speed or direction of action can be changed optically by the following methods:

Skip framing: By printing only some of the frames of the original, action is speeded up.

Double framing: Each frame can be printed twice or more to slow down the action. To change silent speed footage shot at 16 fps to sound speed (24 fps) every other frame must be printed twice. Multiple framing does not result in perfectly smooth action—unlike shooting at a higher speed in the camera, which slows up action smoothly.

The freeze: Shots can be lengthened by repeating a frame over and over. Action can be stopped, or stopped and started through use of multiple framing.

The pictorial element can be changed:

Multiple exposure: Images are superimposed by exposing

the film with one shot and then another. If done with two shots the procedure is called double-exposure, and if three are used, triple-exposure, and so on. With multiple exposure a dark tone superimposed on a light tone yields a light tone. Thus, multiple exposure generally works better with dark scenes than with light. Multiple exposure can be done in the final printing if you use A&B rolls (see p. 107).

Bi-pack exposure: This is a form of superimposition in which one image is exposed through the other. When this method is used, a light tone on a dark tone yields a dark tone. The results of bi-packing can be approximated by sandwiching the two shots to be bi-packed in a viewer. The resulting image will be very close to the bi-packed image. Bi-packing is usually more expensive than double-exposure.

Superimposed titles: Titles can be superimposed ("supered") on a scene. The titles can be black or white or any color. Drop shadows can be added to make the letters stand out from the background.

If you wish the titles to be superimposed in black lettering and your final printing is to be made with a negative, it is possible to superimpose the titles while printing your A&B rolls, treating the titles as a double-exposure. White titles, which are more common, cannot be done this way. If you are using a negative, you must plan to make a master positive to obtain superimposed white lettering, and then make a dupe negative to cut into your final printing rolls. If your final printing will be made with reversal film, then you can cut in the titles in the A&B rolls to have white lettering. However, if you wish to have black lettering superimposed, then your film must go through the intermediate stage of a dupe negative. Of course, if the titles are not superimposed on another scene, then they can be made either black or white on negative or reversal without any intermediate stages.

The optical effects produced by an optical house can cost a good bit of money depending on the complexity of effects you desire. You are charged for all the masters and dupes needed to achieve your effect beyond the particular charges for the effect itself. An optical effect can cost you from $10 to many thousands of dollars.

To have work done at an optical house, you supply the film original and *detailed* instructions as to what you want. The house returns your original material and the effect you ordered on another strip of film that will have the same wind (emulsion orientation) as your camera original so that the effect can be cut into the final print roll. The effect will be a different generation from the original.

Generations

The term *generation* is used to specify how far any print is removed from the original. A copy of the original is known as a first-generation print. Every time a copy is made from a copy another generation is added. A copy of a copy of the original is a second-generation print. If the original is negative and a freeze is made by first making a fine-grain master, the freeze will be second generation on the dupe negative. It will then be cut in with the original. If we then make a dupe neg of the whole film, starting with a fine-grain master, and then make a print, our freeze on the final print is, by this stage, fifth generation, though the rest of the print is third generation.

With each new generation the print loses definition and becomes grainier. There is a noticeable difference in quality from footage used from a different generation print or negative. The smaller the gauge, the more visible this difference. Even in Hollywood films when you see a sudden change in graininess and quality you can anticipate some special optical effect. Stanley Kubrick in making his Cinerama movie *2001: A Space Odyssey* went through a great deal of pains to give the whole film a first-generation look.

The change of quality will not be as noticeable if we try to keep all the shots in the scene of the same generation. If, however, the sequence is of great length, it will surely not be worth the expense. Any effects that can be done directly in final printing should certainly be done there. Though they often are not done as precisely as when made by an optical house, it may not be worth the quality lost in the final print by adding generations to insist upon this greater precision in the effect.

Optical houses charge a lot for their work, and the inexperienced filmmaker should be warned that his desire for "opticals" can cost him more money than all his other expenses combined.

Optical houses tend to be finicky about their work, and because it is usually so complex, the risk of error is increased. If the mistake is theirs they will rework it for you at no cost until they get it right. You should demand meticulous craftsmanship from them; you are paying for it.

Small optical houses may give you more attention and lower prices than the big, established houses. They often let you experiment and be present during optical printing. Rarely will the bigger optical labs allow you to do this.

Homemade optical printer

If you want to attempt to make optical effects by yourself, it is possible. In the July, 1967, issue of the *Canyon Cinema News,* a very inexpensive optical printing stand that you can build yourself was described for 16mm use. It requires a reflex camera for accurate framing and focusing. Some means of focusing to very close distances is necessary. The most versatile method is an extension bellows, though extension tubes or some macro lenses might be adequate. The lens must focus close enough to give a 1:1 reproduction ratio. You obtain this by photographing the subject at a distance twice the focal length of the lens. At 100mm (four inches) a 50mm lens will produce a subject the same size on the film as it is in actuality. In order to have some working space between lens and the film to be reproduced, you should use a 75mm lens or longer. The film that is to be rephotographed should be held in an old projector with a low-wattage bulb (rated at 3200° Kelvin if you are working with color). The motor for the projector will not be needed, but some way of advancing or retarding the film frame by frame will have to be worked out. A cable release should be used to expose each frame to avoid the risk of camera movement.

The diagram (see Fig. X) illustrates the setup suggested in the *Canyon Cinema News.* The f/stops engraved on the lens barrel are no longer accurate when the lens is used at close distances (closer than four times the focal length of the lens). A light-meter reading taken off the film in the projector gate requires an exposure compensation. The formula is:

$$\frac{(\text{Distance of lens to film})^{2}}{(\text{Focal length of lens})^{2}} = \text{Exposure increase.}$$

When the reproduction ratio is 1:1, exposure compensation is two stops of additional light.

Some errors in exposure of the original can be corrected, and with the aid of color correction filters, the color balance of the original can be changed.

The optical printer allows you to make fades and dissolves of any length, multiple exposures, freeze frames mixed with action, reprints of the same footage superimposed on itself (but several frames out of phase with itself), and many other effects. Robert Nelson's film *The Grateful Dead* was made using this type of printing arrangement. The film cost him under $100. Had it been done at an optical house, it would have cost him several thousand dollars, and he probably could not have communicated the ideas for his complex arrangements to a technician at an optical house. In any case,

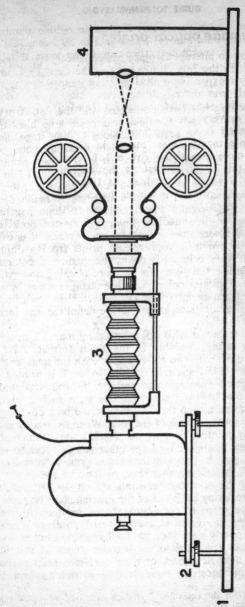

Fig. X. *A homemade optical printer*: The baseboard (*1*) is grooved so the camera can be moved forward and back to change image magnification. The camera is mounted on screw adjustment (*2*) so the camera may be raised or lowered. A bellows (*3*) is used so that the lens can focus down to a 1:1 or 1:2 reproduction ratio. The light source (*4*) projects light through condensers to the converted projector, which holds the already exposed film. You must devise a way to advance the film in the projector one frame at a time.

this printer allows you to try out an incredible number of ideas for very little money. You ought to be aware that optical printing is enormously time-consuming since it is done frame by frame.

Final printing

When editing has been completed and the edited original roll (or rolls) is ready for final printing, it goes back to the lab. You must make several decisions at this stage, among them whether to use your original to make all your prints, thus ensuring the highest quality for your release prints but endangering the original with excessive handling. (You may wish to make release prints from a dupe negative.) If the original was reversal film, the dupe negative is made directly from it. If the original was a negative, a dupe negative is made from an intermediate fine-grain master positive. If many prints (more than seven) are to be made, it is usually less expensive to take your release prints from a duplicate negative. If your original is color, the quality of color from an internegative * is likely to be more pleasing and you are able to make greater color-balancing changes scene by scene in printing from an internegative. Nevertheless, even in color work added generations lower picture definition and increase grain.

The advantages of A&B roll printing are many. This type of printing is rarely available in the 8mm format. A&B roll printing is done with two rolls of film, each the total length of the final film. First one roll, say the "A" roll, is printed. The printing stock is then rewound and the "B" roll is printed. Of course, if the "A" and the "B" rolls were each completely made up of shots, then the final film would be a double-exposure of what was on each of the rolls. When we want a shot to be normally printed, then we put black leader (film that lets no light pass through it) on the other roll opposite to where the shot occurs. In this way the shot is printed normally.

When all the odd-number shots of the film are on the "A" roll and all the even-number shots are on the "B" roll, with black leader taking the place of the missing shots on each roll, the rolls are prepared for *checkerboard printing*. Almost all A&B printing in 16mm is checkerboard printing. When the rolls are properly prepared, the final print will not show any of the splices (physical joins) between shots. If printing is done from a single strand, or when a spliced print is shown, there is a disconcerting jump or flash at every splice. Since

---

*The term for the equivalent of "dupe negative" when the original is color reversal film.

this does not occur with checkerboard printing, it is also known as *invisible-splice printing*.

If other printing rolls are needed for some effect (for example, multiple images), then the next roll would be called the "C" roll, then the "D" roll, and so on. The laboratory charges extra for each additional roll needed to make the final print. Single-strand printing is, therefore, less expensive than A&B roll printing.

A&B roll printing opens up the possibility of adding several effects to the film in the final printing stage—for example, fades, dissolves, and multiple images. If white titles on a totally black background are placed on one of the rolls opposite a shot, then in the final print the titles will be superimposed on the shot. If we are printing reversal, then the titles will appear white on the shot. If we are printing negative, the titles will be black on the shot because of the reversal of tonalities.

Depending on the type of printer your lab has, if you do not print using A&B rolls you may not be able to insist on scene-to-scene timing and color correction. The Bell & Howell Model C Color Printer is capable of making scene-to-scene changes from a single-strand printing roll. The Model C printer allows you when printing from A&B rolls to make effects of different lengths on the same printer roll. It also allows for a radical change in printer light from one scene to its successor, which helps if one shot was overexposed and the next underexposed. Unfortunately, even if your lab owns this printer, it may not be available for your work, especially if your work is not in color. You must be explicit in questioning your lab because they dislike having to admit that their equipment is more limited than that belonging to some other lab. A lab may claim, for instance, that it is capable of making scene-to-scene correction from a single-strand printer roll when it can only change the printer light slowly at the end of one scene and the start of another rather than instantaneously between scenes. Such a limitation might mean the second scene of the two would show optimum density only after a second had elapsed into the shot. In some cases it might not matter, but with two scenes which require very different printer lights the effect could be disturbing.

Even if your original has been printed from A&B rolls, you may encounter the problems of scene-to-scene corrections from a single-strand printing roll if you make a dupe negative or internegative of the whole film, since it will be printed on a single roll. The lab often goes to some trouble to be sure that the dupe can be used to get final prints without any scene-to-scene changes of color balance or light.

Some laboratories offer a variation of A&B printing called

zero printing. Zero printing offers the possibility of avoiding cutting your original. For example, the shot in the original might be 10 feet long, and you might only want 3 feet in your final cut. If you wish to use the same shot in two different films, and the shot lengths differ in the two films, you can zero print, avoiding the expense and loss of quality involved in making masters of the shot. You should consult your lab to see if they offer the service, since very few do. They will give you instructions in preparing your rolls for zero printing.

The answer print

The first print that you order will be what is called an *answer print* or a *first-trial print.* It is usually about three cents more per foot than *release prints.* You will have to pay an additional amount if you use A&B rolls (about two and a half cents). When the print is timed, a lab technician known as *the timer* marks each scene with a printer-light number. The higher the number the more light is sent through the film. Some labs notch the film at each light change; others use different systems. Notching is not consistent from lab to lab, so you cannot expect one lab's notches to cue another's machine. When printing color, the timer also marks what color filters are needed to achieve the best color balance.

You are charged for fades and dissolves made on the first answer print. The charge is about $1 per fade and $2 per dissolve. On subsequent prints no charge is made for fades and dissolves unless you decide to add new ones.

After you receive your first answer print, you evaluate it. First of all you must determine that the original has been properly cut. The first answer print may be the first check you have. It should show no unexpected photographic defects such as bad scratches or mottle. The source of any defect should be checked out with the lab. If it is their fault, they should reprint the defective sections for you without charge. Above all you must check the work of the timer. If there are no scene-to-scene corrections, then the printer light and color filtration (when applicable) should be the best quality possible throughout the whole roll. If there has been scene-to-scene correction, you must evaluate each shot to make certain that it has been properly corrected. If there have been mistakes, as there almost certainly will be, then you must go over the film shot by shot with the timer telling him which scenes are right, which are too light, and which too dark. If the film is color, you must also tell him which scenes are off color.

If your film requires unusual timing or color balancing for

special effects, you ought to be present with the timer when the film is first timed. The timer will evaluate each scene to give what he thinks is a normal rendition. If you wish your shot to deviate from the normal, you must give him special instructions either in writing or while he is working with the film.

The timer looks at the first answer print and marks what corrections he thinks the film will need. If he is skilled and you do not require unusual effects, his corrections should be adequate, and you need not go over the film with him.

The second print you order may still have mistakes on it and it is a good idea to evaluate each scene again. You should expect an adequate print on the second or third try. Occasionally the timer hits target on the first print, but it usually takes him a few tries to make all the shots correct. The first successful print is called a *release print*.

Labs have a sliding scale to determine the price for release prints. Usually if you order more than one the price per foot drops. The price drops even further when more than five prints are ordered at a time.

IX. Problems of Color Filming

Color balance

Film speed for black and white films is usually rated for daylight (outdoor) light and tungsten (incandescent) light. Usually the difference is inconsequential. Tungsten is normally about one-fifth of a stop slower. The nature of the light source is not of great importance for black and white filming; for color it is crucial. The human eye compensates for the difference between tungsten light, which is more yellow and red than the relatively blue daylight. Color film will reproduce colors accurately only when it is properly balanced for the specific light source illuminating the subject. The color quality of most light sources can be rated in terms of color temperature, expressed in degrees Kelvin. The higher the color temperature, the bluer the light source. The lower the color temperature, the redder the light source. Color films are usually balanced for daylight (about 6000°K) or tungsten at 3200°K (though Kodachrome II Type A is balanced for 3400°K). If any of these films is used with a light source different from the type it was balanced for, color reproduction will be very poor. There will be a strong color cast over the entire picture.

Color filming in daylight

Color temperature is less critical in daylight. Ideal balance is achieved when the subject is illuminated by sun and sky. When the subject is in open shade (illuminated only by a blue sky) the image will be a bit blue. Most of this blue cast can be eliminated by using a UV or skylight filter. A #85 filter, which converts tungsten-balanced film to daylight-balanced film, has a UV filter built in.

If the final print can be color-corrected (or balanced) shot by shot (called scene-by-scene color correction), the changes encountered outdoors can usually be altered in the final printing. The most important exceptions to this are the red light at the time just after sunrise and just before sunset. If you shoot two hours from sunrise or sunset, there is no problem. Otherwise, it is very difficult to correct for this red cast properly. For one thing, as the sun sets the light changes from red to redder rapidly, thereby demanding constant correction. If you are shooting at sunset, you probably want some redness to suggest the time of day. Unfortunately, the red light will always show more on the film than it does to your eye. The use of a color temperature meter and experimentation is the best possible course. You can shoot sunsets and sunrises themselves as subjects without all this worry, since the viewer can tolerate the great range of color change involved. But filmed flesh tones are familiar to him and must be acceptably rendered. If the subject is not being illuminated directly by the setting sun but by the sky, you will not encounter so great a drop in color temperature.

On the whole, daylight film will properly render a subject illuminated by window light alone. However, if the room is of a strong, dominant color, it may impart color of that cast to the film.

Unless some special effect is desired, lights of different color temperatures should not be mixed, for both cannot be balanced at once. Thus, when the subject is illuminated by window light, incandescent light in the room should be avoided. Indoors the tungsten lights used should be of the same wattage, as their wattage affects color temperature. The new, faster color films allow you to shoot interiors by available light. Even so, ordinary incandescent or fluorescent bulbs may affect color balance disastrously, though exposure is satisfactory.

Color filming with incandescent light

The lower the wattage of regular household light bulbs, the lower their color temperature, and the warmer (redder) the subject will reproduce. When the color temperature goes below 2800°K, film balanced for 3200°K may look yellowish-brown. A 100-watt household bulb has an approximate color temperature of 2850°K; a 500-watt bulb is about 2950°K. A change of 100°K at this point on the scale is easily noticeable. The matter is further complicated since normal tungsten lights blacken with age, lowering even further the color temperature. A drop in the line voltage at the light source means a further loss in temperature. Normally the loss of one volt results in a 10°K drop. Line voltage tends to drop during peak hours of use in the community. Extension cords can lose voltage in transmission of power.

In emergencies, and when an off-color balance is acceptable, you can shoot using household bulbs. You should change the bulbs to the highest wattage possible, and plan on scene-to-scene color balancing (assuming your lab offers it) to correct for some of the cast. Colored lampshades should, of course, be removed.

The best artificial lighting for color film is the quartz-iodine variety (see pp. 87–8). Lights of this type do not blacken with age and are more efficient than tungsten. Though they are obtainable with a rating of 3200°K (correct for most indoor color emulsions), a drop in the line voltage will lower their color temperature. If the voltage drop is consistently more than 10 volts (measure it with a voltmeter at the light itself), use a lamp rated at 3350° or 3400°K tungsten. Some built-in reflector-type bulbs, which can be used with the inexpensive Lowel-lite kit (see p. 87), are rated at 3200°K. Since these bulbs blacken with age, new bulbs should always be used.

Whenever you use bounce light, take care not to point it at a colored surface unless you want the illumination to be so colored. White walls and ceilings will usually be sufficient, but reflectors made for photographic use or sheets of aluminum foil are best. The foil should be wrinkled so it reflects light evenly.

Color filming with window light

Available light from a window may produce too much contrast in the room for an acceptable result unless all the action occurs at approximately the same distance from the window. Supplementary lights should be added to avoid this problem, but regular incandescent is useless here, since its color temperature is radically different from daylight. When you wish to use a fill light (see p. 82) inside, two solutions to the problem exist. You can change the color temperature of the window light by properly filtering it. Gelatin filter rolls of #85 filter (or MT-2 sheets) are placed over the window light to lower its color temperature to 3200°K. Neutral density filter rolls can also be added to lower the amount of entering window light. The other solution, which is simpler and more practicable, is to use lights that have color temperature approximating that of the entering daylight. Other than arc illumination, which is expensive to use and requires a lot of equipment, the best solution is to filter incandescent light. Blue photofloods can be purchased from most camera shops. Though they do not yield a very good color temperature match, they are acceptable for many uses. Quartz-iodine lights with a dichroic filter are an even better solution. A dichroic filter is a fairly expensive (about $20) glass filter which converts a 3200° or 3400°K lamp to approximate daylight color balance.

Color filming with fluorescent light

Filming color film under fluorescent light is extremely difficult and should be avoided whenever possible. Either change the location or turn off the fluorescent lights and light the interior yourself. When you must film by fluorescent lighting you will need either additional light or you must use the proper filter on your lens.

Fluorescent light yields pictures with a strong blue-green cast and weak reds. Color temperature meters cannot be used to evaluate fluorescent light. These lights vary over a great range in color from brand to brand (even from lamp to lamp of the same brand) with age, voltage changes, and according to the length of time they have been switched on. If you cannot make a test, use a 50R (red) filter with color film balanced for tungsten. Type 7242 EF film should be rated ASA 50 when used with the 50R filter.* The light should be on for at least 10 minutes before shooting to avoid color changes as the lamp warms up.

If you want a solution which is not dependent on filtration, use daylight film (or tungsten film balanced for daylight) and bounce some incandescent light onto the scene so that it mixes with the fluorescent light. This improves color rendition by adding yellows and reds to the subject. The light should be bounced off a white ceiling or wall. Any part of the subject not illuminated by the bounce light reproduces with the blue-green cast typical of fluorescent-light filming.

If the subject is directly illuminated by incandescent light (such as a sun gun) in such a way that whatever fluorescent light is hitting it is overpowered, then tungsten-balanced film may be used, and the fluorescent light disregarded.

Filming with fluorescent light has another possible disadvantage for both color and black and white films. If exposure is less than 1/60th of a second (at 24 fps, with a shutter opening of less than 145°—such as on the Bolex and Canon Scoopic), you will very likely get a picture in which there is a slight pulsating of the light. If exposures are for longer than 1/60th of a second, it is less likely that you will see this pulsating.

Color filming from a television receiver

If you wish to film from a television receiver, you should balance your film for daylight to get the best color rendition.

---

* Special filters for shooting color under fluorescent light are available. Consult the film manufacturer for suggested filters and exposure compensation.

If you film from a television tube, the scanner or rollbar movement will be picked up by your camera if it is filming at standard speeds. If you slow down the camera, in which case the action will project as speeded up, you can get rid of the bar movement. If the camera exposes each frame for more than 1/30th of a second, the bar will go unseen. On most cameras this is about 15 fps or slower. On a reflex camera with a rotating mirror the rollbar can actually be observed through the viewfinder while the camera is running.

X. Filters

In filming, especially if you are working in color, you will often have occasion to use a filter. Filters can be screwed onto most lenses with the aid of an adapter ring. Glass filters are fairly expensive, and each of your lenses may be of a different diameter and require a filter of its own size. If your camera has a matte box, less expensive gelatin filters can be used. A filter in a matte box covers almost any lens you are using regardless of the lens size. Some cameras and lenses provide a way to place the filter inside the camera close to the film plane. Gelatin filters can be cut down to fit the place provided. Filters should be clean and free from scratches wherever they are used.

Filters should be of high quality. Poor filters, especially low-quality glass filters, can reduce the quality of the image significantly. When filters are used behind the lens, the focus of the lens is changed slightly. If you have a reflex camera whose focusing image passes through the filter, you need not worry. If the focusing image does not pass through the filter, as on Angénieux zooms with auxiliary viewfinders, or if your camera is not reflex, then you had best use filters in front of the lens.

Filters should be stored in a cool, dry place. They change color with age and should be checked at intervals against a new filter. Discard a discolored filter as it will no longer deliver predictable or desirable results.

Filter factors

Filters absorb a certain amount of light, and, therefore, you must compensate in your exposure for the decrease in light reaching the film. Manufacturers usually suggest a *filter factor* for each filter calculated for the particular film you are using. The filter factor represents the number of times the normal exposure must be increased. A filter factor of two means an increase of one whole f/stop. Every time the filter factor is doubled, an additional stop of exposure is required. For a factor of four you open the lens two stops wider than for normal exposure.

When you are using a filter, you can take a normal exposure reading, find the suitable f/number, and then compensate for the filter by opening the aperture a suitable amount. As an alternate method, one which should be used especially if your camera has a built-in exposure meter which does *not* read through the lens, you can divide the filter factor into the ASA number and then proceed as though there were no filter. If the filter factor is three (an exposure increase of one and a half stops) and the ASA of the film is 125, then we divide 3 into 125 and get an ASA of 40 (a close enough approximation). If your camera has a meter that monitors the light from behind the lens, there is no need to make any compensation since your meter will do it automatically. You should realize, however, that this built-in compensation on behind-the-lens meters is less than ideal for arriving at the correct exposure with a filter.

If two or more filters are used, their factors should be multiplied. This figure will not be accurate if both filters cut out some of the same wavelengths of light. The multiplying works if you are using a neutral density filter in combination with another filter, or with color filters whose multiplied factor is below 40.

The following sections describe all-purpose filters for black and white and color films.

Neutral density filters

A *neutral density filter* is a gray filter which cuts down the amount of light hitting the lens. Since it affects all colors equally, it can be used with color film without changing relative color values. It is useful if you wish to use high-speed film in bright light or when you want to use a wider aperture to decrease depth of field. Each multiple of .30 in the number describing a neutral density filter means that it cuts down required exposure by one stop (e.g., ND .90 cuts exposure by three stops).

Neutral density filters can be ordered in combination with other filters, so that one filter performs the function of two.

Polarizing filters

Polarizing filters must be able to be rotated when mounted on the lens. The effect of light polarization can be observed by looking through the filter and rotating it. Polarized light is progressively decreased as the filter is rotated. A polarizing filter only works with light that is polarized, such as sunlight, and with reflections on glass and water. (Not all reflected light is polarized.) The polarizing filter acts just like a neutral density filter when there is no polarized light in the subject being filmed.

The polarizing filter does not affect color rendition. Using one is the best way of darkening the sky without changing the other colors on the film. The filter has one serious disadvantage for outdoor cinematography: the amount of light it cuts depends entirely on the angle at which polarized light hits the filter. The effect is most pronounced when the filter and light are at right angles. In a camera pan, part of the sky may appear to have a different tonality from the rest of the sky. With color film a polarizing filter can be used to darken the sky (other methods are discussed below for black and white film), but at a very limited number of angles if the sky is to be kept at one constant tonality.

The amount of reflection from certain surfaces can be controlled, sometimes entirely eliminated, by using a polarizing filter. Observe the reflection while looking through and rotating the filter (on a non-reflex camera) or while looking through the reflex camera's viewfinder and rotating the filter to see how the reflection is affected.

No single filter factor can be given for the polarizing filter since the amount of light it cuts out depends on the degree of rotation. Normally a filter factor of three (one and a half stops) obtains when sunlight is not at a right angle to the lens. If it is to obtain a darker sky, use a filter factor of four to six (two to two and a half stops). Behind-the-lens meters compensate fairly well for the exposure changes required for neutral density and polarizing filters.

Diffusion filters

There are *diffusion filters* available for softening hard lines, frequently used to flatter a woman photographed close-up. The result is usually obvious and corny.

Fog filters

Harrison *fog filters* can be used to create a fog effect in a scene. There are "regular fog" and "double fog" filters. Both types come in varying gradations, simulating light to heavy fog. These require no exposure compensation. The regular fog filters create a halo around highlights and decrease image definition. Double fog filters do neither. If you plan to use diffusion or fog filters, make preliminary tests.

Filters to protect the lens

Clear optical glass of good quality in a filter holder protects your lens from dust, wind, and rain. Many photographers leave a UV or skylight 1A filter over their lenses for protection. Light loss is inconsequential.

Filters for black and white film

The filter will lighten its own color and darken its complement. A red filter will darken green foliage and lighten red lips. When using a filter you must consider *all* the important colors in the subject and decide how they should be rendered in gray tones. You may successfully darken a blue sky with a red filter, but you may have unhappily made someone's lips too light. Filters should be experimented with before they are used for serious work. When in doubt, use little or no filtration rather than falsify your subject's appearance.

The most common uses of filters in black and white filming are for haze penetration and for sky darkening. Haze and ultraviolet light, common features of distant landscapes, will adversely affect your photographic image. Unlike fog or mist, which no filter can penetrate, the visual effect of haze can be decreased. Visible haze decreases as heavier yellow, orange, and red filters are used; the greatest penetration is achieved by a heavy red filter. Yellow, orange, and red filters will also darken the sky.

In much black and white photography, correct exposure for the subject will give you a pale, washed-out, and cloudless sky. A sky darkened too much (by using a heavy filter) will have a phony, heavily dramatic quality. The bluer the sky, the easier it is to darken it and the less filtration needed. When the sky is overcast or misty, filters will not be very effective. The sky near the sun and on the horizon is often almost white and does not respond to filtration. If the film is overexposed, the filter effect may be largely lost.

If you wish to bleach a blue sky, a blue filter will do the trick.

Filters for color film

Color film, to give good color rendition, must be used with illumination of the type for which the film has been balanced (see p. 110). When the light is off balance, filters may be used over the lens to promote good color. A set of color compensating (CC) filters may be purchased with a color temperature meter to balance the film for almost any type of illumination.

Color temperature meters are most useful for evaluating tungsten light. Many give the reading in degrees Kelvin and state the identifying number of the filter required to achieve a proper color balance. The meter should be pointed at the light source, never pointed at the subject.

Color temperature meters are most valuable when used in conjunction with color compensating filters. If in a lighting setup using bulbs rated at 3200°K you take a reading and discover that the color temperature is 3100°K (perhaps because of a voltage drop), the chart with the meter (or on its scale) tells you to correct with a Kodak #82 filter or a Spectra CT 1 T filter. You are thus able to avoid the slightly red cast that would otherwise appear on the film.

Black and white filters should not be used with color films unless some exaggerated effect is desired, such as an all-blue or all-red picture.

A skylight 1A or UV filter can be used to tone down the blue cast from shadows and snow that often appears in the color image when using daylight-balanced film.

A #85 filter will allow you to use film balanced for 3200°K outdoors. It can be combined with a neutral density filter such as the 85N3 (#85 filter plus a ND .30) if the cameraman wishes to use high-speed color film at a wider aperture outside. A #85 filter has a UV filter built in.

If you wish to use film balanced for 3200°K with photofloods (3400°K), a Kodak 81A filter can be used. Film balanced for daylight can be used with photofloods with a Kodak filter 80B, and with 3200°K lamps with a Kodak 80A. Daylight film used with tungsten illumination requires a high filter factor and often results in inferior color reproduction.

Filter factors and filter recommendations are usually included with a data sheet that comes with the filter. Additional information can be acquired from the film or filter manufacturer.

XI. Picture Editing

Editing, or the selecting and arranging of shots into sequences and sequences into a film, is widely held to be the most important element in filmmaking.

To the earliest filmmakers the whole film was one single shot and all significant action had to be built into the one shot. As time went on, it became clear that a shot could be placed after another and the viewer would accept that the action in both shots was occurring in the same space. The placing of one shot next to another is called a *cut;* it is the abrupt ending of one shot and the immediate beginning of the next. Editing is often called *cutting.* The cut refers to both the actual physical joining as well as to the effect on the screen.

Perhaps the most important concept of editing, the one which defines film space and film time, is that a cut from one shot to the next can give the viewer the illusion of continuous space and time within the film's action. The most-often cited example of this, an example that teaches us much about film acting, comes from the Russians. We have one shot of an actor which lasts several seconds. We divide the shot into two parts, alternately placing a shot (i.e., cutting in a shot) of a bowl of soup, a girl who is in pain, and a gun. When the sequences were shown to Russian film students, they all remarked on the fine acting of Mosjoukine (a famous actor of the time)—how in the first shot he looked hungry, in the next pitying, and in the last afraid. Yet he had the same expression on his face in all three cases. The three-shot sequence is a key to much of narrative film editing: we see the actor looking, we see what he sees and how he reacts. (Hitchcock's *Rear Window* was almost entirely done using this simple device.) The audience accepts all three shots as occurring in the same space and time, though the shots may have been taken miles and years apart. A little girl looks at something off-camera, we cut to an explosion, and the viewer accepts that she is looking at the explosion. Peter O'Toole once noted with horror that within two cuts equaling eight seconds of footage in *Lawrence of Arabia* he had *actually* aged two whole years!

How do we go from one time sequence to another? The

usual way at one time was to use a fade, a dissolve, or a wipe. These are often called the punctuation marks of film. A fade is generally used to denote a longer passage of time or a more definite end of a series of events than a dissolve. The length of a fade or a dissolve can be varied to make further time or space distinctions. In *parallel editing*, when two series of events supposedly occurring simultaneously are intercut (e.g., the perils of the heroine and the attempts of the hero many miles away to reach her), the sequences may be connected with a wipe in which one image pushes the other off the screen.

In the last few years it has become fashionable to dispense with these punctuations and to use the cut to divide sequences. This again raises the problem of how to distinguish the cut within a sequence from a cut that divides sequences. Of course, the filmmaker may want to blur that distinction or he may want to fool or confuse the viewer as Resnais did in *Last Year at Marienbad*. If the filmmaker wishes his continuity to be immediately clear, he may separate sequences by explicit changes in locale, lighting, or costumes, add a line of expository dialogue, or cut in a change in weather or even in background noise.

The 180° rule

For the moment we will limit the discussion of film space to that which is within one location and one time—in other words, the simple sequence. To achieve a film space that is realistic, that the viewer will accept as a continuous space in time, there are some simple rules you may observe. The chief one is sometimes called the *180° rule:* If we draw an imaginary line through the main action, all the camera shots must be on the same side of that line. (See Fig. XI)

Another way of putting this is that all screen directions should be the same in any given space. *Screen direction* is whatever direction, right or left, the actor is looking at or moving toward, described from the audience point of view. Screen direction should be preserved unless the actor himself turns or changes direction.

To illustrate this, consider a conversation between two people, A and B, looking at each other. A is at the right looking at B, who is at the left looking at A. If we were to draw a line through the action, from A to B, and to keep all our camera positions on one side of that line, we would always preserve screen direction. A is looking left in any shot on one side of the line. If we were to cross the line, A would

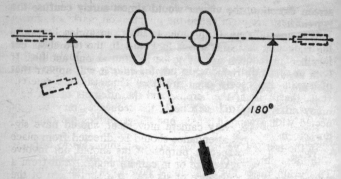

Fig. XI. *The 180° rule:* If we draw a line through the main action, any camera position on one side of the line will preserve screen direction.

be looking right, and we would have changed screen direction and possibly confused the audience.

The viewer will accept shots from many different vantage points, heights, and distances, and will incorporate them into an unambiguous representation of a real space. But when the above rule is violated, relationships of people and objects may be obscured.

If the camera itself crosses over the line during a continuous shot, the change is acceptable. When someone changes from one space to another, as in going out of a house, changing of screen direction may work unambiguously. However, it is important to avoid an effect in which the actor leaves at the right and enters a new scene from the right, because it may look as if he has returned to the same place. If a person is looking or walking directly toward or away from the camera, his screen direction is neutral, and such shots can be cut without danger of confusion with shots of either right or left screen direction.

It is typical in "chase" pictures for both pursuer and pursued to move in the same screen direction so as to heighten the illusion of a chase. When cutting between subjects that are about to make contact, opposite screen directions are used consistently for each. If the cavalry is shown riding from the right, the Indians will always be shown riding from the left. TV coverage of a football game is similar. All the cameras are usually kept on one side of the field. One team is always moving to the right, the other to the left. If the camera position were to cross the 180° line of action, changing screen direction, the viewer would almost surely confuse the two sides.

We can see, then, if someone is shown in a close-up looking right and someone else is looking left, the two shots cut together make them appear to be looking at one another. If both are looking right, when cut together it will appear that they are looking in the same direction.

Cutting and pacing

Every cut, like every camera movement, should have significance. Audience attendance should be directed from place to place for some specific purpose. Cuts should not involve slight changes in image size or in camera angle. A cut from a person filmed at a distance of six feet to a shot taken of the same subject at five feet would be meaningless and inefficient. The subject would jump a little closer but no new information would be revealed to the audience. If cutting is to appear smooth, it must be logical, informing without making the viewer conscious of the cutting by means of unnecessary changes in angle or position.

The length of shots, how much of an action is shown, the length of sequences, and how they are juxtaposed all contribute to the timing or pacing of a film. Unnecessary intervals can be cut out for faster pacing. Events can be stretched or condensed in the cutting, allowing the editor to exercise tremendous control over the sense of time that the audience experiences.

The cut-away

The *cut-away* is a shot supposedly taking place at the same time as the main action, but not directly involved in the main action. The most common variety of cut-away is the *reaction shot*. This is simply a shot of a person reacting to the main action as listener or spectator. Cut-aways, when properly used, do not interfere with the integrity or continuity of the main action. They are often useful for overcoming continuity gaps when footage is not sufficient in this respect.

A *cut-in* or *insert shot* shows some detail of the main action other than actors' faces. If someone looks into a box, a close-up of what he sees is an insert shot.

Cut-aways and insert shots are the two easiest manners of stretching or condensing actual time to give the film different time. If we cut between a race and the spectators' reactions, we often lengthen the actual time of the race. If we cut away for part of a movement, when we cut back we may have cut out a large chunk of action.

Continuity editing

We can distinguish two common methods or styles of continuity editing (narrative film editing). The first is a more subjective style in that it attempts to give the viewer a notion of how things appear to the participants in the film action. This is the three-cut method mentioned above in the Russian experiment with the actor. This sequence of three cuts is often preceded by a general establishing shot which takes in the whole scene and tells the viewer where he is and what the general spatial relations between things and people are. Alfred Hitchcock is perhaps the most accomplished practitioner of this technique.

The second method dispenses with point-of-view shots and in its simplest form consists of an establishing shot, medium shot, and close-up. In the first method, the cutting has a built-in rationale. The establishing shot is the objective view of the scene. Cuts away from the person to objects or people are assumed to be what the person is looking at in the scene.

Both methods of editing tend to be pedestrian, and divergences from them may gain the filmmaker a certain power. For example, a scene completely done in close-ups would be disorienting in a way that neither of the above two methods could be. If every scene has been introduced with an establishing shot, its omission at the start of a new sequence or at a new location might add a sense of mystery or at least convey some feeling of *difference*.

To restate the importance of motivation in filming or editing: you should always know the answer to the questions "Why did you cut here?" or "Why did you pan there?" Cuts have a forward motion; they tend to speed action along in a way that a continuous shot cannot.

When a *match cut,* a cut between shots of the same subject in what is to appear a precisely continuous time span, is used, the rule is to cut on motion to minimize viewer awareness of the cut. Cutting on subject movement helps cover up slight mismatches from one shot to the next, since the action is what draws the attention of the viewer. To give the editor some freedom in cutting, action should be overlapped as much as possible from one shot to the next if you plan continuity editing. If a person walking up a flight of stairs stops to tie his shoelace, we might want to film it in two shots. The first might be a medium shot, and then we cut to a close-up of his hands tying the lace. For the first shot it is important to film the action past the point where the shot should be cut and to begin the second segment with a part of the action al-

EQUIPMENT

1. *(left)* DOUBLE PERFORATED 16MM FILM. Motion picture film is composed of a series of still photographs *(frames)*. The area between successive frames is called the *frame line*. On 16mm film the frame line should be at the center of the film's perforations. A latent edge-number can be seen on the left side of the film. *(right)* SINGLE PERFORATED 16MM FILM. An optical sound track can be seen on the side opposite the perforations. *(David Hancock)*

2. *(left)* 16MM MAGNETIC FILM. Sound is transferred to magnetic film for editing purposes. Through wear, small scratches appear on the edge of the film. If not very deep, they do not affect sound quality. *(right)* 16MM MAGNETIC STRIPED FILM. The edge of the film can be coated with oxide for the reproduction of magnetic sound. Not all sound projectors are capable of playing back magnetic sound. A balancing stripe of oxide should be on the perforation side of the film to guarantee smooth film transport during projection. *(David Hancock)*

3. SUPER 8 CAMERAS are small and often highly automated. (A) The Bell & Howell Focus-Tronic offers a form of automatic focusing. *(Bell & Howell)* (B) The Bolex 155 Super 8 offers a zoom lens which will focus down to very close distances. *(Paillard, Inc.)* (C) The Kodak Instamatic M12 is very inexpensive, has a fixed focus lens, and is exceptionally small. *(Eastman Kodak Co.)* (D) The Kodak Ektagraphic 8 offers through-the-lens exposure readings and a zoom lens, as do the Bell & Howell and the Bolex. *(Eastman Kodak Co.)*

4. 16MM CAMERA—BOLEX H-16 REX 5. Reflex viewing employing a partially silvered mirror. 100′ internal capacity. 400′ magazine can be added, but it makes the camera awkward. Three lens non-divergent turret. Automatic threading. Illustrated with 10mm, 25mm, and 75mm lenses with preset diaphragms. The lenses above are all fitted with lens shades. Special "C" mount lenses are needed for reflex Bolexes for focal lengths less than 75mm. Shutter has a 130° opening. Spring-wound motor with 16½′ run. Can take single frames. Camera speeds from 12-64 fps. Variable shutter. Fades and dissolves can be made in the camera. The rubber eyecup prevents stray light from entering the viewfinder when your eye is pressed against it. Many accessories are available for the camera. *(Paillard, Inc.)*

5. 16MM CAMERA—BOLEX H-16 M-4. Non-reflex camera shown with 17-85mm Pan Cinor f/2 zoom lens. Through-the-lens viewing through auxiliary finder built into the lens. Focusing is not done on a ground glass but with a built-in rangefinder. Single lens turret will accept any "C" mount lens. Auxiliary finder, which fits onto side of camera, is parallax corrected for lenses from 10mm to 150mm. Camera accepts 100" internal loads. Camera speed from 12-64 fps with spring-wound motor with a run of 16½'. Single-frame exposures. Automatic threading. *(Paillard, Inc.)*

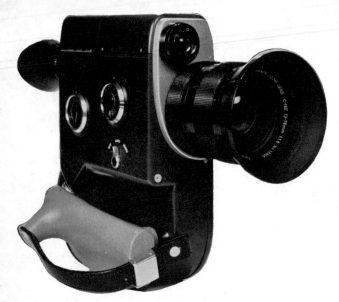

6. 16MM CAMERA—CANON SCOOPIC. Camera has a built-in 13-76mm Canon zoom lens with a very fast maximum aperture of f/1.6. The illustrated lens is fitted with a lens shade. Electric film drive powered by a nickel-cadmium battery within the camera body. The built-in exposure meter with automatic diaphragm has a manual override. Since the exposure meter does not read through-the-lens, parallax problems arise. Reflex viewing with the partially silvered mirror in front of lens diaphragm, so viewing is always wide open. The image is focused on a microprism screen in the center of the viewed image—a system common in Super 8. Some may find microprism focusing more difficult than ground glass focusing. Automatic threading. Filming speeds of 16, 24, 32, and 48 fps. The built-in handgrip is very convenient. *(Canon U.S.A., Inc.)*

7. 16MM CAMERA—CINE-KODAK K-100 TURRET CAMERA. Three lens non-divergent turret with auxiliary viewfinder for each lens. Spring-wound motor can be run up to 40′ on one winding. Parallax adjustments are made by using a set of crosshairs seen through the viewfinder. Camera speeds from 16-64 fps. *(Eastman Kodak Co.)*

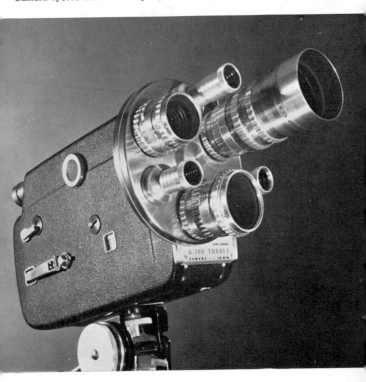

8. 16MM CAMERA—BELL & HOWELL 70-DR. Three lens non-divergent turret with matching auxiliary lens for viewing with parallax correction. Spring-wound motor can run up to 22′. Camera speeds of 8, 12, 16, 24, 32, 48, and 64 fps. 240° shutter opening. Accepts "C" mount lenses. Some models can be run forward or reverse. Some models accept up to 400′ magazines. Critical focuser magnifies a portion of the image for focusing when the lens is swung out of position. The 70-DR is a very rugged camera and has many accessories available. *(Bell & Howell Co.)*

9. 16MM CAMERAS—ARRIFLEX 16 S *(top)*; ARRIFLEX 16 M *(bottom)*. Reflex viewing with rotating mirror and full ground glass focusing. Arriflex S has provision for internal 100′ load. Both cameras are shown with 400′ magazine and matte box. Electric motor. Divergent three lens turret. Extremely rugged. 180° shutter. Registration pin guarantees an exceptionally steady image both in forward and reverse filming. The professional standard for 16mm silent filming. Very wide range of accessories are available. *(Arriflex Corp. of America)*

10. DIVERGENT TURRET. Arriflex S showing a divergent three lens turret. A wide-angle lens can be used without picking up the edge of a long lens. (*Arriflex Corp. of America*)

12. (*right*) 16MM CAMERA—BEAULIEU R16ES. Camera is shown with a 12-120mm Angénieux f/2.2 zoom lens with crank. The pistol grip is a very useful accessory to ease camera holding. The camera features a guillotine mirror shutter for reflex viewing, with full ground glass focusing. Electric film drive. Newer models are available with batteries built into the handgrip. The Model 16B will accept 200′ magazines. All models are exceptionally light in weight. Through-the-lens exposure readings. Single-framing is possible. Though the camera is not noiseless, there is a provision for cable sync-sound. Non-divergent three lens turret. Camera speeds from 2-64 fps. Film rewind. The camera is not easy to load and it is somewhat difficult to clean the aperture. (*David Hancock*)

11. BODY BRACE. Prenzell body brace is shown supporting an Arriflex S to minimize hand-held camera movements. The cameraman's right hand is gripping the follow-focus knob on the lens in shooting position. (*David Hancock*)

13. 16MM CAMERA—ARRIFLEX BL. Features similar to Arriflex M, but it is also self-blimped. Primarily used when sound is being recorded synchronously with the picture. (*Arriflex Corp. of America*)

14. 16MM CAMERA—GENERAL CAMERA SSIII. Self-blimped. Primarily used when sound is being recorded synchronously with the picture. Relatively light for a camera that runs silently. Built to rest on the cameraman's shoulder. Viewing through Angénieux zoom lens with auxiliary viewfinder. Takes various size magazines up to 1200′. Shown with 400′ magazine. This is a more radical example of the many conversions that make the Auricon Cine-Voice sound-on-film camera more flexible.

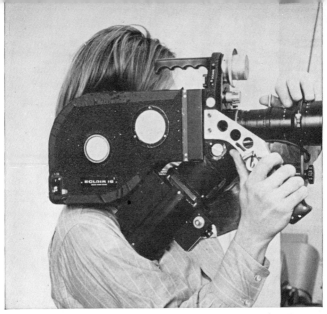

15. 16MM CAMERA—ECLAIR NPR. Rotating mirror for reflex viewing with full ground glass focusing. Camera is noiseless. Primarily used for synchronous sound shooting. The camera is built to rest on the cameraman's shoulder. The grip is custom built. *(David Hancock)*

16. 16MM CAMERA—FILMING WITH SOUND. Cameraman *(left)* is shooting hand-held with an Eclair NPR. Soundman *(right)* is using a Nagra III NPH tape recorder with Sennheiser 804 shotgun microphone with a homemade windscreen. Subject is shooting hand-held with a Bolex. *(National Educational Television)*

17. Lens mounts—*(left)* Arriflex bayonet-type mount. *(right)* Screw-in "C" mount. Most cameras with interchangeable lenses accept "C" mount lenses. Arriflex cameras only accept lenses in an Arriflex mount. The "C" mount is less rugged than the Arriflex mount. *(David Hancock)*

18. A selection of different focal length lenses. Illustrated are Kinoptic lenses ranging in focal length from 12.5mm to 500 mm. Generally, the longer the lens, the longer its focal length and the narrower the field of view it covers, that is, the larger any particular object will be rendered on the film. *(Karl Heitz, Inc.)*

19. THE KINOPTIC SUPER-TEGEA F/1.9 1.9MM LENS. An incredible wide-angle fish-eye type lens. The lens covers a field of view of 197°, seeing a little behind itself. (*Karl Heitz, Inc.*)

20. 8MM ZOOM LENS—ANGÉNIEUX 8-64MM F/1.9 ZOOM LENS. Lens has a zoom lever. Rear lens cap is shown. It protects the rear element of the lens when the lens is not mounted on a camera. (*Angénieux Corp. of America, Inc.*)

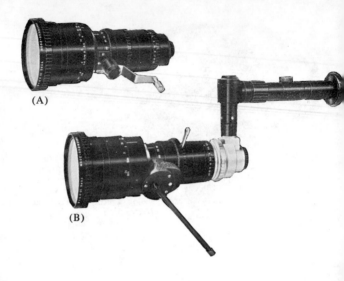

21. 16MM ZOOM LENSES. (A) Angénieux 9.5mm-95mm f/2.2 zoom lens with crank. (B) The same lens with zoom levers and auxiliary viewfinder. (C) Angénieux 12mm-120mm f/2.2 zoom lens with through-the-lens exposure meter and automatic diaphragm. (*Angénieux Corp. of America, Inc.*)

(C)

22. ZOOM LENS SUPPORT. An Angénieux 9.5mm-95mm zoom lens on an Eclair NPR is shown with a zoom lens support. Heavy zoom lenses, especially in "C" mount, should have a zoom lens support. (*David Hancock*)

23. SUPER 8 FILM CARTRIDGE. A light-tank film cartridge used in Super 8 cameras. Loading is simple and automatic. There is no need to thread or handle the film. However, most cameras using Super 8 cartridges cannot make dissolves or superimpositions. The few that can are only able to make effects of limited length. (*Eastman Kodak Co.*)

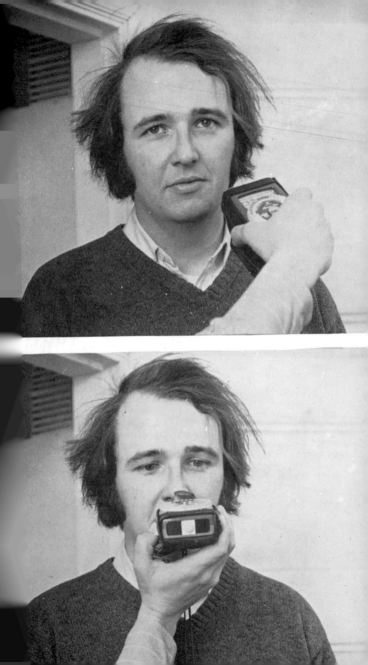

24. *(left)* A REFLECTED-LIGHT READING. Care must be taken to avoid reading any shadow cast by the meter. The exposure will normally be increased one stop over the reading, since the meter is reading average Caucasian skin. *(David Hancock)*

25. *(below left)* AN INCIDENT LIGHT READING. With the incident light attachment in place, the meter is placed at the subject and pointed *toward* the camera in order to measure the light falling on the subject. In this case no exposure compensation need be made. *(David Hancock)*

26. *(below)* AN INCIDENT LIGHT READING. The Spectra meter has a large photosphere which is pointed toward the camera. The photosphere or hemisphere is like a small face which measures the light striking the subject from all directions and compensates for the amount of effective exposure given by each kind of light. The Spectra directly indicates the required f/stop. Incident light readings are often helpful when there is danger of stray light hitting the meter and influencing the reading. *(David Hancock)*

27. EXPOSURE METERS. *(left to right)* The Weston Master II with case—an older version of a commonly used Selenium meter, used primarily for reflected-light readings. The Gossen Luna-Pro—a highly sensitive CdS meter, used primarily for reflected-light readings. It does have a built-in incident light attachment which is fairly good. The Spectra Universal meter—used primarily for incident light readings. It features a large photosphere and is the standard professional incident light meter. *(David Hancock)*

28. The Honeywell Pentax 1/21 spot meter. A reflected-light meter which reads a very small part of the subject. Its field of measurement is only 1°, and its field of view is 21°. Spot meters are often helpful in very difficult lighting situations. *(David Hancock)*

29. The Weston Ranger 9. A Cadmium-sulfide type meter. The meter is primarily for reflected-light readings, but a built-in incident light attachment is fairly good. *(Weston Instruments, Inc.)*

30. TRIPODS. *(left)* A fairly light metal tripod can usually support a light camera such as the Beaulieu. The pan-and-tilt head is useful for setting up shots but will not usually yield smooth camera movement during a shot. *(below)* The heavier wooden tripod has a fluid head. This tripod will accommodate the heavier 16mm cameras and give smooth pans and tilts. The tripod legs are mounted on a *spider* with clamps to hold the legs stationary on a hard surface. *(David Hancock)*

31. HI-HAT. The tripod head is placed on a hi-hat when the cameraman wishes to shoot from a few inches off the floor. *(David Hancock)*

32. CHANGING BAG. A portable darkroom. Film that must be handled in the dark is placed in one end of the double-lined, double-zippered bag, and hands are placed in the appropriate sleeved holes at the other end of the bag. *(David Hancock)*

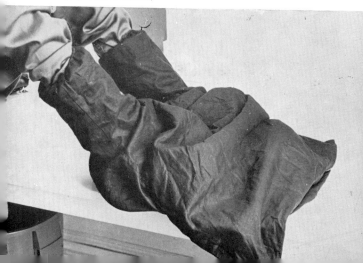

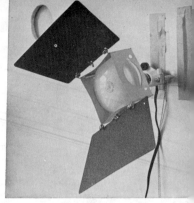

(A)

33. LIGHTS. (A) LOWEL-
LITE with barndoors and
wall bracket. The black
flaps (barndoors) prevent
stray light from hitting the
camera lens. Lowel-lite fixtures are extremely light
and can be attached to
walls with gaffer's tape. The
fixture takes R-40 reflector
bulbs. (B) COLORTRAN
QUARTZ LIGHTS mounted on
stands. Quartz lights offer
many advantages over reg-
ular tungsten lights. The Quartz-King Dual "650" *(left)* has a spot and
flood position. The Mini-Lite "10" *(right)* has a very wide, even pattern,
making it a good fill light. Both of the illustrated Colortran units are
light in weight. (C) THE SYLVANIA SUNGUN is a battery operated 30 volt
portable light. In this case, power is supplied with the Dana Fuller
Silver Cadmium battery belt. *(David Hancock)*

(B)

(C)

34. 16MM ACTION VIEWER. On this viewer the film has a relatively complicated path. The fewer parts the film comes into contact with on the viewer, the better. This viewer delivers a fairly sharp and steady picture. *(David Hancock)*

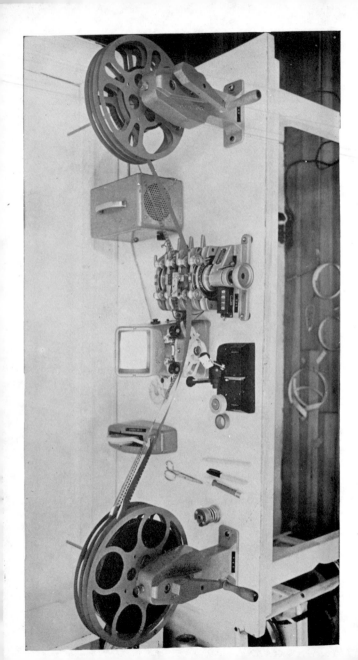

35. *(left and below)* 16MM EDITING BENCH—equipped for double system sound. The sound and picture reels are mounted on long shafts attached to the rewinds. The screws on top of the rewinds adjust the amount of friction drag during rewinding. If picture alone were being edited, only the rewinds (with short shafts), viewer and splicer would be necessary. The Moviscop viewer has a very simple film path and puts little wear on the film. In front of the viewer is a Rivas straight splicer. It uses either roll 16mm sprocketed Mylar splices or precut splices. The illustrated Moviola synchronizer to the right of the viewer keeps sound and picture in exact synchronization. Picture is loaded on the synchronizer behind the sound. In the illustration, the synchronizer has four gangs. The sound is on the second gang. The sound head on the second gang is attached to an amplifier-speaker to reproduce sound. *(David Hancock)*

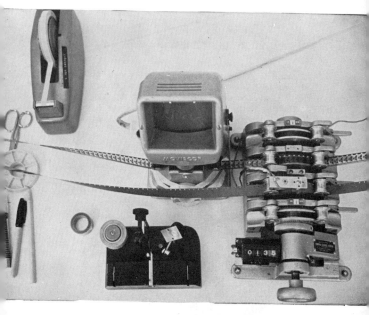

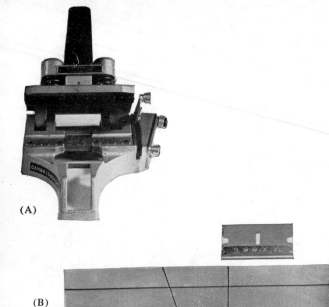

(A)

(B)

36. SPLICERS. The guillotine splicer (A) has a high initial cost, but the splices themselves are inexpensive. Tape splices can be made on a splicing block (B) with the aid of a pair of scissors and a sharp razor blade. This is a difficult way to splice. *(David Hancock)* Cement splicer (C), Griswold Film Splicer Jr. Model 8 & 16mm. *(Neumade Products Corp.)*

(C)

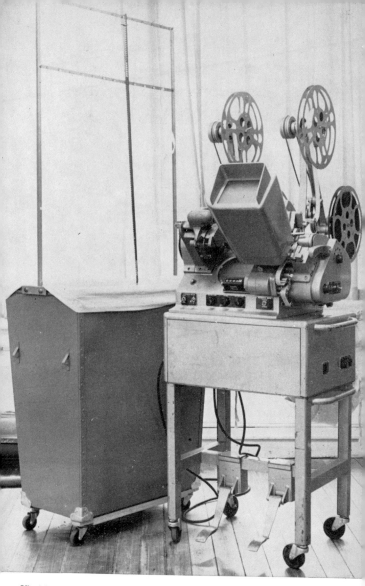

37. 16MM-16MM MOVIOLA EDITING MACHINE. For editing double system sound and picture. At the left of the Moviola is an editing bin, which is useful for storing shots. Individual shots are suspended from pins. (*David Hancock*)

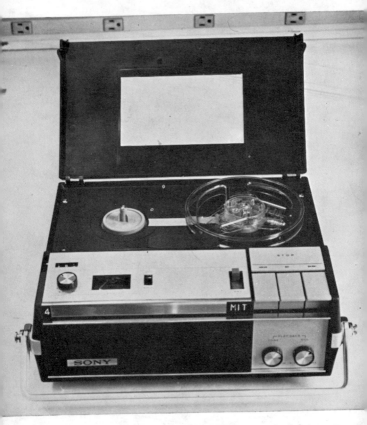

38. TAPE RECORDER—SONY 800. A portable battery-operated tape recorder. *(David Hancock)*

39. TAPE RECORDER—NAGRA IIINPH. A portable battery-operated tape recorder. A studio quality machine which can be used for shooting synchronous sound with an appropriate camera. *(David Hancock)*

40. Siemens double system "2000" sound projectors. The 16mm magnetic sound is loaded on one side, and the picture is loaded on the other side. Synchronization is preserved in both forward and reverse. The unit illustrated at the left has a synchronous motor. These models have been discontinued and replaced by the more rugged and expensive Sonorex interlock projector. The Bauer P6 Studio and the Palmer Interlock are also available double system projectors. *(Arriflex Corp. of America)*

FOCAL LENGTH, PERSPECTIVE, EXPOSURE, DEPTH OF FIELD

41. This series of shots (A)–(G) is taken from the same camera position, about 14′ from the couple. Each shot is marked with the approximate focal length of the lens used in the 16mm format. To arrive at the approximately equivalent 8mm focal length, divide the 16mm focal length in half. In 8mm the series of shots (A)–(G) would be about 4.5mm–50mm. With the shorter focal lengths, the couple looks farther away. As we use longer lenses, the reproduction ratio becomes larger, we start to lose depth of field, and the couple appears closer. Perspective is the same in the whole series of shots since subject-to-camera distance is constant. The range of focal lengths shown is about the same as that of a 10:1 zoom lens. *(David Hancock)*

(A) 9mm

(B) 12mm

(C) 17mm

(D) 35mm

(E) 45mm

(F) 65mm

(G) 100mm

42. As we move farther from the subject and use longer lenses we start to notice a flattening of perspective (foreshortening). The gravestones appear to be piled one on top of another, with little distance between them. *(David Hancock)*

43. As we move in closer to the subject with a wider angle lens, perspective becomes exaggerated. Shooting upward, figures appear to be taller and stronger.

44. In these three pictures we have kept the subject the same size in the frame but have varied the focal length of the lens used and the subject-to-camera distance in order to illustrate changes in perspective. In the 9mm shot (A), the nose is elongated and the ears seem to be far back. The 100mm shot (C) gives us a flatter perspective than the 17mm shot (B). In the 100mm shot, the ears appear to be much closer to the front of the face, and the chin seems smaller. *(David Hancock)*

(A) 9mm

45. In order to get maximum depth of field, we want to stop the lens down as far as possible (A). If we open up the lens we get less depth of field. (B) was taken with the lens five stops wider open than in (A). When we have a small amount of depth of field, the plane of critical focus stands out more clearly. (*David Hancock*)

(A)

(B)

(A)

(B)

46. If we compare the overexposed photograph (C) with the better exposed photograph (A), we see the former has no differentiation of tones in the sky. The shadows on the road are washed out and barely discernible. The snow shows no small bright areas with surrounding shadows—only large expanses of undifferentiated white. In the under-exposed photograph (B) we lose shadow detail. The shadows become undifferentiated black. The brighter areas of the scene are depressed, and we get no good whites. The scene appears to be more of a night scene. *(David Hancock)*

(C)

47. If you are shooting negative film, it is important to learn what a properly exposed negative image looks like. The negative in the upper left (A) is the best exposed. The negative below it (B) is underexposed. It will appear thin and light. A lot of detail will be missing in the shadow areas. The overexposed negative (C) often looks good to the inexperienced eye. Overexposure can be recognized by very dense (dark) sections which cover the brighter areas of the subject. (*David Hancock*)

(C)

ready completed in the first shot. This is insurance against mismatching shots because some bit of the action was missed or destroyed. The editor will be given the choice of whether to cut before, during, or after the action. Obviously, extreme care must be exercised to see that everything in the scene stays the same from one shot to the next (position of limbs, clothes, hair, facial expression, position of objects, etc). If the actor ties his right shoelace in the first shot, it must be the lace of his right shoe in the second shot.

Jump-cutting

In recent years, largely because of the influence of Jean-Luc Godard, it has become the fad to dispense with match cuts and use *jump-cuts*. Jump-cutting used to be the foremost demon of the editing room. Any poorly made match cut was called a jump-cut. The most common type of jump-cut used today is the simple cutting out of footage that would otherwise give the sequence normal continuity. Much more rarely used is the type of jump-cut in which camera viewpoint changes very slightly on the cut, giving the impression of a jump in the action.

The mechanics of editing

In order to edit you need some way of viewing the film and some way of cutting it up and putting it in a new order. You do this with a film viewer, a set of rewinds, and a splicer.

Film rewinds

For 8mm, rewinds tend to be flimsy and cannot accommodate much film. The rewind handles can be gripped between only two fingers, which increases fatigue. 16mm rewinds are usually much more solid. The type with the handle which can be gripped with the palm should be selected. (See Plate 35)

For 16mm, a useful accessory to the rewind is a friction adjuster, a knob which adjusts the amount of drag or tension. It is particularly useful when you are working with original film, for it prevents the film from turning by itself and touching the editing bench. Improperly mounted rewinds may start to turn by themselves very slowly, and if you must step away from the bench for a moment, you may return to find film all over the floor. When you are working with a separate track of sound or conforming the original with the workprint, you should have a rewind with a shaft long enough to accommodate more than one reel.

Rewinds should turn easily and move the film along

quickly without much cranking of the handle. 16mm rewinds should be able to handle 2000 feet of film at a time.

The reel is attached to the shaft by sliding the *key* (the square hole on the center of the reel) onto the rewind shaft, where there is a peg which locks into the key of the reel. A hinged end keeps the reel from slipping. For editing 16mm, get double-keyed reels (i.e., reels with keys on both sides). Single-keyed reels are used primarily for release prints. When more than one reel is used, a clamp holds the additional reels in place. (The Moviola spring clamp is the best I have found.)

The rewinds should be attached rigidly to a board for a less permanent editing setup, otherwise to a solid table. You must mount them on an exact line so as to avoid wear on film being wound onto reels at an angle. The rewinds should be spaced sufficiently far apart so that all the other editing equipment can be placed between them with adequate room (viewer, splicer, and, in more sophisticated setups, synchronizer and sound reader). (See Plate 35) They should not be so far apart that the film cannot be comfortably rewound with one hand while the other hand holds the opposite reel and adjusts drag so the film does not come off the feed reel and onto the take-up reel too quickly and spill.

The rewinds should be placed on a table within reach of where you will sit to edit. If you plan to work for long periods at a time, it is a good idea to invest in a comfortably padded stool.

A frosted viewing box is best built into the table between the rewinds. When the light in the box is switched on, individual frames and edge numbers can be easily read. A gooseneck lamp will help you avoid eyestrain when you are working at the editing table for long periods.

A solid pair of 16mm Neumade rewinds can often be purchased used for $10 to $15. A good pair of new rewinds, such as are made by Hollywood Film Company or Moviola, costs around $50.

The action viewer (action editor)

The *viewer* should present a crisp, sharp, bright image. (See Plates 34, 35) It should allow no nonmoving part to touch the film. Its viewing screen should be of sufficient size so that the image can be easily seen at normal reading distances. If the film is left in the gate, it should not overheat and burn the film. You should be able to wind the film through it at a fairly rapid rate (though not as fast as when simply rewinding). It should be easy to load and should allow you some simple means of marking a frame while it is on the viewing screen. A focusing device and a frame-line adjusting device are standard features on a viewer.

It is most important that the viewer design be simple to avoid its scratching the film, especially if the original is to be viewed. For its simplicity of loading and its scratch-free operation, the Moviscope has become the standard in 16mm editing, even though other viewers have larger and sharper images. The Moviscope costs around $125. Other adequate 16mm viewers can be purchased new for about $60. Any used viewer should be carefully checked to make certain that it is in proper working condition and does not scratch film or overheat. Most viewers read properly (that is, they render the image unflipped, right side up) when the film is run left to right. This is standard. Occasionally you find a 16mm viewer which reads properly when the film is run right to left. This idiosyncrasy does not cause any insuperable problems.

Viewers are excellent devices for quickly rearranging shots into the desired order or for quickly searching footage to find particular shots.

Since film is generally cranked through the viewer by hand, it is difficult to maintain the proper projection speed. It is therefore somewhat difficult to judge the length of a shot with a viewer. Timing and pacing are easier to judge from a screen projection than they are from a viewer.

Most viewers employ a prism for projecting the image onto the viewer screen, and consequently the viewer image is never as sharp as one thrown by a good projector. Image sharpness and focus should not be decided using the viewer.

For the most part, 8mm viewers are far less expensive and far inferior in quality to 16mm viewers (though for prices akin to those paid for 16mm viewers you can get comparable quality). 8mm rewinds usually have a maximum capacity of 400 feet. 8mm film must be handled with greater care than 16mm. It is more likely to twist and break, and it spills (unrolls) more often.

Splicers

There are four basic types of splicers: Mylar splice perforated, Mylar splice unperforated (guillotine), cement splice, cement splice heated (hot splice). (See Plates 36B, 36C, 37) The two main groups, cement and Mylar, each have advantages that are worth understanding.

A cement splice is made by overlapping a very thin section of the two pieces of film to be joined and dissolving the base of one into the base of the other (emulsion and bond must be scraped off one of the two). The two pieces of film become one, though the film becomes thicker at the join where the overlap occurs. The bond on a properly made splice is very strong. (See Appendix B) On projection the splice can be seen as a little jump and flash, since part of the overlap cuts into a small part of the top of one of the frames. When a negative is so cut and then printed, the splices are light and show up more than on a print of cut reversal where the splices are dark.

Cement splices can be used in A&B printing to achieve invisible splices (see p. 106). For all printing work cement splices are preferable because they cover up less film area and are thinner than Mylar splices. Furthermore, when the film is cleaned, the splices will hold. Mylar splices are removed by the best methods of cleaning (ultrasonic cleaning). When magnetic film is used (see p. 157) cement splices are inferior as they cause drops in the sound level. When you use a cement splicer, you lose a frame every time you make or change a cut.

Mylar splices are a relatively new method of making a film join. The two ends to be joined are butted against each other and a piece of Mylar tape (much like ordinary cellophane tape) is put across the two shots, preferably on both sides. No frames are lost when the tape is peeled off and another shot cut in. No part of a frame is scraped off so there is no flash in projection. However, the splice, being much thicker than ordinary film, throws the image out of focus for an instant when the spliced frames go through the gate. Even though the Mylar tape is transparent, the frames on either side of the splice can easily be seen to be different.

No film cement is needed for a Mylar splice. It can be made much faster than a cement splice and requires much less skill to make properly. Mylar splicing is therefore preferred for cutting workprint. Cement splices go through some projectors better and are less noticeable than Mylar splices. They should be used for splices on your original if it is to be used for printing. There is a special opaque white Mylar tape for sound splicing. It is thicker and makes a strong splice even when used on only one side (which is the rule in splicing magnetic film).

Mylar splicers cut either on a diagonal, sometimes used for sound cutting, or on a straight line along the frame line, which is usual for picture cuts, or on a curve, which is an alternate way of making a picture cut. A curved splice has the advantage of joining a greater area of the two shots, resulting in a stronger splice. Often, however, the curved splice cuts into the picture area and can be seen. The greater

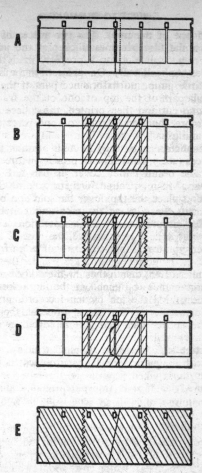

Fig. XII. *Splices:* The cement splice (*A*) is an overlap splice. A small part of one shot overlaps a small part of the next shot. Splices *B*, *C*, *D*, and *E* are tape splices in which no overlap is used. *B* and *C* are splices using clear tape for picture cutting and heavier white tape for sound. Generally, the picture is spliced on both sides, while sound is always spliced on the base side only. The edges of *B* are smooth because either a guillotine splicer, precut splicer, or a pair of scissors was used to cut the splice. The edges of *C* are jagged because it was cut with the built-in cutter on the splicer. *D* illustrates a curved splice. Sometimes 16mm magnetic film is cut with a diagonal splice *E* to minimize the pops on the sound track which often appear at sound cuts.

strength afforded by a curved splice is not really needed in the 16mm format, though it may be of some advantage in 8mm. The straight splice is standard. (See Fig. XII)

There are three basic ways of making Mylar splices in both 8 and 16mm: by using unperforated Mylar tape, roll Mylar, or precut Mylar.

The *guillotine splicer* uses unperforated tape. Generally speaking, the best tape is Mylar tape. Tapes such as ordinary cellophane tape usually become brittle and are harder to peel off when changing cuts. High-quality guillotine splicers, usually distributed by professional motion picture stores, cost about $175 for 16mm and $225 for super 8. Both cut the film and have good registration pins for holding the shots to be spliced. You place the tape over the join and pull down a lever which cuts the edge of the tape and punches out the sprocket holes simultaneously. The operation is very fast. Even though the splicer is expensive, the cost of the individual splice is very low, about one-fifth of a perforated tape splice. However, guillotine splicers are fragile; they go out of alignment more often than other high-quality splicers. The splicer sometimes fails to punch out the film's sprocket holes adequately. Finishing the job by hand costs a great deal in time. When the splicer is operating properly, the results are excellent. The splicer can also be employed to repair torn perforations very well.

The guillotine splicer can be supplied with a diagonal cutter for use with magnetic film. This cutter will not cut fewer than several frames when trimming the head of a shot. Generally speaking, a guillotine splicer is probably not worth the investment required, since it so often fails to fulfill its function properly.

Presprocketed Mylar comes either in rolls (single- or double-perforated), which costs about $6 for 66 feet (about a penny a splice), or precut (though Quicksplices, or the preferred Kodak Presstapes), which costs about two cents a splice. Kodak Presstapes bought in bulk cost about a penny and a half per splice. The precut variety (made primarily for amateurs) makes splices which are superior to roll Mylar splices. The tape is thinner and easier to remove and it never overlaps the sides of the film as roll Mylar may do. (If this should happen, use scissors to trim the sides of the splice to avoid projector jams.) Precut tape requires less skill to apply properly.

Splicers for presprocketed Mylar consist of a cutting device and a set of registration pins to align the film properly. Splicers which accommodate roll Mylar also come with a tamper to press the tape down easily and a cutter to tear the Mylar from the roll. Splicers of this type fall into one of two price ranges: under $10 or over $150. The cheaper versions often do not make well-registered splices. An important exception is an *editing block* (butt-splice block) which costs between $10 and $25. Splices of very high quality can be made with an editing block and a razor blade, but a great deal of practice is needed.

Cement splices are very inexpensive but you need a constant supply of fresh cement. Hot splices made by a cement splicer with a heating element are made more quickly and help seal the weld, but they raise the price you will pay for the splicer from about $30 to over $200. Cement splicers are divided into types that make so-called positive splices and negative splices. Negative splices are made with a smaller overlap than positive splices and take slightly less time to make since less scraping is involved. A well-made negative splice should be as strong as a positive splice. But poorly made, a positive splice will be stronger because of its greater overlap.

To prepare A&B rolls a cement splicer is needed which makes one of the cuts on the frame line. The other cut is made in the picture area. It is essential that the splicer be properly aligned, otherwise, a scrape line will be visible on the print. (See Appendix B for more discussion of cement splices.)

Other editing equipment

A *film bin* is a very handy accessory. (See Plate 38) Basically it is a barrel with a linen bag inserted. Suspended above the barrel is a roll of pegs or clothespins on which strips of film can be placed. As shots are cut out of rolls they can be placed on the pegs for eventual reordering.

You will need cans, reels, and a place to store them. If your amount of 16mm film is great, you will find it well worth the money to add a *tight-wind* attachment to the rewinds, which will enable you to dispense with many of your reels. Film can be stored without a reel by winding it tightly around a core (usually obtainable from your laboratory). One or two *split reels* should be purchased so that the tight-wound film can be placed in them for use. Two-inch cores are used for camera raw stock in long lengths. For editing, use three-inch cores. When film is shipped from labs in long lengths, it is usually shipped on cores to save postage expense.

You should use a grease pencil to mark the film, for it can be easily wiped off. White or yellow are the clearest colors. Special film cloths or a felt cloth and film cleaner (such as

Kodak or Ecco 1500) are available to keep the film relatively clean and supple. If the film is brittle when it returns from the lab and it chatters when projected, it is called *green film*. The lab probably omitted to lubricate the film. It should either be returned or treated with a film cleaner which contains a lubricant.

Whenever you are working with the original, you should wear white film gloves. A dozen can be purchased for a couple of dollars. Keep handling of the film to a minimum, especially if it is negative film or Ektachrome Commercial (ECO Type 7252). Professional filmmakers tend to make a ritual of the careful handling of the irreplaceable camera original. Any scratch or cinch mark on the original may stay with the film for its lifetime, and the dust or grit that touches the original can cause scratches.

Leader

Film leader can be purchased from your lab or the film manufacturers. The least expensive leader is called *lightstruck* leader. It is undeveloped film, usually yellowish-white in color. It is used for replacing damaged footage in the cut of the film (a practice termed *slugging*) so that you know how much film has been damaged. Several feet of leader should be attached to the *head* (beginning) and *tail* (end) of every roll. This protects the film and serves as the threading footage used in loading the projector. It can be written on to note information about the roll. Every roll of film should have identifying marks written on its head and tail leader so they can be read when the film is wound on a reel. A non-water base dry marking pen should be used to write on leader. Sanford Sharpies or Magic Markers work well and can be purchased in various colors. Black is clearest for most uses.

Leader has a base and emulsion like other types of film. The dull side is the emulsion and the shiny side, the base. If you touch the film with your lips, they will stick to the emulsion side and not to the base. The leader should be attached to the film, emulsion to emulsion and base to base.

In 16mm there is both single- and double-perforated leader. If a roll has any single-perforated film in it, the leader must be single-perforated on the same side. If the *whole* roll is double-perforated, then double-perforated leader may be used. If double-perforated leader is used with single-perforated film in one roll, it is easy to load the projector incorrectly and rip up the single-perforated film.

Starex leader has no emulsion. Both sides are made of film

base. Unlike lightstruck leader, it will not shrink much with age. It is available in a wide range of colors that are useful for various systems of coding. For example, you may use one color for tail leader and another for head leader.

Cutting shots

As noted before, shots should always be spliced emulsion to emulsion and base to base, otherwise, at the point of change the shot will go slightly out of focus and will change in direction; its mirror image will be projected. If you wish to change the direction of a shot, you can have the lab make a master or a dupe of the shot. If the shot is flipped when cut into the final printer rolls, it will be slightly less sharp than the original. If this does not bother you it can be done, but only if you have used double-perforated film.

When the film is put into its approximate sequence, the result is called a *rough cut*, first *assembly*, or *rough continuity*. When the film appears to be smooth in its cut, it may be termed a *three-quarter cut*. When the film is edited in its final form, it is known as a *fine cut*.

Workprinting

Making a workprint or cutting copy of all your footage is wise since the camera original will be kept safe from dirt, scratches, and splicing mistakes. Unfortunately, workprinting is expensive. A 16mm workprint from negative film costs between three and five cents per foot, and from reversal film it costs between four and seven cents a foot. Color costs between eight and thirteen cents per foot. Many people make a very rough cut of the film and have that alone workprinted. This is easiest to do when the original is reversal film, since you can judge positive shots more easily than negatives. Reversal film is more resistant to scratches than negative film and does not show dust as noticeably.

If a cut workprint is made, the original must be matched to it. In 16mm, the latent edge-numbers on the original can be printed through to the workprint. It is important to check that this has been properly done and that they can be easily read. 8mm film has no edge-numbers, so have both original and workprint marked with the same machine edge-numbers. A few labs offer this service. When there is some problem with latent edge-numbers on 16mm rolls, matching machine numbers should be printed on original and workprint.

Handling film

The proper care and handling of film will greatly extend its life and usefulness. When handling original film, do not allow dust, scratches, or fingerprints on the surface. It should always be handled with white editing gloves, which are available from most film laboratories. No film should ever be wound so tight as to cause *cinch marks*. These usually appear as diagonal scratches on the film. They can be caused by pulling to tighten film at the end of a loose-wound reel or by pushing down on core-wound film. If you get dust on original material to be used in printing, have it ultrasonically cleaned by your laboratory just before they make a print. Any of the standard film cleaners such as Kodak film cleaner and lubricant or Ecco 1500 will remove dust from a print. Dampen a lintless pad (preferably of felt) lightly with the cleaner. The pad should sandwich the film as it is slowly wound from one reel to another. Make sure the cleaner fluid has evaporated before it reaches the take-up reel. The pad should be cleaned often so that it cannot build up a layer of grit which will scratch the film. Change the area of the pad which comes into contact with the film frequently.

If there is white or black sparkle on a print made from the original, the negative may have been improperly cleaned. If so, the dust on the negative can be removed by the laboratory and subsequent prints will be free of sparkle. Make sure your laboratory cleans your film ultrasonically before printing. Since ultrasonic cleaning removes all adhesives, tape splices cannot be so cleaned. If you have tape-spliced your printing material, be sure to notify the lab so that they may use an alternate method of cleaning your film.

Scratches

In screening a print for the first time it is important to look for scratches. Scratches can come from the camera when the film was shot, from the lab developer or printer, from the way the film was handled, or, most commonly, from the projector. Base scratches can usually be buffed so they do not print or project. There are laboratories that specialize in film rejuvenation which can buff your film to remove base scratches. If the scratch is on the emulsion side, there is little you can do about it. If a scratch appears on a print from the original and the physical scratch is not on the print itself, you can usually tell if the scratch is on the base or emulsion of the original. Emulsion scratches let light pass through them,*

* Unless the print is allowed to get dirty, in which case the emulsion scratch fills up with dirt and light no longer passes through.

whereas base scratches diffract light and do not let it through. Therefore, if the scratch projects as white and the original is negative, it is a base scratch. If black, it is an emulsion scratch. If the original is reversal and the scratch projects white, then it is an emulsion scratch. If it projects black, it is a base scratch. If the scratch is annoying and it is a base scratch, then for a few cents a foot it can be put through scratch removal.

Dust on a print will project as black. If there was dust on original reversal, then prints from that original will also show black dust spots. Dust on negative original will print through as white. White sparkle is much more noticeable and annoying than black dust spots.

Do not put film on bent reels. The projector and action viewer should not scratch, overheat, or put undue stress on the film. If the film is stored on cores, use three-inch cores rather than the two-inch cores on which camera original is wound in darkroom loads. Film should always be kept away from extremes of temperature and humidity. It should *never* be stored near a radiator or in a car trunk or glove compartment in warm weather.

Film cans are useful for storing film, since they offer protection from dust. When film is mailed it should be carefully packed so the reels do not bend and the film does not cinch.

XII. Preparing the Original for Printing

If a workprint was used for editing, the original must be conformed to the workprint before final printing. This is a very delicate and time-consuming task. Extreme care must be taken not to get dirt, fingerprints, or scratches on the original. White editing gloves should always be used when handling original. Splices must be well made since a break in the film during printing can have disastrous results. If you can afford to, leave the matching of workprint and original to a professional. Many laboratories offer the service and there are people outside the lab who specialize in this work. Costs vary from $75 to $175 per 10-minute reel.

Marking the workprint

There are certain conventional markings made on the workprint to aid the cutter in his task. Every splice in the workprint signals the cutter to make a cut. However, you may often make a cut and then decide to extend the shot. The usual mark to designate an unintentional splice to be ignored by the cutter is two short parallel lines across the unintentional joint. (See Fig. XIII) All such marks on the workprint are usually made with a yellow or white China marker.

FIG. XIII

UNINTENTIONAL SPLICES

The workprint (or sometimes its sprocket holes) often tears during editing. Blank leader is usually used to replace the damaged sections. The exact number of frames damaged are replaced. If the section replaced is within a shot, the unintentional splice sign should be put at each end where the leader joins the picture. (See Fig. XIII) If the leader ends where the shot ends, an arrow from the shot to the leader is drawn with the arrowhead at the point where the next shot begins. (See Fig. XIV)

FIG. XIV

EXTENDED SCENE

In order to effect fades and dissolves, the printing rolls must have special marks placed on them and be cut in certain ways. The workprint must be thus marked so that the cutter is made aware of what you intend. Fade-outs are marked by two lines extending from the edge of the film at the point where the fade is to be started, converging to a point at the place the fade-out is to end. (See Fig. XV) A fade-in is the same sign in reverse. (See Figs. XVI and XVII) A dissolve is

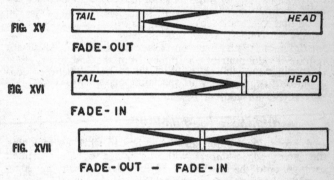

FIG. XV

TAIL   HEAD

FADE-OUT

FIG. XVI

TAIL   HEAD

FADE-IN

FIG. XVII

FADE-OUT — FADE-IN

created by the superimposition of the successive shots, one fading in, the other fading out. Since the workprint must be the same length as the final print, some frames of workprint must be cut out. For example: on a 48-frame dissolve, 24 frames at the tail of the first shot and 24 frames at the head of the second shot should be removed from the workprint. The dissolve should be indicated by a diagonal line going from the beginning of the dissolve, across the picture area from one edge of the film to the other, ending at the picture join. The diagonal line should be repeated on the other end of the join. (See Fig. XVIII)

FIG. XVIII

DISSOLVE

Double-exposure or superimposed titles (white titles can be superimposed when making a reversal print and black titles can be superimposed when making a positive print from a negative) are marked by cutting in a few inches of workprint of the superimposed titles at the beginning and the end of the double-exposure. A wavy line should be drawn through the whole length of the double-exposure. (See Fig. XIX)

FIG. XIX

DOUBLE - EXPOSURE

Fades on negatives, dissolves, and superimpositions demand that you do A&B roll printing, which is currently available only in 16mm format. Not all printers can make fades when printing from reversal single strand. Most labs can make only one length effect on any one printing roll. At these labs you must choose the length that *all* the fades and dissolves will be on that roll. Some labs can only do effects of one set length, usually 48 frames. A few labs do have machines that allow for different length effects on the same printer roll. Most labs require a minimum of 54 frames from the end of an effect to the next straight cut, and at least 12 frames between consecutive dissolves. You should check with your laboratory before you cut your original.

Matching edge-numbers

A professional cutter always prefers to work by matching the latent edge-numbers with the image of them printed through onto the workprint. If for some reason the edge-numbers have not been printed through, or in the case of 8mm film where there are no latent edge-numbers, machine-printed edge-numbers can be used as a way of matching workprint with original.

Latent edge-numbers are the most accurate aids. You should make sure that every shot has a latent edge-number on it. Since one appears every 20 frames (twice every 16mm foot), shots shorter than 20 frames may not have an edge-number. Unless some notation is made, the cutter will have no way of finding the matching original for that shot. To avoid this problem, you can put a thin piece of masking tape on the film, noting how many frames it is removed from the preceding edge-number.

Sometimes matching has to be done by eye; the cutter has to inspect the picture on the workprint and find the matching picture on the original. This is more difficult of course when the original is a negative or in 8mm format. Matching pictures by eye is laborious and time-consuming. When the correct shot is found, it is best to find a frame showing some movement, for consecutive frames display the greatest difference when the subject is in motion. Once one frame of work-print is matched with one frame of original, it is simple to find the first and last frame to be cut with the aid of a synchronizer. (See p. 158)

Leader

A standard type of leader is attached to the head of each printer roll. The older standard leader is called Academy leader or old SMPTE leader, and the picture countdown is marked in feet. It is being replaced now by the new SMPTE leader which is marked in seconds. Your lab can usually supply leader for you in the correct wind, and give you a diagram for properly preparing head and tail leader for final printing.

Lining up the optical track

If you have an optical sound track to be printed with your film, it must be lined up with the printer rolls so that the lab can place it properly alongside the picture. In 16mm, optical sound is placed 26 frames before the corresponding picture. While editing, sound is usually kept opposite its corresponding picture (*editorial sync*). When printing, the leader on the sound track must be marked for *projection sync* so that the sound will be advanced 26 frames.

If a bleep tone was put at the head of the sound track (see p. 163), and new SMPTE leader was used on the picture, the bleep tone should be across from the single frame marked #2. If this is done, it will be easy to align optical sound with the picture. The bleep will be easily seen on the optical track as a group of heavy lines lasting for approximately one frame. The frame with these sound modulations can be placed opposite the #2 frame on the SMPTE leader on the printing rolls (editorial sync), advanced 26 frames into projection sync, and a printer start mark put opposite the printer's start marks for the rolls of cut original. If you are printing A & B rolls, the printer start marks should be opposite each other on the A & B picture rolls and 26 frames to the left on the optical sound track.

See Appendix D for a discussion of conforming original with workprint.

XIII. Sound

The filmmaker has to cope eventually with the problem of sound. There is a certain snobbism among some film historians that celebrates the silent film. Silent films were rarely shown without any sound at all. They usually were run with at least a piano accompaniment, and sometimes a full orchestra for the more spectacular films. Silent films are often shown today without sound, and most viewers find them hard to sit through for that very reason. Even the whirring of a projector is better background for a silent film than a silent room. Many avant-garde films made today are silent. The filmmaker may think of this as a way of emphasizing the cinema as a visual medium. Obviously it is, but it does not follow that sound is not a useful or even a necessary adjunct to the visual.

The cost of sound and the way it is recorded depend to a great degree on the type of sound your particular film requires and how standardized you wish the final print of your film to be. For example, if you wish to make a 16mm sound film that can be screened anywhere, your print must have what is called an optical sound track. On the other hand, if you alone will be showing the film, then the most bizarre Rube Goldberg device may suffice for the playing of your sound accompaniment.

Synchronization

Synchronization is the correspondence of the sound with the picture. If your sound track is on the film physically, the synchronization of picture and sound will always be the same from showing to showing, assuming that the projector has been properly loaded. If the sound is not physically on the film but played on a separate machine, the synchronization of picture and sound will vary from showing to showing unless sophisticated and expensive devices are used. Often the difference will be very marked. It is important to understand why, for the answer also explains why sound taken with a simple recorder while you film will not be properly synchronized with the picture. For example, if you film and record someone's speech, on playback the words will not match his lip movements. Since the two machines (in this case a tape recorder and the projector) are run by different motors, and the motor speeds will vary independently of each other, they will run at different speeds. They will also warm up to running speed at different rates. The standard tape for home recorders (¼-inch wide) stretches and slips, changing its length as it is played. The tape may be as much as 20 percent out of phase with the film. This means if the film lasts ten minutes, the tape may be finished in eight minutes. If the same machines are used both for recording and playback, differences of this magnitude will not be encountered, but the difference may still be considerable even with high-quality equipment, as much as 3 percent. For *lip synchronization,* the correct joining of words and the lip movements that produced them, accuracy has to be within two frames or the image appears to be *out of sync.* For a one-minute shot, tolerable synchronization inaccuracy is less than one-tenth of 1 percent. Consequently, an independently running projector and tape recorder (or camera and tape recorder) cannot possibly give you sound which is highly synchronized with the picture unless special precautions are taken (which are discussed in the chapter on synchronous sound).

Optical track

The standard sound track on a 16mm release print is an *optical track.* (See Plate 1) This is a photographic image of sound modulations which run down the side of the 16mm film. Optical sound prints must be single-perforated since the optical track is on the edge opposite the sprocket holes. The optical sound track must be printed on the film at the same time the picture is printed. Optical sound cannot be added to an already existing print. An optical sound track can be played on virtually every 16mm sound projector in the world.

Magnetic track

Many projectors made since 1964 offer the option of a *magnetic sound track.* With this method a strip of magnetic coating is placed on the film at the same place where the optical track would go, and then the sound track is recorded onto the magnetic striping. Magnetic sound is potentially capable of higher-quality reproduction than optical sound. Furthermore, magnetic sound can be added to an already existing print. Even a double-perforated 16mm print can have magnetic striping added. However, the coating is much narrower and a good deal of sound quality is lost. Magnetic sound tracks, unlike optical tracks, can be erased. This means the sound track can be changed without your having to make another print. But it also means you may lose your sound track altogether if the print comes into contact with a strong magnetic field.

When only one or two prints are to be made, a magnetic sound track may be less expensive. Otherwise, optical tracks are less expensive. The major advantage of optical 16mm sound, other than its cost, is that it is the worldwide standard. If you have a magnetic track on your film, there is no guarantee that you can show it on any sound projector that happens to be available. And you may not be able to sell prints as easily or enter your print in certain film festivals.

In 8mm you have a choice of magnetic or optical sound. However, neither has been standardized. Regular 8mm and super 8 optical sound is of much lower quality than 8mm magnetic sound.

Separate sound tracks

The least expensive method of adding sound to a film is by playing it separately on a tape recorder. Acetate base ¼-inch tape should be used in preference to polyester (Mylar) tape, since acetate tape will break under strain whereas polyester tape will stretch. Tape stretch can cause the length of tape to change from showing to showing. If the sound is played on a separate tape recorder, there can be no close synchronization of picture and sound. No attempt should be made to match dialogue or sound effects like a door slam with the picture. Music and narration demand the least precise synchronization between picture and sound. Some projectors and tape recorders have a rheostat device which can slow or speed one of the motors to bring the diverging sound back into approximate synchronization. This method will not work well for lip synchronization.

If the sound is played on a tape recorder, you cannot expect anyone else to be able to show your film accurately. Such a nonstandardized method basically limits showing of your film to the times when you are free to screen it yourself, unless synchronization between picture and sound can be very loose.

A further sophistication of the above method is to take the separately recorded ¼-inch tape and place it on the film either optically or magnetically. The chief advantage of this method is that it is standardized so that the relationship between picture and sound will remain constant from showing to showing.

Magnetic stripe

If the sound is to be put onto a magnetic stripe on the edge of the film (see Plate 2), you can transfer the sound from the tape recorder to the film by yourself. However, as mentioned above, magnetic sound is not as standardized as optical sound, and in 16mm format you have no guarantee that your film can be played on just any 16mm sound projector.

In order to be able to transfer the sound, the print must be magnetically striped. The cost is three to six cents per foot for the striping. *Prestriped film,* raw stock with the magnetic stripe already applied, though less expensive, has the disadvantage of causing unnecessary wear on the camera during shooting. Striping should be done by a reliable lab or through Kodak, because a magnetic stripe applied in an inferior manner can lead to a considerable deterioration in your final sound quality. You will require a projector that can record sound magnetically onto the film. Such projectors are fairly common in super 8, and can be rented for about $15 per day in 16mm. It is important that the magnetic sound precede its corresponding picture by 56 frames in 8mm, 18 frames in super 8, and 28 frames in 16mm. At the present time these are the standard lengths that will guarantee proper play on most magnetic sound projectors. You will need a jack from the tape recorder output to the projector input. The recording should not be *overmodulated*, recorded with the volume control too high, or sound distortion will result. If the volume control is too low, an excessive amount of tape noise will be heard on playback. If a take is not satisfactory, you can try again. Magnetic striping sound can be erased in the same way as ¼-inch tape can be erased. Unless your projector has a very special device, you cannot record sound on top of sound. That is, you cannot record once and then record again and expect the first sound to come through. If you try this, your first sound track may be completely erased.

You can also record directly from live sound onto the magnetic stripe using musicians, narration track, or sound effects. It is essential that you place the microphone in a different room from the projector so that projector noise is not picked up on your sound track. You will have the advantage of achieving a closer synchronization, since you can see the film while recording, and give the performers their cues. Dialogue synchronization is well-nigh impossible, however, without several takes of short duration.

You can combine live sound with sound from the tape recorder or you can feed several tape recorders into the projector simultaneously. By adjusting levels properly, you can mix several tracks together. This gives you a great deal of control over your ultimate sound track. Below we will discuss a more sophisticated method of mixing or re-recording (see p. 162).

Making the optical track

If you wish to add sound to the film using the standard 16mm method, you must do it via an optical track. This method can also be used in 8mm. The optical track must be made by a laboratory. The lab makes a separate film which has no picture image but only the photographic image of your sound along the edge. When you make a print, the print is run through the printer once for the visuals and again to add the sound. You must tell the lab whether your camera original is reversal or negative, because the optical track differs for the two types of film. Most labs need an optical track in the same wind as the picture. If the picture is an original, a "B" wind optical track is required. If the picture is an internegative, most likely an "A" wind optical track will be used. The optical track master itself costs from six to ten cents a foot. Some labs make no additional charge for the printing of the sound on each print. A few charge an additional one or two cents per foot for the sound.

In order to get the optical track made, you supply your lab with a ¼-inch tape of your sound. Unless a more expensive system (discussed below) is used, the sound may not synchronize with the picture in the same way that your tests show. Since the tape playback machine the lab uses is different from yours, and since your projector is almost certainly not running at exactly 24 frames per second, there may be changes in the positioning of the sound in relation to your picture. With magnetic striping, you could make tests directly on the film, and retransfer if there are any major errors. However, with optical sound you do not find out the results until you have invested in the optical master and a print. There is no way to correct an error at this point without cutting the optical master and making another print. So unless synchronization between picture and sound is not very critical in your film, and if you can't afford the alternate methods discussed below, optical sound is very likely too risky for you to attempt. Of course, if your equipment is of high quality, then the change in synchronization will not be as great as the change from low-quality machines. In any case, you should not expect great synchronization accuracy.

16mm magnetic track

Problems of synchronization could be overcome if there were a way to guarantee the speed at which the sound is recorded and played back. Film has sprocket holes which guarantee that it stays the same length permanently. If the sound had sprocket holes, then we could match one frame of picture with one frame of sound and be able to maintain exact synchronization. This can be done by transferring the sound from regular ¼-inch tape to *16mm magnetic film*. (See Plate 2) Doing this involves a very different method of dealing with sound and opens up radically different possibilities. We will deal with this method in the chapter on sound editing (Chapter XVI).

XIV. Sound Recording

Tape recorders

Tape recorders come in all sizes and prices. For field recordings, a battery-operated portable model is particularly useful. A good portable tape recorder adequate for most film uses should cost $100 or more. (See Plate 37) In the chapter on synchronous sound we will discuss the higher-quality portable recorders.

Microphones

The weakest component in a medium-priced tape recorder is usually the microphone supplied with the machine. It is most often a very inexpensive piece of equipment, well below the quality of the tape recorder itself. If you wish to get better sound you should buy another microphone compatible with your tape recorder. The microphone impedance and the impedance of the microphone input on the tape recorder must be matched.

The *omnidirectional microphone:* This is a microphone which accepts sound coming from all directions. It has a fairly limited use in film work, though it is useful for some types of music recording, and gives a good sense of presence for recording crowds.

The cardioid microphone (unidirectional): The level of any sound recorded with this microphone varies depending on the direction from which the sound comes. Sounds from the rear do not get picked up as well as sounds from the front. It can therefore be used to better isolate sounds from background. It can be pointed at sounds to pick them up better, and is particularly good for dialogue. It is perhaps the best overall microphone, and is the best choice if you can only purchase one. The pickup pattern differs from one brand to another. Cardioid microphones cost from $20 to several hundred dollars. When the pattern is very narrow, the microphone is called a shot-gun or ultradirectional microphone.

Shot-gun microphones: These are long and expensive microphones costing several hundred dollars. (See Plate 13) Their prime purpose is to pick up dialogue when there is a fair amount of background noise or when a group of people are being recorded with one microphone. The acceptance pattern is narrow on this microphone, and when it is relatively near a person talking it will isolate his voice fairly well from the background. However, the microphone cannot perform miracles and will only isolate sounds when the sounds are closer to it than to background sounds or if they come from a different direction from sounds in the background.

Lavalier microphones: These are very small microphones that cost from $50 to over $100 and are used suspended from the neck of the person being recorded. They can be worn concealed under clothes and can easily pick up the speech of the wearer. The voice of people other than the wearer will lack the volume and presence recorded from his speech. The MKH 125 Sennheiser lavalier microphone does pick up voices other than the wearer's with good quality, but it is very expensive. Lavalier microphones reproduce only the middle frequencies well and therefore should never be used for recording music. They are often used in conjunction with wireless (or radio) microphones. A *wireless microphone* consists of a radio transmitter and a receiver. The microphone sends its signal to the transmitter, which in turn sends the signal to the receiver, which sends it into the tape recorder. Transmitter and receivers can be miniaturized. (High-quality ones cost over $500 and are about the size of a cigarette pack.) A transmitter can be concealed with a lavalier microphone on a person. This is especially helpful when you take sound with the picture, for you can obtain good presence without placing a microphone so close to the speaker as to limit your camera angles.

Tape speed

Sound to be used for 16mm film is usually recorded at 7½ ips. Little quality is gained by recording at a higher speed because you would lose that quality in transferring the sound to the film. Speech can be satisfactorily recorded at 3¾ ips but music should be recorded at 7½ ips. The faster the speed of the tape, the easier it is to edit. If you plan to do accurate editing on ¼-inch tape, then record the sound at 7½ ips.

Tape

The tape available for your recorder will most likely be offered in varying thicknesses. The thickest tape (1.5 mil) can be purchased in a low print-through (or master) tape. *Print-through* is the sound from one turn of the tape that has "printed" on the next turn. You can notice it when there are loud noises and low background noise. Thinner tapes (1 mil and .5 mil) allow greater print-through but offer a proportionately greater amount of playing time.

Recording

Overmodulating (overrecording) results in sound distortion which lowers intelligibility of speech and music fidelity. Almost all tape recorders have some provision to indicate that you are overmodulating. On the less expensive machines, a light may flash when you are overrecording, or two moving lights may touch or overlap when overrecording. On bet-

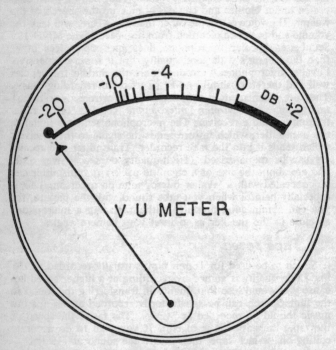

Fig. XX. *VU meter:* When the needle goes above 0db in the black region (red on some machines), you are overrecording the sound, and your tapes will be distorted. The volume control should be turned down.

ter machines there is usually a VU meter. (See Fig. XX) When the meter does not move, it means that the sound you are recording is too low (or not recording at all). When you replay the tape, its own hiss and other electronic noise will sound annoyingly loud. Normal recording should take place in the –20 to 0db range on a VU meter. Average speech should be recorded between −14 and −8db. When the needle goes above 0db, the tape is overloading and distortion will result.

Before and during recording, the sound should be monitored with a good set of earphones (headsets). Not all recorders have provisions for monitoring the sound through headsets. This is a very important feature if you wish to get good sound. The headsets should be comfortable and should cut out a good deal of background sound so that you have no trouble distinguishing the recorded sound from the live sound. Good-quality headsets usually cost about $30. Since they are normally stereo, you will need an adapter plug to convert them to monaural.

You should learn to distinguish good from bad sound while monitoring through the headsets. It is worthwhile to experiment with various microphone positions to hear the differences. You will find that moving the microphone closer to the speaker enables you to lower the volume control and thereby cut down the background noise. Moving the microphone closer by half the distance lowers the background noise by four times.

When recording out of doors or when you are moving the microphone, you will sometimes pick up wind noise, either a low rumbling sound or a static-type crackle. Avoid this by placing the microphone behind a wind breaker or purchase a windscreen. In emergencies, a nylon sock pulled over the microphone may help cut down wind noise without hurting other sound. Acustofoam wrapped around the microphone often works very well. Some microphones have a built-in filter which cuts off frequencies below a 100 or 50cps. Since most wind noise is of low frequency, this cut-off filter will often help quite a bit. These filters are usually not of very high quality. A high-quality in-line filter used to cut off the low frequencies can be purchased for under $50 and these often completely cut out wind noise.

The soundman should try to anticipate extreme volume changes so as to avoid over- and under-recording. When an audience is about to applaud, the soundman should turn down his volume control, and thereby avoid distortion. A few tape recorders have a record mode called "automatic record." When the recorder works in this mode, the machine itself compensates to avoid overmodulation. However, the overall recording quality will not be the highest, and should not be greatly relied upon.

When microphones are hand-held as opposed to being placed on a stand or boom, hand noises may record on the tape. Any hand or wire movement at the recorder's connection to the microphone will cause annoying crackles on the tape. You must not move your hand along the microphone while recording but must keep the same grip on it throughout the take. If a small length of the microphone wire is looped in your hand, this will prevent wire noise when you turn the microphone to follow a sound.

Sound not taken to synchronize exactly with the picture is called *wild sound*. Wild sound can be taken at the same time the picture is taken, or separately. When sound is recorded to synchronize exactly with the image, allowing dialogue synchronization with lip movement, it is known as *synchronous sound* (or *sync sound, lip synchronization,* or *sound sync*).

XV. Synchronous Sound

Almost all American feature films, and many documentaries, are shot with synchronous sound. Synchronous sound equipment has been available for a long time. However, until the end of the 1950's it was extremely heavy and cumbersome.

Camera

Technological advances brought about the introduction of light 16mm cameras capable of taking synchronous sound. For the first time, the filmmaker could record the sound and images of people simultaneously without complicated setups, following his picture wherever it went and filming it, if he wished, without a script, directly from life. This method of filming is sometimes called *cinéma-verité* or direct cinema. Of course the portable 16mm camera can also be used for scripted films (such as, for example, the Canadian film *Nobody Waved Goodbye* or *Faces*) but we will discuss the principal importance of this type of filming: its use for *cinéma-verité* documentary. What applies to the documentary will apply to the scripted film as well, but the filmmaker has much greater technical control of such aspects as lighting, camera movements, and tripod shooting when he shoots from a script with actors.

Synchronous sound demands different equipment both in shooting and editing from that required for silent shooting.

The camera: The camera has either to have a synchronous motor or a governor motor which puts out a *sync signal* (or sync pulse). Cameras with a sync pulse are most popular now because of their greater availability and lower cost. If the camera has a synchronous motor, the tape recorder must be equipped with a *sync-track generator*. No connection need be made between camera and recorder; thus, the cameraman and soundman can move around independently. A reliable system of this sort is usually extremely expensive and either custom-made or relatively bulky. One good, compact conversion converts a $2,000 Auricon into a cableless camera-tape-recorder combination for an additional few thousand dollars. (See Plate 14) This type of setup can be rented for about $50-$100 per day.

Some cameras (e.g., the Auricon and Mitchell) can record the sound directly on the film. They use what is called *single-system sound* recording. The disadvantages of single-system recording are its lower sound quality and the difficulty of editing it. Since the sound precedes the picture by 28 frames when on a magnetic stripe, picture and sound cannot be cut at the same place. If you are using a workprint, you have to transfer your sound anyway, thereby giving up most of the simplicity of single-system recording. The single system's great advantage is speed and accurate synchronization. Its primary use is to shoot footage in the evening for the 11:00 P.M. news show. Because its use is so limited, we will not discuss this type of sound system in further detail but will confine ourselves to the *double system* of recording, whereby the sound is not recorded on the film but on a tape recorder.

The cameras capable of shooting synchronous sound handheld can be divided into two groups. The cameras in the first group are expensive (usually costing more than $4,000), heavy (more than 14 pounds), and are virtually noiseless when running. These accept 400-foot loads of film. Cameras in this group include the Arriflex BL, Eclair NPR, and the Bolex Pro 16 camera. In the second group, the cameras are less expensive (around $1,500), fairly noisy, and lighter (under seven pounds). These usually accept only 100-foot loads (though some have provisions for longer lengths at increased price). Cameras in this group include the Beaulieu RC-16, Bolex H-16 Rex 5, and a modified Canon Scoopic. Cameras in both groups have motors which put out a pulse that can be picked up by suitable tape recorders to guarantee picture-sound synchronization. Most all the cameras have through-the-lens focusing. The only important exception is the Auricon Cinevoice conversion (a standard conversion done by many professional camera stores) which relies on an auxiliary viewfinder supplied with a zoom lens. The Beaulieu, Arriflex, Bolex Pro 16, and Eclair have a rotating mirror shutter which is preferable to the half-silvered mirror available on the other cameras mentioned.

Only the larger cameras are *self-blimped* (run silently). Some cameras have a provision for a *barney*, a leaded cover for the camera which cuts down some of the camera noise. A silently running camera is a great advantage as any camera running noise will be picked up on the sound track. If you are shooting without actors, people are made aware that you are filming if they hear the disruptive camera noise. If you use one of the noisier, smaller cameras, you will probably only be able to shoot outdoors (where sound doesn't carry well), keeping the camera several feet from the microphone, or if indoors, using the camera in a different room from the microphone.

If you use a directional microphone fairly close to the person speaking (or a lavalier microphone), the noisy camera will not pose so great a problem.

When filming sync sound without a script, you should have as much film in the camera as possible. Because of weight limitation, a 400-foot load has become the most common. Normally at least two 400-foot magazines are used. One is on the camera and the other is loaded (often by an assistant) and ready to use when the first runs out. You will usually need more than two magazines if different types of raw stock are used (one low speed, the other high speed), if a magazine jams (unfortunately not an infrequent occurrence), or if you have no assistant.

A zoom lens is essential if you are shooting without a script and have to anticipate action. The standard lens has become the Angénieux 12-120mm zoom lens, both because of its high quality and its long zoom range (10:1). Lenses with shorter zoom ranges usually do not have as wide an angle length as 12 mm, except for the Angénieux and Zeiss 12.5-75mm lenses, which lacks the longer focal lengths available with the 12-120mm lens. A fairly new Angénieux lens, the 9.5-95mm lens may replace the 12-120mm as the standard lens for hand-held shooting. Its wide angle increases the lens' versatility considerably, and 95mm is the most you need in length when shooting hand-held, for close-ups, or focusing. For other uses, even 95mm is too long for steady hand-held shooting. This lens focuses down to two and a half feet, whereas the 12-120mm lens can focus only to five feet, a limiting factor in crowd situations or cramped quarters, such as an automobile. The 9.5-95mm does have some disadvantages: It is more than a pound heavier, is somewhat larger, and seems to be a bit more fragile than the 12-120mm lens.

For synchronous sound in super 8, the Bell & Howell Filmosound offers a relatively inexpensive system. It is a special camera and cassette tape recorder with a connecting cable. Due to the difficulties of editing, and because it is not a standardized system, its main use can only be amateur. Nevertheless, it is the simplest and most economical way to get lip synchronization in 8mm.

Several disadvantages should be noted. For about the first second of every shot there is no sound. Further, only 3.3 minutes (one 50-foot roll of processed footage) can be shown continuously. In the magazine *Popular Photography*,

June, 1969, an editing system is described which partially overcomes some of these drawbacks. However, the editing is somewhat complex, and does not allow very much manipulation of picture in relation to sound.

Tape recorder

You will need a tape recorder fitted with a provision for recording a sync pulse. Nagra, Uhrer, Perfectone, Stellavox, and Tandberg all make portable, battery-operated models that can be used for sync sound. (See Plate 40) Prices range from $500 to over $1,000. A whole sync rig, with a camera like the Eclair NPR and a Nagra tape recorder, with all necessary accessories, can usually be rented for less than $100 per day. The Nagra III NPH, which costs over $1,000, has become the standard of *cinéma-verité* shooting because of its exceptional high quality, light weight, and rugged design. The newer Nagra IV will no doubt continue this tradition.

Cableless sync

Most double-system sound is recorded with a sync cable connecting camera and tape recorder. The cable feeds the sync pulse from camera to tape recorder. If the camera is fitted with a synchronous motor, then it is possible to hold sync without any physical connection. When the camera is not run off AC current (such as is found in most house circuits), synchronization of the motor is maintained from a signal generated by either a tuning fork or crystal. A matched tuning fork or crystal (that is, one that vibrates at the same rate) feeds a signal into the tape recorder (the *sync-track generator*). This guarantees sync.

Cableless sync is generally less reliable than sync guaranteed by the cable. Cableless systems generally add weight and bulk to the camera. However, when freed from the sync cable, the cameraman and soundman are much more mobile. Further, they no longer have to worry about people tripping over the connecting cable.

There are cableless sync systems which rely on a wireless microphone to transmit the sync pulse from the camera to the tape recorder. Except under good conditions, the radio signal is too unreliable to be depended on. If sync fails, all your footage may be unusable. You are betting a great deal on the reliability of your sync system.

Several cableless sync systems rely on both the camera and the tape recorder running off AC current. Here portability is sacrificed, since you are attached to an electric outlet.

Microphone

The choice of a shot-gun microphone usually narrows down to the Sennheiser 805 and the Electro-Voice 642. The Sennheiser is of higher quality, but the difference is lost when the sound is put on a 16mm optical track. It has a somewhat narrower acceptance angle than the Electro-Voice, and may be preferred for that reason. However, it is more sensitive to wind noise, hand noise, and car ignitions. The use of a windscreen and in-line hi-pass filter will remedy this to a large extent. The Sennheiser requires batteries because it is a condenser microphone, whereas the Electro-Voice, a dynamic microphone, does not.

Slate

In a properly working system, the picture and sound will be in sync throughout each shot. The editor will have to find one point on the picture which matches the appropriate point on the sound for each shot. When he does this, the rest of the shot will be in sync.

To facilitate syncing (or syncing up—pronounced "sinking"), each shot should have a *slate*, a visual cue on the picture with an easily identifiable corresponding cue on the sound track. The traditional way of slating in studio productions is to use a slate board and clapper stick. On a small blackboard is written the name of the production, cameraman, shot number, roll number, and any other useful information. It has a stick which can be raised and hit against the top of the blackboard. When the camera comes up to speed (this usually takes less than a second), someone calls out the roll and take numbers while the camera is photographing the slate board. The clapper stick then is brought down, making a dry, hollow sound. The editor can easily see the exact frame at which the stick hits the board and hear the exact point on the sound track where the stick hits, giving him the point of correspondence between sound and picture that he needs. All field-slating systems work basically on the same system. The Arriflex and the Eclair offer an automatic clapstick when a cable is used between camera and tape recorder. When the camera comes up to speed, a light flashes inside the camera, fogging several frames, and an audible bleep is picked up by the Nagra. As an alternate method, which can be used even when there is no physical connection between camera and tape recorder, a pad containing shot numbers can be tapped against the microphone and the number spoken into the microphone.

After each shot, one page is torn off, revealing the next shot number.

The simplest method of all for making a slate is to hit the microphone with your hand. The microphone should be tapped cleanly, but not too hard as this can damage some microphones. Some people use a light on the microphone or tape recorder and it simultaneously puts a bleep on the Nagra. Usually the light is too weak to show up in sunlight, and slates are often missed because of this.

You will encounter situations in which it is inconvenient to slate when doing so might disrupt the subject action. The only type of slate which does not demand any additional movements on the part of the crew is the automatic clapper discussed above.

When shooting from a script, you'll find it is more convenient to slate at the beginning of a shot (*head slate*); without a script it is usually easier to slate at the end of a shot (*tail slate*). If you use tail slates, the last shot on every roll will not have a slate (*runout shot*). Shots without slates are very difficult to sync, for the editor must read the lips of a speaker, and then find the corresponding sound. With practice this becomes easier.

XVI. Sound Editing

If a great deal of sound is to be edited or if the sound is synchronous, the sound must be sent to a sound studio for transfer to 16mm *magnetic film*. Magnetic film is exactly like camera film, except that oxide, like that used on ¼-inch tape, replaces the light-sensitive emulsion on camera film. The standard practice is to record on the edge (*edge track*) of the magnetic film. Some older recorders record in the center (*center track*).

Sound transfer

If the sound is synchronous, the studio must be informed. If the sound is wild (if it has no sync signal recorded on it), this too should be noted. The sound can either be transferred *flat* (without *equalization*) or it can be equalized for 16mm magnetic film. Properly equalized sound will reproduce better. *Filtering* emphasizes some frequencies at the expense of others. Some unwanted background sounds might be reduced and a voice made more intelligible. Transfer costs about $25 an hour for studio time. It usually takes about 50 minutes to transfer a half hour of sound. The magnetic film raw stock costs about two cents a foot, slightly less if you supply it to the studio. Therefore, transfer plus materials costs about four cents per 16mm foot.

It is often possible to buy used 16mm magnetic film at a considerable saving. If there are splices in the magnetic film, you will not be able to record as well over the splices. When a splice hits the recorder head, it lifts slightly off the head causing a momentary loss in gain (volume). This can be particularly annoying in music, but is also noticeable with speech. If the splices on the used 16mm magnetic film are few, it could be worth using it if you can afford some momentary dips in volume. The tape will have to be erased before you use it, and this must be done with a bulk eraser. Instructions for the erasing of tape should be followed carefully.

Sound studio services

Sound studios provide many services. They will transfer

film to magnetic striping on film for you. The recording will be of higher quality than obtained by using a projector to do the recording. Sound studios will also record sounds for you —music, dialogue, or narration. They will also post-dub. This is a rather complicated and slow process for adding dialogue to a film requiring lip synchronization after the film has been shot. (See *American Cinematographer Manual*, pp. 535–8, for a description of post-dubbing.) Studio time ranges from $45-$125 per hour. It is often possible to find small studios or local filmmakers who have the requisite equipment and will perform these services at far lower costs.

When the sound is returned from the sound studio, it is usually broken down into rolls that match the camera rolls. If the sound is synchronous, it is then synchronized with the picture, either by using an action viewer-sound reader-synchronizer combination or an editing machine like the Moviola 16mm-16mm machine. (See Plates 35, 37)

The synchronizer

A *synchronizer* is used to keep your film and sound track (or tracks) in the same relation to each other as you move from one part of the film to the next. (See Plate 35) It consists of two or more rigidly attached sprocket wheels mounted on a revolving shaft. The sound and picture are loaded onto separate wheels and they are kept in synchronization as the sprocket wheels engage the perforations on the picture and magnetic films. A *sound head* can be mounted onto one of the *gangs* (sprocket wheels), which, when hooked into an amplifier and speaker, will read (reproduce) the sound track. The film viewer is then placed a standard number of frames away from the sound reader. A point of synchronization is found and the picture placed in the viewer with the corresponding point in the sound track placed under the sound reader. The film is then cranked with the rewinds and kept in synchronization as long as the number of frames between viewer and sound reader remains constant.

Since you are cranking by hand, the speed of the sound will change. It takes considerable skill to keep the sound at a constant rate around 24 fps. Both because of speed variations and poor quality in the sound-reproduction system, the sound is often reproduced barely above an intelligible level. Only someone familiar with the track will be able to understand it easily. Nevertheless, most editing can be done using this system. If there are additional gangs on the synchronizer, additional sound heads can be added if you wish to hear two or more sound tracks together.

The Moviola

The 16mm-16mm *Moviola* editing machine is the standard 16mm sound editing machine in the United States. (See Plate 37) It sells for over $2,500, but may be rented for $10 a day or from $100 a month and up. It consists of a motorized viewer placed next to a motorized sound reproducer. The machine is upright. The picture is loaded on one side and the magnetic film on the other. A shaft connects the picture head to the sound head. The two can be *interlocked* so that they run together. Or the coupler can be disengaged so that either the sound or the picture can be run separately. This is very helpful when synchronizing rushes since it is possible to change the relationship between picture and sound quickly. The Moviola runs at sound speed to give much better sound reproduction than the synchronizer-viewer combination. However, the reproduction system is not of very high quality, and you should not judge sound quality from it.

Additional sound heads can be added to the Moviola for reproducing more than one sound track in synchronization.

Moviolas tear film or put undue stress on the perforations when the machine is improperly adjusted. If this should happen, check the machine at once.

Editing tables are similar to the Moviola except the film and sound are run horizontally. They generally reproduce sound better than a Moviola and they rarely tear film. The editing process is much faster on a table since you can more easily splice on the editing table than on a Moviola. The picture and sound can be advanced and retarded at much greater speeds on the editing tables. However, picture reproduction is not usually as good as on a Moviola, and editing tables are very expensive. In the past they have not been popular in the United States because they break down too often. Recently the Steenbeck, a German editing table, has been introduced; it seems to be of exceptionally high quality and very reliable. Unfortunately it costs more than two Moviolas. Tables are much bigger and heavier than Moviolas and are rented only for long periods of time at a very high rental fee.

Synchronizing rushes

When the rushes are synchronized, the editor either cuts the sound to match the picture, cutting out wild sound and *plugging* (adding leader) to those sections of picture without sound (sometimes called *wild picture* or MOS); or he can plug the picture for the wild sound, if the wild sound is important and should be heard when the rushes are screened or previewed. Double-system sound can be shown on a Moviola or on a double-system projector like the Siemens which sells for under $2,000 and can be rented for around $35 a day. (See Plate 40)

If there are no slates, usually a Moviola or editing table like the Steenbeck must be used to be able to read lips and sync them by experiment (moving the sound backward and forward). If there are clear slates, a viewer-sound recorder-synchronizer combination will probably suffice for synchronizing picture and sound.

Care of the magnetic film

Pictures can be marked with a grease pencil, but you should never use grease pencil on the oxide (dull) side of the sound. The wax will accumulate on the playback head and seriously lower the sound reproduction quality. It is also difficult to remove grease pencil from track.

Leader should be attached to the sound track with the leader base joined to the magnetic film's oxide side and the magnetic film's base to the leader emulsion. This prevents the soft emulsion from wearing off and collecting on the playback head. Single-perforated leader should be used for magnetic film, both at the head and the tail, to ensure proper loading of the sound. Single-perforated leader should also be used when plugging parts of the sound track. When double-perforated leader is used for plugging, it often causes unwanted sound to be reproduced. This is not serious at the editing stage, but if the sound is mixed (re-recorded), the noise may show up in your final film.

Anything that might catch on the recorder's playback head and gum it up (such as adhesives) should not be put on the oxide side of magnetic film. Easily visible black dry-mark ink (such as in felt-tipped pens) is the best to use since it does not injure the playback head or affect sound quality. Adhesives and oil can be removed from oxide with tape-head lubricant or alcohol. Never use tape-head cleaner; it will dissolve the oxide.

Start marks

When the rushes have been synchronized or when any sound has been properly layed in next to the picture, a *start mark* should be placed on picture and sound at a corresponding point of synchronization on the head leader of each. A start mark is simply an "X" used to load picture and sound in synchronization. When we load the sound and picture to play in sync, the start mark tells us where to line them up. The start mark should be a few feet in from the beginning of the head leader, and a few feet before the first frame of picture or sound.

Degaussing

When working with magnetic tape you have to be careful that none of your equipment becomes magnetized. Scissors, splicers, recorder heads, and reels can all become magnetized and affect your sound adversely. When a recorder head becomes magnetized, you must raise the volume control to record adequately. When scissors or splicers become magnetized, they may add a click to your sound track when they are used to make a splice. If you start to hear clicks at sound cuts, it probably means that your splicer is magnetized. You can test for this by taking unrecorded magnetic tape, splicing it, and listening for clicks when the tape is played back. If any equipment is magnetized, it must be *degaussed* (*demagnetized*) at once. You can purchase small pencil degaussers to do the job; however, it is considerably easier with a bulk degausser. Instructions should be followed carefully and the equipment should be tested again as described above to make sure it has been properly degaussed. An improperly used degausser can increase the magnetization of the equipment.

Machine edge-numbering

If synchronous sound has been used, when the rushes have been synchronized they are usually sent to a lab for machine edge-numbering. This costs between one-half and one cent per foot. The lab lines up the corresponding picture and sound, guided by the respective start marks, and puts the same numbers on each. Most edge-numbering machines use from one to three code letters followed by four numbers. You must tell the lab what letters and numbers to use. You may want to have all of one production coded with the same series of letters.

When picture and sound have corresponding edge-numbers, editing is made easier. Instead of having to line picture and sound up in a synchronizer, the editor makes the corresponding picture and sound cuts by lining up the machine edge-numbers. Also, he can check synchronization at any point in the film very quickly by running picture and sound through the synchronizer, making sure the edge-numbers correspond. You will rely a great deal on these edge-numbers while editing, and it is important that you make sure they were applied properly and that the rushes were properly synchronized.

Continuity editing

In editing synchronous sound film for continuity, you have several special problems. Not only the picture, but also the sound must flow smoothly. Sometimes you will not have enough picture for the sound you need and vice versa.

To achieve sound continuity, background levels must match and the sound quality must be approximately the same on either side of the sound cut. When volume changes at a sound cut, it can often be adjusted at the mix when the sound is re-recorded. If background levels do not match, a piece of room tone might be used to bridge the cut, or it might be put behind both pieces of sound. *Room tone* is simply the background noise of any environment. Each location has its own special sound, so you should record some room tone at every location where sound is taken. Room tone can often be used to bridge gaps where no dialogue is needed but the picture lacks any sound. A complete absence of sound is most unnatural and noticeable.

When you do not have adequate picture for the required sound, you usually use a cut-away, normally a reaction shot. In documentary shooting with sound it is very important to get cut-aways for just this reason. A typical, often weak, television device is to cut to the hands of the speaker. Shots of people listening to him are usually far superior.

The mix

If the sound track for the finished film is going to be complicated, or if there is a synchronous sound track, you will probably need what is called a *mix* (or *re-recording*) session. The cost for a mix at the best studios ranges from $50 to $125 an hour. Ten minutes of film may take from thirty minutes to two hours or more to mix, depending on the complexity of the sound track, the skill of the mixer, and how fussy you are about the result.

Most dialogue sound is put on one or two tracks. Separate tracks are used for narration and music. One to three tracks may be used for sound effects and room tone. The mixer adjusts levels for each of the different tracks, and equalizes and filters them differently to get the best sound possible. He can also add echo to a voice or make a voice sound as if it is coming over a telephone or PA system. He can make it seem far away, though rarely can he bring it closer (give it greater presence).

Whenever one sound is to melt into another, they must be put on separate tracks with at least one foot of overlap and preferably more. Sound dissolves are often used to match picture dissolves or to introduce a new sound slowly into a sequence. Sound fades are used similarly to match picture fades or to remove a sound from a sequence slowly.

Sound loops are sometimes made from room tone to increase the tone's length. A loop is a length of film with its head spliced to its tail. It is put into one of the sound dubbers and played continuously so that the sound mixer can patch into it at any time. Loops should be at least four or five feet long and the point where the splice is made should be carefully chosen so the sound cut is not obvious. The sound studio will often transfer loops to 35mm magnetic film, which is less likely to break.

All the tracks must be synchronized with each other and with the picture. When magnetic film has been used this is easy since the sprocket holes on the magnetic film guarantee sync. Each track should be marked with a start mark corresponding to the start marks on all the other reels of track. Usually the start mark on the picture is punched so it shows up clearly on projection. A small piece of tape with adhesive on the back that has a high-frequency signal recorded on it (*bleep tape*) can be put on the sound start mark to check that the tracks have been loaded in proper relationship to each other. If the punch mark projects at the same time that all the bleeps sound in unison, we know that the tracks are synchronized with each other and with the picture. Any bleep not in unison indicates that a track has not been properly loaded. The bleep tone also serves to align the optical track with the edited original before they are to be printed together. The bleep tone appears on the optical sound track as a series of regular modulations about one frame long.

Most mixing studios have a footage counter and you should supply the mixer with a *cue sheet* (or *log*) that tells him at which point each track has sound as opposed to blank leader on it. Fades and dissolves of sound and/or picture should also be marked. Most studios and mixers demand that all footage numbers be given in 35mm footage. There are calculators that will help you do this, or use a synchronizer with a 35mm and a 16mm footage counter. These can be rented. Sixteen 16mm frames are equivalent to one 35mm foot, and two 16mm feet are the equivalent of five 35mm feet.

The easiest log to make is one that has a column for each sound track and one for the picture. Every time a track has sound on it draw a vertical line with a 35mm footage number at top, giving the footage from the start mark and a 35mm footage number at the end. The sheets should be large and continuous with corresponding footage numbers in each column. No matter how carefully you make up your log, the mixer will most likely rewrite it for his own use. What is most important is that you have clearly marked what sound is on what track and where. This saves valuable time.

More time can be saved, especially with a difficult mix, when the studio is equipped with reversible dubbers or reproducers. These make up a *rollback system* which enables the mixer to stop at any point in a reel, go back, and re-record. He can simply erase any mistakes he has made. (In the old system the whole 10-minute reel had to be done over to correct mistakes.)

The result of the mix, the complete mixed sound track, is usually delivered in one of three forms: a ¼-inch tape with a sync signal recorded on it, a 16mm magnetic film, or a 16mm optical master track in the correct wind for your printing system. The mix studio may supply you with one of these at no additional charge. It is generally a good idea to get the ¼-inch master tape and the master optical track.

The optical track will have to be properly lined up with the cut rolls of original film before it is sent to the laboratory for final printing. If the original is reversal and you decide to make an internegative, a different wind may be required on your optical master track, depending on the type of printing equipment your lab has available. Some color reversal printing systems require a negative rather than a positive optical sound track. Check with the lab as to whether they require a negative or positive optical track and what wind it should be for your particular printing material.

Epilogue

Showing the film

The completed film with optical or magnetic sound track will ultimately be shown to people on a projector. Since pacing, image quality, and the impact of the film will depend to a great extent on how large the image is when projected, it is wise to look at the film during editing as often as possible on a projector. The film will often appear completely different when projected to some size. Close-ups will appear *very* different, as will long shots. The pacing of the film will be different. It takes considerable skill to be able to look at a film on a viewer and imagine how it will look on the screen.

Unfortunately, the screening of a film is much like the playing of a piece of music. There are good performances and bad. There will be good projections and bad ones. Sound that is perfectly intelligible on one projector will be totally impossible on another. The picture will appear bright and crisp under some conditions and dull and washed out under others. When the projector has been properly maintained, and the room where the film is to be shown is dark and has reasonable acoustics, variations from screening to screening will not be so great. However, 16mm and 8mm films are rarely shown under uniformly good conditions.

The darker the room, the better the projected image will appear. Stray light in the room will decrease image clarity and crispness and seriously impair picture contrast. The screen should be in good condition and have no wrinkles. It is important that the screen be parallel to the film as it passes the projector gate or part of the image will be out of focus.

If the projector lens is not clean, again crispness will suffer and picture contrast will be lowered. The projector should be clean, and the projector gate checked to ensure that there are no emulsion deposits that may scratch the film. Dirt in the aperture will show up at the edges of the projected image. If the print itself is not clean, dust will appear at the edges of the frame while the film is being projected.

Several feet of head and tail leader should be attached to the print to ensure that none of the film itself gets damaged during rewinding and loading. The leader should be marked so that the print may be identified.

Most modern projectors will hold 2000 feet of 16mm film and no more. Consequently, if your film is longer than 55 minutes, you will want to break it into more than one reel. If you do use 2000-foot reels and you are distributing the film, you had best include a 2000-foot take-up reel, since many people will be supplied with only 1200-foot or 1600-foot take-up reels. If at all possible, it is best to mount the film on reels smaller than 2000 feet, since some projectors will not accommodate that reel size and some of those that do may put undue stress on film wound on very large reels.

The brighter the projector bulb, the better the projected image will look. The larger the image is projected, the more crispness it will lose.

Optical sound reproducers on projectors are often out of alignment. If this is the case, you will not be able to get high-quality optical playback and the machine will have to be sent for repairs. Some projectors allow you to align the optical playback system, and thereby give you control over one of the chief factors responsible for poor sound playback. On Kodak Pageant projectors the fidelity control allows you to adjust alignment in the optical playback system.

The nature of the room will determine sound quality to a large degree. Bare surfaces tend to reflect sound and make it less intelligible. Curtains, carpeting, and people absorb sound, cutting down boominess. Broken-up walls and irregular surfaces tend to improve acoustics.

Some projectors have built-in speakers. If possible, you should plug in an external speaker which can be placed in front of the screen. Built-in speakers are usually of low quality, and, in any case, sound coming from behind the viewer sets up an unnatural separation between sound and picture. Since the projector noise and the reproduced sound come from the same direction with a built-in speaker, it becomes a bit more difficult for the ear to filter out the unwanted projector noise. If possible, place the projector in a separate room to cut projector noise. Some projectors come with a speaker in a separate case which you can place by the screen. This sort is also far better than a built-in speaker.

You should try to show your films to as many people as possible, and you should go with your film to see how audiences react. You may be able to learn a great deal from the audience.

As in all things, it is often hard to find yourself in film. For some, the way is to make their films alone. For others, film is essentially a group enterprise. In film you may be able to find yourself, understand the world, show others what the world really is, and, finally, change it.

APPENDIX A

A Comparison of Running Times and Formats of 8mm, Super 8, and 16mm Motion Picture Films*

RUNNING TIMES AND FILM LENGTHS FOR COMMON PROJECTION SPEEDS

Film Format	8mm (80 Frames per Foot)				Super 8 (72 Frames per Foot)				16mm (40 Frames per Foot)			
Projection Speed in Frames per Second	18†		24		18		24		18†		24	
Running Time and Film Length Seconds	Feet	+ Frames	Feet	+ Frames	Feet	+ Frames	Feet	+ Frames	Feet	+ Frames	Feet	+ Frames
1	0	18	0	24	0	18	0	24	0	18	0	24
2	0	36	0	48	0	36	0	48	0	36	1	8
3	0	54	0	72	0	54	1	0	1	14	1	32
4	0	72	1	16	1	0	1	24	1	32	2	16
5	1	10	1	40	1	18	1	48	2	10	3	0
6	1	28	1	64	1	36	2	0	2	28	3	24
7	1	46	2	8	1	54	2	24	3	6	4	8
8	1	64	2	32	2	0	2	48	3	24	4	32
9	2	2	2	56	2	18	3	0	4	2	5	16
10	2	20	3	0	2	36	3	24	4	20	6	0

(continued on p. 168)

Film Format	8mm (80 Frames per Foot)				Super 8 (72 Frames per Foot)				16mm (40 Frames per Foot)			
Projection Speed in Frames per Second	18†		24		18		24		18‡		24	
Running Time and Film Length	Feet	+ Frames	Feet	+ Frames	Feet	+ Frames	Feet	+ Frames	Feet	+ Frames	Feet	+ Frames
20	4	40	6	0	5	0	6	48	9	0	12	0
30	6	60	9	0	7	36	10	0	13	20	18	0
40	9	0	12	0	10	0	13	24	18	0	24	0
50	11	20	15	0	12	36	16	48	22	20	30	0
Minutes 1	13	40	18	0	15	0	20	0	27	0	36	0
2	27	0	36	0	30	0	40	0	54	0	72	0
3	40	40	54	0	45	0	60	0	81	0	108	0
4	54	0	72	0	60	0	80	0	108	0	144	0
5	67	40	90	0	75	0	100	0	135	0	180	0
6	81	0	108	0	90	0	120	0	162	0	216	0
7	94	40	126	0	105	0	140	0	189	0	252	0
8	108	0	144	0	120	0	160	0	216	0	288	0
9	121	40	162	0	135	0	180	0	243	0	324	0
10	135	0	180	0	150	0	200	0	270	0	360	0

* KODAK Pamphlet No. S-42, reprinted by permission of Eastman Kodak Company, Rochester, New York 14650.

† USA Standard PH22.22-1964

‡ USA Standard PH22.10-1964

TYPICAL RUNNING TIMES OF FILMS

Film Format	8mm				Super 8				16mm			
Projection Speed in Frames per Second	18		24		18		24		18		24	
Inches per Second	2.7		3.6		3.0		4.0		5.4		7.2	
Film Length and Screen Time — Feet	Minutes	Seconds	Minutes	Seconds	Minutes	Seconds	Minutes	Seconds	Minutes	Seconds	Minutes	Seconds
50	3	42	2	47	3	20	2	30	1	51	1	23
100	7	24	5	33	6	40	5	0	3	42	2	47
150	11	7	8	20	10	0	7	30	5	33	4	10
200	14	49	11	7	13	20	10	0	7	24	5	33
300	22	13	16	40	20	0	15	0	11	7	8	20
400	29	38	22	13	26	40	20	0	14	49	11	7
500	37	2	27	47	33	20	25	0	18	31	13	53
600	44	27	33	20	40	0	30	0	22	13	16	40
700	51	51	38	53	46	40	35	0	25	56	19	27
800	59	16	44	27	53	20	40	0	29	38	22	13
900	66	40	50	0	60	0	45	0	33	20	25	0
1000	74	4	55	33	66	40	50	0	37	2	27	47
1100	81	29	61	7	73	20	55	0	40	44	30	33
1200	88	53	66	40	80	0	60	0	44	27	33	20

NUMBER OF FRAMES SEPARATION BETWEEN SOUND AND PICTURE*

	8mm	Super 8†	16mm
Magnetic Track	56	18	28
Optical Track	—	22	26

* Figures given are for reel-to-reel projection in which the sound precedes the picture. A proposed standard places the sound 28 frames behind the picture for cartridge-loaded films.

† Proposed USA Standard Dimensions.

APPENDIX B

HANDLING, REPAIR, and STORAGE of
Eastman Kodak 16mm Motion Picture Films*

TABLE OF CONTENTS

* KODAK Pamphlet No. D-23, reprinted by permission of Eastman Kodak Company, Rochester, New York 14650.

Handling, Repair, and Storage of Eastman Kodak 16mm Motion Picture Films

Everyone concerned with the handling and storage of 16mm films should be interested in prolonging the useful life of these films. After the primary consideration of first-quality processing by a reputable processor, long service for films depends on proper care. The following pages suggest the best methods of handling, repairing, and storing processed 16mm Kodak motion picture films.

POSSIBLE CAUSES OF DAMAGE TO 16mm FILM

1. Dirt in the projector gate and other parts that guide the film through the projector.

2. Improper threading or operation of the projector.

3. Lack of inspection and repair of the film before projection.

4. Improper rewinding of the film. Much damage can be done by rewinding onto bent reels, rewinding too rapidly, overloading the reels, or cinching the film.

5. Use of projection equipment that has worn or defective pulldown claws, gate, sprocket teeth, or other parts that are in contact with the film.

6. Poor splicing.

7. Accidents due to carelessness in handling, such as dropping a reel of film; damage to film cans; breakage during projection.

8. Improper handling of film, resulting in fingerprints, crimping, etc. (Film should be handled by edges only.)

9. Film lubrication needed.

10. Improper storage.

SUGGESTIONS FOR THE PROMOTION OF LONG FILM LIFE

1. The projector gate and other parts that guide the film through the projector should be kept clean.

2. Film should be threaded correctly, and the projector operated properly.

3. Films should be inspected and repaired (if necessary) before use.

4. Films should be cleaned and lubricated properly.

5. Splices should be made with care and accuracy.

6. A long leader should be attached at the start of a reel; a trailer at the end. The leader will protect the first few feet of film from scratches and tears that can occur during threading and start-up. Also, a leader is easy to replace when damaged. Similarly, the trailer protects the last scene from damage that might occur during rewinding and cleaning.

7. Reels should not be filled to capacity. The outside layer of film should be at least ½-inch in from the edges of the flanges. Film from an overloaded reel can be damaged easily, and may not take up properly when projected.

8. Badly bent reels should be discarded.

9. Care should be exercised in rewinding films. The tension should be high enough to produce a tight roll, but not so high that it will cinch the film.

10. Films should be stored at the recommended temperature and relative humidity. Storage in an excessively dry atmosphere can cause film to become brittle and therefore easily broken.

11. Libraries should:

    (a) Include instruction leaflets with each shipment of film to advise customers of the best method of handling.

(b) Refuse rentals to the customers who apparently have caused film damage in the past. This may prevail upon them to provide a competent projectionist and satisfactory projection equipment.

(c) Warn customers that they will be charged for the replacement of film that is damaged while it is in their possession. Some libraries require a deposit for rental films; others insure the films against damage and add the cost to the rental fee.

12. Film should be packed in rigid containers that will withstand rough handling and provide ample protection to the film reels. Reinforced-fiber and light metal cases are commercially available and are excellent for this purpose.

CLEANING AND LUBRICATION

All 16mm films processed in Kodak Processing Laboratories are lubricated, after processing, to insure smooth operation in projectors. This practice conforms with the recommended procedure in the professional motion picture industry.

You can clean and lubricate films by drawing them through soft, lintless cloths moistened with a preparation such as KODAK Movie Film Cleaner (with Lubricant). This should be done whenever a film becomes dirty. If a film is unsteady and noisy during the first projection, it may not have been lubricated at the processing laboratory you have selected (non-Kodak). In this case, the film should be lubricated not only to reduce noise, but also to prevent film damage during use.

Cleaning cloths of the following types are usually satisfactory: a good grade of Canton flannel, a short- or medium-pile rayon or nylon plush, or a soft cotton batiste. These should preferably be white, undyed, and free of fabric fillers and additives for stiffening or improvement of feel. In case of doubt, the cloths should be laundered before use.

To clean film, place it on a rewind and thread the leader strip onto a take-up reel. Rewind the film, drawing it between two cloths that have been moistened with the cleaner/lubricant. Constant light pressure with one hand assures continual contact between the film surfaces and the cloths. This operation must be performed slowly enough to permit the cleaner to evaporate *completely* before the film reaches the take-up reel.

Frequent remoistening of the cloths is recommended because the solvent evaporates rapidly.* To avoid scratching the film with accumulated dirt particles, it is advisable to re-fold the cloths often, so that clean areas only will be in contact with the film. If streaks are noticed on the film after lubrication, they can usually be removed by buffing with a soft cloth.

Any color that appears on a cloth used for cleaning Kodak color film can be disregarded. It is a film-surface accumulation, not a part of the dye in the image.

KODAK Film Cleaner and KODAK Movie Film Cleaner (with Lubricant) are satisfactory for cleaning both film to which KODAK SONOTRACK Coating has been applied, and pre-striped sound film.

Methyl chloroform is a solvent that is safe to use on Kodak film having SONOTRACK Coating or on Kodak pre-striped film, but it may have an adverse effect on other magnetic sound stripes.

Another lubricant that gives good results consists of 0.1 gram of a wax, such as PE Tetrastearate (Pentaerythritol Tetrastearate), Practical Grade,† in 100ml of a solvent such as CHLOROTHENE.‡

If the film has a magnetic sound stripe, a test should be made on a discarded piece of the film before cleaning it with a solvent, or before applying a lacquer. This is to be certain that the solvent in the cleaner or lacquer does not dissolve the binder in the magnetic stripe. In case the stripe softens or smears, another type of cleaner or lacquer will have to be used.

NOTE: Water detergent cleaners are not recommended for color films because under certain conditions they can cause fading of the dyes.

SPLICING

The splicing of motion picture films is not a complicated procedure, but a great deal of damage can be caused by poorly made splices. A good splice can be made by either of

---

* KODAK Movie Film Cleaner (with Lubricant) manufactured since January 1952, does not contain carbon tetrachloride (the vapors of which are highly toxic). Even so, the cleaner should be used with adequate ventilation. If used for more than a few minutes at a time, forced-air ventilation should be provided. No matter what type of cleaner is being used, the instructions on the container should be followed.

† Available as Chemical No. P7421, from Eastman Organic Chemicals, Rochester, N. Y. 14603, or as Hercules B-16 Synthetic Wax, from Hercules Powder Co., 910 Market Street, Wilmington, Delaware 19899.

‡ Trademark.

two methods: tape splicing, in which an adhesive tape (KODAK PRESSTAPE) designed especially for the purpose is used; or cement splicing in which the ends of the film to be spliced are fused, or welded together.

Either PRESSTAPE or cement splicing, properly done, affords a satisfactory splice. Cement splicing may be preferred by those who have occasion to make splices frequently and who have become familiar with that technique. For nonproduction splicing, the PRESSTAPE method is recommended.

Tape Splicing

A modern and simple way to splice 8mm, super 8, and 16mm motion picture film is offered by the KODAK PRESSTAPE Universal Splicer. This is a dry splicer; no cement or water is required. The splices are made with pressure-sensitive KODAK PRESSTAPE.

This method provides a strong, durable bond and the film can be projected immediately after a splice has been made. The heat from the projector lamp will cure the splice, making it even stronger. Even if the film is not projected for some time, curing will take place within three or four weeks.

Cement Splicing

Film cement contains a solvent that fuses the film ends together. A cement of good quality, such as KODAK Film Cement, should be used.

Directions furnished with your splicer should be followed in scraping and cementing the film. When the film is placed in the splicer, the emulsion (dull) side must be up. It is important that both the emulsion and the coating under it (the binder) be removed completely from the section of film that is to be overlapped in the splicer. Next, the cement should be applied evenly, in a thin layer. The back of the overlapping film strip should be pressed quickly on top of the scraped area. After the splicer has been closed and reopened, excess cement should be wiped off.

Principle of Cement Splicing: Illustrations on pages 177–178 show the principle involved in cement splicing of motion picture film.

Structure of Motion Picture Film: Film has several layers (Figs. 1 and 2, page 177). These include:

1. Flexible film *base* provides a strong and durable support.

2. *Emulsion* coating consists chiefly of gelatine. In this layer is suspended the silver or dye that forms the photographic image.

3. A microsopically thin layer, or *binder,* between the *base* and emulsion coating, binds these two layers tightly together.

CEMENT SPLICING OF MOTION PICTURE FILM

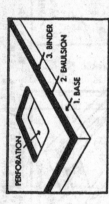

Figure 2 — 1. The flexible film base provides a durable support. 2. The emulsion coating consists chiefly of gelatin, in which is suspended the silver or dye image. 3. A thin layer, or binder, between the base and emulsion binds them tightly together.

Figure 4 — The emulsion and binder coatings should be moistened with water. This softens the emulsion slightly so that it can be removed easily. The moistened surface should be dry before the film cement is applied.

Figure 1 — If a small section of motion picture film were to be magnified to great size, we should see that the film is made up of more than one layer. In the above illustration the thickness of the various layers is exaggerated.

Figure 3 — It is impossible to cement the base side of one piece of film to the emulsion of another. The emulsion and binder must first be completely removed so that the two film base surfaces can come in direct contact with each other.

Figure 5 — To make a welded splice, the two top layers—emulsion and binder—should be completely removed. The base side of the other film may have oil on it, picked up from projection. This must be removed before a good weld can be made.

Figure 6 — A good motion picture film splice is actually a weld. When a perfect splice is made, one side of the film base is dissolved into the base of the other film. With most splicing apparatus this requires from 10 to 20 seconds.

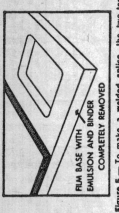

Figure 7 — If any emulsion or binder remains on the base in the area where the splice is to be made, a good weld will not result and the splice may not hold.

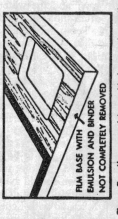

Figure 8 — Scratching or gouging the prepared film base near the emulsion edge should be avoided. Such scratches (A) weaken the weld and may cause the film to break at this point. Fine abrasive scratches are not serious.

Preparing the Base Side: The base side, or undersurface, of the film that will be overlapping in the splicer may have oil on it, picked up in projection; also, some films are made with a thin coating on the back. If a good weld is to be made, the oil and base coating must be removed.

To remove oil or similar foreign material, the back of the film should be wiped first with a dry cloth. Further rubbing with a cloth moistened with alcohol is often effective. Should these simple measures fail, it will be necessary to apply film cement to the base and then wipe it off with a soft cloth. Cement applied to the base side should be about equal in amount to that used in making a splice. It should be wiped off completely as soon after application as possible.

The use of abrasives on the back of the film is not recommended unless it is absolutely necessary, since there is a danger that the abrasive particles will spread through the roll and scratch the film.

Pretreatment of Old Film: If film is old, it may be necessary to pretreat the back surface of the film support with film cement, as described above.

Removing Emulsion: For a good splice, the two top layers—emulsion and binder—must be removed completely from the film to be overlapped in the splicer. Magnetic sound stripe in the splicing area must also be removed. This will leave the top of the support bare to be surface-dissolved, or fused, into the back of the film to which it is to be attached.

Usually, the emulsion and binder coatings should be moistened with water and the water allowed to soak in for a few seconds to soften the coatings before the film is scraped (Fig. 4, page 177). Too much water can damage the emulsion adjacent to the splice. The prepared area should be wiped with a clean, dry cloth or brush before cement is applied, to make sure that any moisture and emulsion particles are removed.

Dry scraping should not be attempted unless the splicer and scraper are especially designed for it; otherwise, the film may tear at the perforations or near the edge. Any torn section should be cut off and a new surface prepared.

Scrapers on most splicers are equipped with guides that control the depth of the scraping and the width of the area from which emulsion is to be scraped. On some, the amount of pressure applied and the number of scrapes determine the depth. The scraper should have sharp working edges and it should be free of emulsion debris from previous use.

It is best to scrape with light strokes at first, then gradually increase the pressure until the emulsion and binder are completely removed (Fig. 5, page 178). If too much pressure is applied too fast, the perforations may become torn and the base gouged. Film that is scraped too deeply will be weakened and is likely to break at the splice.

Film Cement: Film cement is a chemical solution that is capable of dissolving film base. Besides a solvent, it contains other chemicals that stabilize its action. If film cement is exposed to the air, the solvent will evaporate, the cement will become thick and gummy, and it will usually not make a satisfactory weld. For these reasons and for convenience, the bulk supply of cement should be kept in a stock bottle, and a quantity sufficient for immediate use in a well-stoppered working bottle.

Applying Cement: The cement should be applied by brush to the prepared surface—enough to wet the complete splice area, but not so much that it will run outside the splice when the two films are pressed together. It is important that you close the splicer, and bring the two areas of film into contact as soon as possible after applying cement (seconds count!) and keep them under pressure for 10 to 20 seconds.

The body and viscosity of most modern film cements are such that little or no cement will be squeezed out of the weld when splices are made properly. If too much cement is used, however, the excess will be squeezed out of the weld. This must be wiped off immediately with a soft cloth. Otherwise it may adhere to and leave a smear on the preceding or following convolution of film in the reel, causing damage, distortion or cockle. Also, any magnetic stripe will be dissolved.

Films that have become very dry or that have been rolled on small-diameter reel hubs sometimes have so high a curl that splicing is difficult. Such films can be held under pressure in the splicer 30 seconds or longer after the cement is applied, in order to allow the splice to develop more strength.

The finished splice should be rubbed firmly with a soft cloth held over the finger. This will give added assurance of a better splice and compensate for any non-uniformity of pressure applied by the splicer.

Checking the Cement Splice: A good splice has sufficient strength after 20 seconds so that the film can be removed from the splicing block and wound onto the reel at normal tension. Although it is possible to project the film immediately, it is best to allow time, at least two hours, for the welded area to cure.

Each splice should be examined for quality. A good splice is fully transparent; bubbles and hazy areas indicate a poor splice.

Causes of Unsatisfactory Cement Splices: If emulsion or binder remains on the base in the prepared area (Fig. 7, page 178), a good weld cannot be made. Also, excessive scraping, scratching, or gouging of the prepared film base will weaken the base and can cause the film to break.

A splice may not hold if there is too great a delay in bringing the film ends into contact after applying cement.

The film may buckle at the splice after a short time if too much cement is applied (this can cause difficulty when the film goes through the projector gate). If too little cement is used, the weld will not be completed over the whole area of the splice and the splice will not last long. Such splices should be repaired because the edges will remain loose and may tear easily. Failure of a splice that apparently has had the proper amount of cement applied may be due to inadequate preparation of the base side, or to the use of a type of cement not suited to the film base.

Practice Splice: It is advisable to make practice splices with scrap film; this is a good way to learn the "feel" of the process.

Splicing KODAK White Movie Leader to Film: The simplest and most effective way to splice white leader to film is to use a "cement wipe." Either side of the leader can be joined to the base side of the film. However, if the film or leader (or both) has perforations on only one edge, the leader must be placed on the splicer with the perforations in the proper position.

The leader should be placed on the splicer in the same position as the part of the film that is to be scraped. Instead of being scraped, the portion of the leader that is to be overlapped by the film should be brushed with film cement, then immediately wiped with a clean cloth to remove the coating from the area that is to be overlapped. Cement should then be applied a second time to the leader, and the splice completed.

Splicing Film That Has a Magnetic Sound Track

When PRESSTAPE splices are made on film having a magnetic sound stripe, the tape should be trimmed on one edge with scissors before application, so that it will not cover the sound track.

Cement splices on film having a recorded magnetic track cause some loss in signal level due to the mechanical separation of the coated film from the magnetic head at the splice. This effect is minimized in correctly made splices because the butt is toward the tail end of the film and the splice is made on the side of the film with the sound stripe.

If the steel scraper or cutter in the splicer becomes magnetized, a noticeable click will be heard in films on which the sound has been recorded magnetically prior to the time the splice is made. If this proves to be a problem, the splicer should be demagnetized, or all editing should be done before the sound is recorded.

NOTE: Film that has an optical sound track should be spliced in the same way as film with *no* sound track because the optical sound track is essentially a part of the film emulsion. The use of blooping ink is recommended on optical sound film splices to eliminate the possibility of light leakage and to prevent consequent pops or clicks.

STORAGE

Film Cans

Films should be stored in film cans or boxes. These containers protect films from damage, dirt, and dust, and they help assure scratch-free projection.

Storage Cabinets

All modern 16mm films are on safety base and can be stored on wooden shelves or in wooden cabinets. However, most libraries store film on metal shelves or in metal cabinets made especially for this purpose.* Such metal cabinets are usually supplied with adjustable shelving to accommodate standard-size reels. The film cans should be stored on edge for easy access.

Storage Conditions

Storage cabinets should be separated enough to permit free circulation of air on all sides. Storage areas should be located on the intermediate floors of buildings, never in damp basements or on the top floors of uninsulated buildings, which may be too hot. Also, film should be kept away from steampipes, radiators, hot-air ducts, and other sources of heat and humidity.

Film storage and handling areas should be kept as free as possible from dust and dirt. Ideally, such rooms should be supplied with conditioned and filtered air. Precautions should be taken to prevent the entrance of dust and dirt through ventilators, heating ducts, and windows.

All Kodak and Eastman motion picture films are made on safety base, which the National Board of Fire Underwriters

---

* Manufacturers of such equipment include: General Fireproofing Company, 413 E. Dennick Avenue, Youngstown, Ohio 44501; Lyon Metal Products, Inc., 1933 Montgomery Street, Aurora, Illinois 60505; Neumade Products Corporation, 250 West 57th Street, New York, New York 10019.

has determined presents somewhat less of a fire hazard than does the same form and quantity of common newsprint. The information herein applies to the storage of such films. Any film made on nitrate base is flammable and therefore dangerous to store. Information on the building of vaults and the proper storage of nitrate film * can be obtained from the National Board of Fire Underwriters, 85 John Street, New York, N. Y. 10038. It can also be found in the KODAK Data Book, *Storage and Preservation of Motion Picture Film,* available from Kodak dealers.

Black-and-White Films

Ideally, 16mm black-and-white films in active use should be stored at a relative humidity of 40 percent and a temperature of about 70 F, but temperatures up to 75 F or 80 F and a relative humidity between 25 and 60 percent are acceptable. If other conditions of storage are necessary for an extended period of time, the film should be checked frequently for signs of trouble.

The storage of 16mm films presents no special problem in the parts of the United States that have moderate climatic conditions. However, if the relative humidity exceeds 60 percent for any length of time, the storage room must be dehumidified. If extremely dry conditions prevail so that the film can become brittle, humidification is necessary.

Dehumidification: Storage in high relative humidity is likely to result in the growth of mold or fungus, the formation of objectionable shiny marks on the emulsion surface (ferrotyping), and rust or corrosion on metal reels and cans. Mold growth is encouraged by high relative humidity and frequently becomes a serious problem with any humidity above 60 percent. The use of an electrically operated refrigeration-type dehumidifier is recommended.† The storage area should be relatively airtight, and the walls should be coated with paper-laminated aluminum foil to minimize vapor transfer. The humidistat should be set to maintain a relative humidity of about 40 percent.

NOTE: If fungus growth is observed on the film, KODAK Movie Film Cleaner (with Lubricant) should be used.

* Nitrate films have not been manufactured by the Eastman Kodak Company since 1951.

† Carrier Corporation, Carrier Parkway, Syracuse, New York 13201; Frigidaire Division, General Motors Corporation, 300 Taylor Street, Dayton, Ohio 45401.

Humidification: If the film becomes brittle and curly as the result of dry conditions, damage in handling or in projection is likely. If necessary, controlled humidification must be employed to keep the air in the storage space at the proper humidity. The correct amount of moisture can be added by mechanical humidifiers.* It is advisable to remove the film from cans and store the open reels on edge, on open racks with spaces of ½ inch or more between reels. Such storage will permit air circulation both horizontally and vertically. The humidifier should be controlled by a humidistat set to produce about 40 percent relative humidity.

Color Films

Since Kodak and Eastman color films were first introduced, many improvements have been made in the stability of the dyes. However, all dyes are fugitive to some extent and they change in time. Heat, moisture, and light are the three factors that most affect the permanence of dyes. For maximum permanence, therefore, processed films should be stored where it is cool, dry, and dark.

High relative humidity can cause change in color images even if films are stored in the dark, or are refrigerated. The effect of high relative humidity is especially pronounced if it is accompanied by high temperature.

Prolonged storage in an atmosphere of excessively high relative humidity can cause mold and other growths that are particularly harmful to color films.

Both excessive heat and light from the projection lamp tend to accelerate dye change. However, the projection time per frame is so short on standard motion picture projectors that no harm results from normal projection.

A relative humidity of 25 to 40 percent and a temperature of 50 F or lower are best for storage of processed color films. However, Kodak color films can be expected to have a useful life of many years if shown with care in good projection equipment and stored at ordinary room temperature (70 F) and a relative humidity below 50 percent. Extreme desiccation must be avoided, as it renders the film brittle and subject to breakage.

---

* Fresh'nd-Aire Company, Division of the Cory Corporation, 3200 West Peterson Avenue, Chicago, Illinois 60645; Parks-Cramer Corporation, Newport Street, Fitchburg, Massachusetts 01420; Walton Laboratories, 1188 Grove Street, Irvington, New Jersey 07111.

Film with a Magnetic Sound Track

Film with a magnetic sound coating on which sound has been recorded should be stored observing the same precautions that apply to the storage of any other safety motion picture film. Heat and humidity cause deterioration of the film and, to a certain extent, of the magnetic track. A magnetic sound track, as far as is now known, is as permanent as the film base to which the coating has been applied. Storing the film in a metal container, such as a film cabinet or an aluminum or steel film reel, will not adversely affect the recorded sound. The film must not be stored near a permanent magnet or near electrical wiring that carries a heavy current.

Long-Term Storage

If valuable black-and-white film is to be stored for a long period of time, it is quite important that the relative humidity be held between 40 and 50 percent and the temperature be kept below 80 F. Color film should be stored at a relative humidity between 25 and 40 percent and at a temperature of 50 F or less.

To achieve and maintain these conditions in some climates, the storage vault should be air-conditioned. The cost of such equipment can amount to several thousand dollars and the installation will add to this figure, but a properly designed system will keep the temperature and relative humidity at the right levels. Information can be obtained from a local air-conditioning engineer.

If no air-conditioned vault is available, a cold-storage or deep-freeze unit can be used. In this case, the films should be pre-conditioned to the recommended relative humidity before they are placed in cans. The cans should be sealed tight with tape to protect the films against the high relative humidity usually present in cold-storage units.

Be sure that you choose a tape which is air- and moisture-tight in order to provide permanent protection. Freezer tape is ideal for this purpose; a good grade of rubber-base surgical tape is recommended also. Both are readily available in most areas.

For long-term storage, the cans of film should be kept lying flat to prevent distortion from the sagging of any loosely wound rolls. The cans should be stacked no more than six or eight high.

TEMPERATURE AND HUMIDITY RECOMMENDATIONS FOR STORAGE

16mm Motion Picture Films	Long-Term Storage		Films in Active Use	
	Temperature (F)	Relative Humidity (%)	Temperature (F)	Relative Humidity (%)
Black-and-white	Below 80	40 to 50	Below 80	25 to 60
Color Films	50 or lower	25 to 40		

If relative humidity exceeds 60 percent for any length of time, dehumidification is required; if relative humidity is below 25 percent and brittleness is encountered, humidification is required.

CONCLUSION

The useful life of 16mm films can be lengthened materially by exercising care in handling and projection, by keeping the films in good repair, and by providing proper storage conditions.

APPENDIX C

Depth of Field Charts

The following depth of field tables are based on a circle of confusion of 1/1000 of an inch. This is the accepted circle of confusion for 16mm work. When focus is very critical, a smaller circle of confusion is used, and the depth of field is less.

To find the depth of field for a particular situation find the chart with the focal length of the lens you are using. Look for the column with the f/stop you have selected and then find the row corresponding as closely as possible to the distance you have focused on. The box where the row and the column meet has two numbers in it. The top number represents the near limit of your depth of field, and the bottom number the far limit. If you subtract the near limit from the far limit, you get the distance that the depth of field covers.

One row on the chart gives the hyperfocal distance for a given f/stop. The *hyperfocal distance* is the smallest possible number such that when the lens is focused at that number all the objects beyond it are in focus (that is, it is in focus to infinity). When you focus at the hyperfocal distance, everything from one-half the hyperfocal distance to infinity is in focus.

When the far limit of the depth of field is given as "INF." all objects to infinity are in focus.

The Kinoptic Tegea 5.7mm f/1.9 lens is an extreme wide-angle lens for 16mm work. Like many other extreme wide-angle lenses its focus is fixed since it has a great deal of depth of field even when used wide open. Below is a special chart for this lens. (*Courtesy Karl Heitz, Inc.*)

TEGEA   5.7mm f/1.9 (fixed focus)

f/stop	near limit	far limit
1.9	19″	INFINITY
2.8	16″	INFINITY
4	14″	INFINITY
5.6	12″	INFINITY
8	10″	INFINITY
11	9″	INFINITY
16	8″	INFINITY
22	7½″	INFINITY
32	7″	INFINITY

DEPTH OF FIELD CHARTS

LENS FOCAL LENGTH = 7 MM

Lens Aperture	F/1.4	F/2	F/2.8	F/4
Hyperfocal Dist.	4′ 6″	3′ 1″	2′ 3″	1′ 6″
Lens Focus (Feet)	Near Far	Near Far	Near Far	Near Far
8″	0′ 7″ 0′ 9″	0′ 6″ 0′10″	0′ 6″ 0′11″	0′ 5″ 1′ 1″
10″	0′ 8″ 1′ 0″	0′ 7″ 1′ 1″	0′ 7″ 1′ 3″	0′ 6″ 1′ 8″
1	0′ 9″ 1′ 3″	0′ 9″ 1′ 5″	0′ 8″ 1′ 9″	0′ 7″ 2′ 7″
1½	1′ 1″ 2′ 2″	1′ 0″ 2′ 9″	0′10″ 4′ 3″	0′ 9″ 22′ 6″
2	1′ 4″ 3′ 6″	1′ 2″ 5′ 3″	1′ 0″ 15′11″	0′10″ INF.
3	1′ 9″ 8′ 9″	1′ 6″ 50′ 7″	1′ 3″ INF.	1′ 0″ INF.
5	2′ 4″ INF.	1′11″ INF.	1′ 6″ INF.	1′ 2″ INF.
7	2′ 9″ INF.	2′ 2″ INF.	1′ 8″ INF.	1′ 3″ INF.
10	3′ 1″ INF.	2′ 4″ INF.	1′10″ INF.	1′ 4″ INF.
25	3′ 9″ INF.	2′ 9″ INF.	2′ 0″ INF.	1′ 5″ INF.

CIRCLE OF CONFUSION = .001" (1/000")

F/5.6	F/8	F/11	F/16	F/22
1′ 1″	0′ 9″	0′ 6″	0′ 4″	0′ 3″
Near Far	Near Far	Near Far	Near Far	Near Far
0′ 5″ 1′ 6″	0′ 4″ 3′ 6″	0′ 3″ INF.	0′ 3″ INF.	0′ 2″ INF.
0′ 5″ 2′11″	0′ 4″ INF.	0′ 4″ INF.	0′ 3″ INF.	0′ 2″ INF.
0′ 6″ 7′ 4″	0′ 5″ INF.	0′ 4″ INF.	0′ 3″ INF.	0′ 2″ INF.
0′ 7″ INF.	0′ 6″ INF.	0′ 5″ INF.	0′ 3″ INF.	0′ 2″ INF.
0′ 8″ INF.	0′ 6″ INF.	0′ 5″ INF.	0′ 4″ INF.	0′ 3″ INF.
0′ 9″ INF.	0′ 7″ INF.	0′ 5″ INF.	0′ 4″ INF.	0′ 3″ INF.
0′11″ INF.	0′ 8″ INF.	0′ 6″ INF.	0′ 4″ INF.	0′ 3″ INF.
0′11″ INF.	0′ 8″ INF.	0′ 6″ INF.	0′ 4″ INF.	0′ 3″ INF.
1′ 0″ INF.	0′ 8″ INF.	0′ 6″ INF.	0′ 4″ INF.	0′ 3″ INF.
1′ 0″ INF.	0′ 9″ INF.	0′ 6″ INF.	0′ 4″ INF.	0′ 3″ INF.

LENS FOCAL LENGTH = 8 MM

Lens Aperture	F/1.4	F/2	F/2.8	F/4
Hyperfocal Dist.	5'10"	4' 1"	2'11"	2' 0"
Lens Focus (Feet)	Near Far	Near Far	Near Far	Near Far
8"	0' 7" 0' 8"	0' 6" 0' 9"	0' 6" 0'10"	0' 6" 0'11"
10"	0' 8" 0'11"	0' 8" 1' 0"	0' 7" 1' 1"	0' 7" 1' 4"
1	0'10" 1' 2"	0' 9" 1' 3"	0' 9" 1' 5"	0' 8" 1'10"
1½	1' 2" 1'11"	1' 1" 2' 3"	1' 0" 2'11"	0'10" 5' 2"
2	1' 5" 3' 0"	1' 4" 3' 9"	1' 2" 6' 0"	1' 0" 44' 5"
3	1'11" 6' 0"	1' 8" 10' 8"	1' 5" INF.	1' 2" INF.
5	2' 8" 31' 8"	2' 3" INF.	1'10" INF.	1' 5" INF.
7	3' 2" INF.	2' 7" INF.	2' 0" INF.	1' 7" INF.
10	3' 8" INF.	2'11" INF.	2' 3" INF.	1' 8" INF.
25	4' 9" INF.	3' 6" INF.	2' 7" INF.	1'10" INF.

CIRCLE OF CONFUSION = .001″ (1/1000″)

F/5.6	F/8	F/11	F/16	F/22
1′ 5″	1′ 0″	0′ 9″	0′ 6″	0′ 4″
Near	Near	Near	Near	Near
Far	Far	Far	Far	Far
0′ 5″	0′ 4″	0′ 4″	0′ 3″	0′ 2″
1′ 2″	1′ 9″	4′ 6″	INF.	INF.
0′ 6″	0′ 5″	0′ 4″	0′ 3″	0′ 3″
1′10″	3′ 9″	INF.	INF.	INF.
0′ 7″	0′ 6″	0′ 5″	0′ 4″	0′ 3″
2′11″	17′ 4″	INF.	INF.	INF.
0′ 9″	0′ 7″	0′ 6″	0′ 4″	0′ 3″
910′ 2″	INF.	INF.	INF.	INF.
0′10″	0′ 8″	0′ 6″	0′ 4″	0′ 3″
INF.	INF.	INF.	INF.	INF.
0′11″	0′ 9″	0′ 7″	0′ 5″	0′ 4″
INF.	INF.	INF.	INF.	INF.
1′ 1″	0′10″	0′ 7″	0′ 5″	0′ 4″
INF.	INF.	INF.	INF.	INF.
1′ 2″	0′10″	0′ 8″	0′ 5″	0′ 4″
INF.	INF.	INF.	INF.	INF.
1′ 3″	0′11″	0′ 8″	0′ 5″	0′ 4″
INF.	INF.	INF.	INF.	INF.
1′ 4″	0′11″	0′ 8″	0′ 6″	0′ 4″
INF.	INF.	INF.	INF.	INF.

LENS FOCAL LENGTH = 9 MM

Lens Aperture	F/1.4	F/2	F/2.8	F/4
Hyperfocal Dist.	7′ 5″	5′ 2″	3′ 8″	2′ 7″
Lens Focus (Feet)	Near Far	Near Far	Near Far	Near Far
8″	0′ 7″ 0′ 8″	0′ 7″ 0′ 9″	0′ 6″ 0′ 9″	0′ 6″ 0′10″
10″	0′ 9″ 0′11″	0′ 8″ 0′11″	0′ 8″ 1′ 0″	0′ 7″ 1′ 2″
1	0′10″ 1′ 1″	0′10″ 1′ 2″	0′ 9″ 1′ 4″	0′ 8″ 1′ 7″
1½	1′ 3″ 1′10″	1′ 2″ 2′ 1″	1′ 0″ 2′ 5″	0′11″ 3′ 5″
2	1′ 6″ 2′ 8″	1′ 5″ 3′ 2″	1′ 3″ 4′ 2″	1′ 1″ 8′ 1″
3	2′ 1″ 4′11″	1′10″ 6′11″	1′ 8″ 14′ 7″	1′ 4″ INF.
5	3′ 0″ 14′11″	2′ 6″ 100′ 3″	2′ 1″ INF.	1′ 8″ INF.
7	3′ 7″ 104′ 0″	3′ 0″ INF.	2′ 5″ INF.	1′10″ INF.
10	4′ 3″ INF.	3′ 5″ INF.	2′ 8″ INF.	2′ 0″ INF.
25	5′ 9″ INF.	4′ 3″ INF.	3′ 3″ INF.	2′ 4″ INF.

CIRCLE OF CONFUSION = .001″ (1/1000″)

F/5.6	F/8	F/11	F/16	F/22
1′10″	1′ 3″	0′11″	0′ 7″	0′ 5″
Near Far	Near Far	Near Far	Near Far	Near Far
0′ 5″ 1′ 0″	0′ 5″ 1′ 3″	0′ 4″ 2′ 0″	0′ 4″ 26′ 0″	0′ 3″ INF.
0′ 6″ 1′ 5″	0′ 6″ 2′ 1″	0′ 5″ 5′ 4″	0′ 4″ INF.	0′ 3″ INF.
0′ 7″ 2′ 0″	0′ 6″ 3′10″	0′ 5″ INF.	0′ 4″ INF.	0′ 3″ INF.
0′10″ 7′10″	0′ 8″ INF.	0′ 7″ INF.	0′ 5″ INF.	0′ 4″ INF.
0′11″ INF.	0′ 9″ INF.	0′ 7″ INF.	0′ 5″ INF.	0′ 4″ INF.
1′ 1″ INF.	0′11″ INF.	0′ 8″ INF.	0′ 6″ INF.	0′ 4″ INF.
1′ 4″ INF.	1′ 0″ INF.	0′ 9″ INF.	0′ 6″ INF.	0′ 5″ INF.
1′ 5″ INF.	1′ 1″ INF.	0′10″ INF.	0′ 7″ INF.	0′ 5″ INF.
1′ 6″ INF.	1′ 1″ INF.	0′10″ INF.	0′ 7″ INF.	0′ 5″ INF.
1′ 8″ INF.	1′ 2″ INF.	0′11″ INF.	0′ 7″ INF.	0′ 5″ INF.

LENS FOCAL LENGTH = 9.5 MM

Lens Aperture	F/1.4	F/2	F/2.8	F/4
Hyperfocal Dist.	8' 3"	5' 9"	4' 1"	2'10"
Lens Focus (Feet)	Near Far	Near Far	Near Far	Near Far
2	1' 7" 2' 7"	1' 5" 3' 0"	1' 4" 3' 9"	1' 2" 6' 1"
3	2' 2" 4' 7"	1'11" 6' 1"	1' 9" 10' 5"	1' 5" INF.
4	2' 8" 7' 7"	2' 4" 12' 6"	2' 0" 85' 7"	1' 8" INF.
5	3' 1" 12' 4"	2' 8" 33'10"	2' 3" INF.	1'10" INF.
6	3' 5" 21' 2"	2'11" INF.	2' 5" INF.	1'11" INF.
8	4' 1" 186' 2"	3' 4" INF.	2' 8" INF.	2' 1" INF.
10	4' 6" INF.	3' 8" INF.	2'11" INF.	2' 3" INF.
15	5' 4" INF.	4' 2" INF.	3' 3" INF.	2' 5" INF.
25	6' 3" INF.	4' 8" INF.	3' 6" INF.	2' 7" INF.
50	7' 1" INF.	5' 2" INF.	3'10" INF.	2' 9" INF.

CIRCLE OF CONFUSION = .001" (1/1000")

F/5.6	F/8	F/11	F/16	F/22
2′ 0″	1′ 5″	1′ 0″	0′ 8″	0′ 6″
Near Far	Near Far	Near Far	Near Far	Near Far
1′ 0″ 36′10″	0′10″ INF.	0′ 8″ INF.	0′ 6″ INF.	0′ 5″ INF.
1′ 2″ INF.	0′11″ INF.	0′ 9″ INF.	0′ 7″ INF.	0′ 5″ INF.
1′ 4″ INF.	1′ 0″ INF.	0′10″ INF.	0′ 7″ INF.	0′ 5″ INF.
1′ 5″ INF.	1′ 1″ INF.	0′10″ INF.	0′ 7″ INF.	0′ 5″ INF.
1′ 6″ INF.	1′ 2″ INF.	0′10″ INF.	0′ 7″ INF.	0′ 5″ INF.
1′ 7″ INF.	1′ 2″ INF.	0′11″ INF.	0′ 8″ INF.	0′ 5″ INF.
1′ 8″ INF.	1′ 3″ INF.	0′11″ INF.	0′ 8″ INF.	0′ 6″ INF.
1′ 9″ INF.	1′ 3″ INF.	0′11″ INF.	0′ 8″ INF.	0′ 6″ INF.
1′11″ INF.	1′ 4″ INF.	1′ 0″ INF.	0′ 8″ INF.	0′ 6″ INF.
1′11″ INF.	1′ 5″ INF.	1′ 0″ INF.	0′ 8″ INF.	0′ 6″ INF.

LENS FOCAL LENGTH = 10 MM

Lens Aperture	F/1.4	F/2	F/2.8	F/4
Hyperfocal Dist.	9' 2"	6' 5"	4' 7"	3' 2"
Lens Focus (Feet)	Near Far	Near Far	Near Far	Near Far
8"	0' 7" 0' 8"	0' 7" 0' 8"	0' 7" 0' 9"	0' 6" 0' 9"
10"	0' 9" 0'10"	0' 8" 0'11"	0' 8" 1' 0"	0' 8" 1' 1"
1	0'10" 1' 1"	0'10" 1' 2"	0' 9" 1' 3"	0' 9" 1' 5"
1½	1' 3" 1' 9"	1' 2" 1'11"	1' 1" 2' 2"	1' 0" 2' 8"
2	1' 7" 2' 6"	1' 6" 2'10"	1' 4" 3' 5"	1' 2" 5' 1"
3	2' 3" 4' 5"	2' 0" 5' 6"	1' 9" 8' 4"	1' 6" 36'11"
5	3' 3" 10' 9"	2' 9" 21' 7"	2' 4" INF.	1'11" INF.
7	3'11" 28' 7"	3' 4" INF.	2' 9" INF.	2' 2" INF.
10	4' 9" INF.	3'11" INF.	3' 1" INF.	2' 5" INF.
25	6' 8" INF.	5' 1" INF.	3'10" INF.	2'10" INF.

CIRCLE OF CONFUSION = .001" (1/1000")

F/5.6	F/8	F/11	F/16	F/22
2' 3"	1' 7"	1' 2"	0' 9"	0' 7"
Near Far	Near Far	Near Far	Near Far	Near Far
0' 6" 0'11"	0' 5" 1' 1"	0' 5" 1' 5"	0' 4" 3' 1"	0' 3" INF.
0' 7" 1' 3"	0' 6" 1' 7"	0' 5" 2' 7"	0' 5" 99' 5"	0' 4" INF.
0' 8" 1' 8"	0' 7" 2' 5"	0' 6" 5' 8"	0' 5" INF.	0' 4" INF.
0'11" 4' 1"	0' 9" 16' 5"	0' 8" INF.	0' 6" INF.	0' 5" INF.
1' 0" 13' 7"	0'10" INF.	0' 8" INF.	0' 6" INF.	0' 5" INF.
1' 3" INF.	1' 0" INF.	0'10" INF.	0' 7" INF.	0' 5" INF.
1' 7" INF.	1' 2" INF.	0'11" INF.	0' 8" INF.	0' 6" INF.
1' 8" INF.	1' 3" INF.	1' 0" INF.	0' 8" INF.	0' 6" INF.
1'10" INF.	1' 4" INF.	1' 0" INF.	0' 8" INF.	0' 6" INF.
2' 1" INF.	1' 6" INF.	1' 1" INF.	0' 9" INF.	0' 6" INF.

LENS FOCAL LENGTH = 12 MM

Lens Aperture	F/1.4	F/2	F/2.8	F/4
Hyperfocal Dist.	13′ 3″	9′ 3″	6′ 7″	4′ 7″
Lens Focus (Feet)	Near Far	Near Far	Near Far	Near Far
2	1′ 8″ 2′ 4″	1′ 7″ 2′ 6″	1′ 6″ 2′10″	1′ 4″ 3′ 5″
3	2′ 5″ 3′10″	2′ 3″ 4′ 4″	2′ 0″ 5′ 4″	1′ 9″ 8′ 3″
4	3′ 0″ 5′ 8″	2′ 9″ 6′11″	2′ 6″ 9′10″	2′ 1″ 26′11″
5	3′ 7″ 7′11″	3′ 3″ 10′ 8″	2′10″ 19′ 8″	2′ 5″ INF.
6	4′ 1″ 10′10″	3′ 7″ 16′ 8″	3′ 1″ 58′ 5″	2′ 7″ INF.
8	5′ 0″ 19′11″	4′ 3″ 55′ 6″	3′ 7″ INF.	2′11″ INF.
10	5′ 8″ 39′11″	4′ 9″ INF.	4′ 0″ INF.	3′ 2″ INF.
15	7′ 0″ INF.	5′ 9″ INF.	4′ 7″ INF.	3′ 6″ INF.
25	8′ 8″ INF.	6′ 9″ INF.	5′ 3″ INF.	3′11″ INF.
50	10′ 6″ INF.	7′10″ INF.	5′10″ INF.	4′ 3″ INF.

CIRCLE OF CONFUSION = .001″ (1/000″)

F/5.6	F/8	F/11	F/16	F/22
3′ 3″	2′ 3″	1′ 8″	1′ 1″	0′10″
Near Far	Near Far	Near Far	Near Far	Near Far
1′ 3″ 4′10″	1′ 1″ 12′ 9″	0′11″ INF.	0′ 8″ INF.	0′ 7″ INF.
1′ 7″ 27′ 7″	1′ 3″ INF.	1′ 1″ INF.	0′10″ INF.	0′ 7″ INF.
1′ 9″ INF.	1′ 5″ INF.	1′ 2″ INF.	0′10″ INF.	0′ 8″ INF.
2′ 0″ INF.	1′ 7″ INF.	1′ 3″ INF.	0′11″ INF.	0′ 8″ INF.
2′ 1″ INF.	1′ 8″ INF.	1′ 3″ INF.	0′11″ INF.	0′ 8″ INF.
2′ 4″ INF.	1′ 9″ INF.	1′ 4″ INF.	1′ 0″ INF.	0′ 9″ INF.
2′ 6″ INF.	1′10″ INF.	1′ 5″ INF.	1′ 0″ INF.	0′ 9″ INF.
2′ 8″ INF.	2′ 0″ INF.	1′ 6″ INF.	1′ 0″ INF.	0′ 9″ INF.
2′11″ INF.	2′ 1″ INF.	1′ 7″ INF.	1′ 1″ INF.	0′ 9″ INF.
3′ 1″ INF.	2′ 2″ INF.	1′ 7″ INF.	1′ 1″ INF.	0′ 9″ INF.

LENS FOCAL LENGTH = 12.5 MM

Lens Aperture	F/1.4	F/2	F/2.8	F/4
Hyperfocal Dist.	14′ 4″	10′ 1″	7′ 2″	5′ 0″
Lens Focus (Feet)	Near Far	Near Far	Near Far	Near Far
2	1′ 9″ 2′ 3″	1′ 8″ 2′ 5″	1′ 6″ 2′ 8″	1′ 5″ 3′ 3″
3	2′ 5″ 3′ 9″	2′ 3″ 4′ 2″	2′ 1″ 5′ 1″	1′10″ 7′ 3″
4	3′ 1″ 5′ 6″	2′10″ 6′ 6″	2′ 6″ 8′10″	2′ 2″ 18′ 6″
5	3′ 8″ 7′ 7″	3′ 4″ 9′ 9″	2′11″ 16′ 0″	2′ 6″ 291′ 4″
6	4′ 2″ 10′ 2″	3′ 9″ 14′ 7″	3′ 3″ 34′ 7″	2′ 9″ INF.
8	5′ 1″ 17′10″	4′ 5″ 37′10″	3′ 9″ INF.	3′ 1″ INF.
10	5′10″ 32′ 4″	5′ 0″ 763′ 8″	4′ 2″ INF.	3′ 4″ INF.
15	7′ 4″ INF.	6′ 0″ INF.	4′10″ INF.	3′ 9″ INF.
25	9′ 1″ INF.	7′ 2″ INF.	5′ 7″ INF.	4′ 2″ INF.
50	11′ 2″ INF.	8′ 4″ INF.	6′ 3″ INF.	4′ 7″ INF.

CIRCLE OF CONFUSION = .001" (1/1000")

F/5.6	F/8	F/11	F/16	F/22
3′ 7″	2′ 6″	1′10″	1′ 3″	0′11″
Near Far	Near Far	Near Far	Near Far	Near Far
1′ 3″ 4′ 4″	1′ 1″ 8′11″	0′11″ INF.	0′ 9″ INF.	0′ 7″ INF.
1′ 7″ 16′ 9″	1′ 4″ INF.	1′ 1″ INF.	0′10″ INF.	0′ 8″ INF.
1′10″ INF.	1′ 6″ INF.	1′ 3″ INF.	0′11″ INF.	0′ 9″ INF.
2′ 1″ INF.	1′ 8″ INF.	1′ 4″ INF.	1′ 0″ INF.	0′ 9″ INF.
2′ 3″ INF.	1′ 9″ INF.	1′ 4″ INF.	1′ 0″ INF.	0′ 9″ INF.
2′ 5″ INF.	1′11″ INF.	1′ 5″ INF.	1′ 1″ INF.	0′ 9″ INF.
2′ 7″ INF.	2′ 0″ INF.	1′ 6″ INF.	1′ 1″ INF.	0′10″ INF.
2′10″ INF.	2′ 1″ INF.	1′ 7″ INF.	1′ 1″ INF.	0′10″ INF.
3′ 1″ INF.	2′ 3″ INF.	1′ 8″ INF.	1′ 2″ INF.	0′10″ INF.
3′ 4″ INF.	2′ 4″ INF.	1′ 9″ INF.	1′ 2″ INF.	0′10″ INF.

LENS FOCAL LENGTH = 16 MM

Lens Aperture	F/1.4	F/2	F/2.8	F/4
Hyperfocal Dist.	23′ 7″	16′ 6″	11′ 9″	8′ 3″
Lens Focus (Feet)	Near Far	Near Far	Near Far	Near Far
2	1′10″ 2′ 2″	1′ 9″ 2′ 3″	1′ 8″ 2′ 4″	1′ 7″ 2′ 7″
3	2′ 8″ 3′ 5″	2′ 6″ 3′ 7″	2′ 4″ 3′11″	2′ 2″ 4′ 7″
4	3′ 5″ 4′ 9″	3′ 2″ 5′ 3″	2′11″ 6′ 0″	2′ 8″ 7′ 7″
5	4′ 1″ 6′ 3″	3′10″ 7′ 1″	3′ 6″ 8′ 7″	3′ 1″ 12′ 5″
6	4′ 9″ 8′ 0″	4′ 4″ 9′ 4″	3′11″ 12′ 1″	3′ 5″ 21′ 4″
8	5′11″ 12′ 0″	5′ 4″ 15′ 4″	4′ 9″ 24′ 5″	4′ 0″ 207′ 2″
10	7′ 0″ 17′ 3″	6′ 2″ 25′ 1″	5′ 5″ 63′ 5″	4′ 6″ INF.
15	9′ 2″ 40′10″	7′10″ 156′ 4″	6′ 7″ INF.	5′ 4″ INF.
25	12′ 1″ INF.	9′11″ INF.	8′ 0″ INF.	6′ 2″ INF.
50	16′ 0″ INF.	12′ 5″ INF.	9′ 6″ INF.	7′ 1″ INF.

CIRCLE OF CONFUSION = .001″ (1/1000″)

F/5.6	F/8	F/11	F/16	F/22
5′10″	4′ 1″	3′ 0″	2′ 0″	1′ 6″
Near Far	Near Far	Near Far	Near Far	Near Far
1′ 6″ 2′11″	1′ 4″ 3′ 9″	1′ 2″ 5′ 8″	1′ 0″ 34′ 8″	0′10″ INF.
2′ 0″ 5′11″	1′ 9″ 10′ 5″	1′ 6″ 154′ 0″	1′ 2″ INF.	1′ 0″ INF.
2′ 4″ 12′ 0″	2′ 0″ 88′11″	1′ 8″ INF.	1′ 4″ INF.	1′ 1″ INF.
2′ 8″ 30′10″	2′ 3″ INF.	1′10″ INF.	1′ 5″ INF.	1′ 1″ INF.
2′11″ INF.	2′ 5″ INF.	2′ 0″ INF.	1′ 6″ INF.	1′ 2″ INF.
3′ 4″ INF.	2′ 8″ INF.	2′ 2″ INF.	1′ 7″ INF.	1′ 3″ INF.
3′ 8″ INF.	2′11″ INF.	2′ 3″ INF.	1′ 8″ INF.	1′ 3″ INF.
4′ 2″ INF.	3′ 2″ INF.	2′ 6″ INF.	1′ 9″ INF.	1′ 4″ INF.
4′ 9″ INF.	3′ 6″ INF.	2′ 8″ INF.	1′10″ INF.	1′ 5″ INF.
5′ 3″ INF.	3′ 9″ INF.	2′10″ INF.	1′11″ INF.	1′ 5″ INF.

LENS FOCAL LENGTH = 17 MM

Lens Aperture	F/1.4	F/2	F/2.8	F/4
Hyperfocal Dist.	26′ 7″	18′ 7″	13′ 3″	9′ 3″
Lens Focus (Feet)	Near Far	Near Far	Near Far	Near Far
2	1′10″ 2′ 1″	1′ 9″ 2′ 2″	1′ 8″ 2′ 4″	1′ 7″ 2′ 6″
3	2′ 8″ 3′ 4″	2′ 7″ 3′ 6″	2′ 5″ 3′10″	2′ 3″ 4′ 4″
4	3′ 5″ 4′ 8″	3′ 3″ 5′ 0″	3′ 1″ 5′ 8″	2′ 9″ 6′11″
5	4′ 2″ 6′ 1″	3′11″ 6′ 9″	3′ 7″ 7′11″	3′ 3″ 10′ 7″
6	4′10″ 7′ 8″	4′ 6″ 8′ 9″	4′ 1″ 10′ 9″	3′ 7″ 16′ 6″
8	6′ 1″ 11′ 4″	5′ 7″ 13′11″	5′ 0″ 19′ 9″	4′ 3″ 53′ 9″
10	7′ 3″ 15′11″	6′ 6″ 21′ 4″	5′ 8″ 39′ 4″	4′10″ INF.
15	9′ 7″ 34′ 1″	8′ 3″ 75′ 3″	7′ 0″ INF.	5′ 9″ INF.
25	12′10″ 387′ 8″	10′ 8″ INF.	8′ 8″ INF.	6′ 9″ INF.
50	17′ 4″ INF.	13′ 7″ INF.	10′ 6″ INF.	7′10″ INF.

CIRCLE OF CONFUSION = .001″ (1/1000″)

F/5.6	F/8	F/11	F/16	F/22
6′ 7″	4′ 7″	3′ 4″	2′ 3″	1′ 8″
Near Far	Near Far	Near Far	Near Far	Near Far
1′ 6″ 2′ 9″	1′ 4″ 3′ 5″	1′ 3″ 4′ 8″	1′ 1″ 12′ 0″	0′11″ INF.
2′ 0″ 5′ 4″	1′10″ 8′ 1″	1′ 7″ 22′ 7″	1′ 3″ INF.	1′ 1″ INF.
2′ 6″ 9′ 9″	2′ 2″ 25′10″	1′10″ INF.	1′ 5″ INF.	1′ 2″ INF.
2′10″ 19′ 4″	2′ 5″ INF.	2′ 0″ INF.	1′ 7″ INF.	1′ 3″ INF.
3′ 2″ 55′ 5″	2′ 7″ INF.	2′ 2″ INF.	1′ 8″ INF.	1′ 3″ INF.
3′ 7″ INF.	2′11″ INF.	2′ 4″ INF.	1′ 9″ INF.	1′ 4″ INF.
4′ 0″ INF.	3′ 2″ INF.	2′ 6″ INF.	1′10″ INF.	1′ 5″ INF.
4′ 7″ INF.	3′ 6″ INF.	2′ 9″ INF.	2′ 0″ INF.	1′ 6″ INF.
5′ 3″ INF.	3′11″ INF.	2′11″ INF.	2′ 1″ INF.	1′ 7″ INF.
5′10″ INF.	4′ 3″ INF.	3′ 2″ INF.	2′ 2″ INF.	1′ 7″ INF.

LENS FOCAL LENGTH = 17.5 MM

Lens Aperture	F/1.4	F/2	F/2.8	F/4
Hyperfocal Dist.	28′ 3″	19′ 9″	14′ 1″	9′10″
Lens Focus (Feet)	Near Far	Near Far	Near Far	Near Far
2	1′10″ 2′ 1″	1′ 9″ 2′ 2″	1′ 9″ 2′ 3″	1′ 8″ 2′ 5″
3	2′ 8″ 3′ 4″	2′ 7″ 3′ 6″	2′ 5″ 3′ 9″	2′ 3″ 4′ 3″
4	3′ 6″ 4′ 7″	3′ 4″ 4′11″	3′ 1″ 5′ 6″	2′10″ 6′ 7″
5	4′ 3″ 6′ 0″	4′ 0″ 6′ 7″	3′ 8″ 7′ 8″	3′ 4″ 9′11″
6	4′11″ 7′ 7″	4′ 7″ 8′ 6″	4′ 2″ 10′ 4″	3′ 8″ 15′ 0″
8	6′ 2″ 11′ 1″	5′ 8″ 13′ 4″	5′ 1″ 18′ 3″	4′ 5″ 40′ 7″
10	7′ 4″ 15′ 5″	6′ 7″ 20′ 1″	5′10″ 33′ 9″	4′11″ INF.
15	9′ 9″ 31′10″	8′ 6″ 61′ 4″	7′ 3″ INF.	5′11″ INF.
25	13′ 3″ 213′ 2″	11′ 0″ INF.	9′ 0″ INF.	7′ 1″ INF.
50	18′ 0″ INF.	14′ 2″ INF.	11′ 0″ INF.	8′ 3″ INF.

CIRCLE OF CONFUSION = .001″ (1/1000″)

F/5.6	F/8	F/11	F/16	F/22
7′ 0″	4′11″	3′ 7″	2′ 5″	1′ 9″
Near Far	Near Far	Near Far	Near Far	Near Far
1′ 6″ 2′ 9″	1′ 5″ 3′ 3″	1′ 3″ 4′ 4″	1′ 1″ 9′ 4″	0′11″ INF.
2′ 1″ 5′ 1″	1′10″ 7′ 4″	1′ 7″ 16′ 6″	1′ 4″ INF.	1′ 1″ INF.
2′ 6″ 9′ 0″	2′ 2″ 19′ 8″	1′10″ INF.	1′ 6″ INF.	1′ 3″ INF.
2′11″ 16′ 7″	2′ 6″ INF.	2′ 1″ INF.	1′ 8″ INF.	1′ 4″ INF.
3′ 3″ 37′ 9″	2′ 8″ INF.	2′ 3″ INF.	1′ 9″ INF.	1′ 4″ INF.
3′ 9″ INF.	3′ 0″ INF.	2′ 5″ INF.	1′10″ INF.	1′ 5″ INF.
4′ 1″ INF.	3′ 3″ INF.	2′ 7″ INF.	1′11″ INF.	1′ 6″ INF.
4′ 9″ INF.	3′ 8″ INF.	2′10″ INF.	2′ 1″ INF.	1′ 7″ INF.
5′ 6″ INF.	4′ 1″ INF.	3′ 1″ INF.	2′ 3″ INF.	1′ 8″ INF.
6′ 2″ INF.	4′ 6″ INF.	3′ 4″ INF.	2′ 4″ INF.	1′ 8″ INF.

LENS FOCAL LENGTH = 18 MM

Lens Aperture	F/1.4	F/2	F/2.8	F/4
Hyperfocal Dist.	29'10"	20'11"	14'11"	10' 5"
Lens Focus (Feet)	Near Far	Near Far	Near Far	Near Far
2	1'10" 2' 1"	1' 9" 2' 2"	1' 9" 2' 3"	1' 8" 2' 5"
3	2' 8" 3' 3"	2' 7" 3' 5"	2' 6" 3' 8"	2' 4" 4' 2"
4	3' 6" 4' 7"	3' 4" 4'11"	3' 1" 5' 5"	2'10" 6' 5"
5	4' 3" 5'11"	4' 0" 6' 6"	3' 9" 7' 5"	3' 4" 9' 5"
6	5' 0" 7' 5"	4' 8" 8' 4"	4' 3" 9'11"	3' 9" 13'10"
8	6' 3" 10'10"	5' 9" 12'10"	5' 2" 17' 0"	4' 6" 33' 2"
10	7' 6" 14'11"	6' 9" 19' 0"	6' 0" 29'10"	5' 1" 200' 7"
15	10' 0" 29'11"	8' 9" 52' 5"	7' 6" INF.	6' 2" INF.
25	13' 7" 150'11"	11' 4" INF.	9' 4" INF.	7' 4" INF.
50	18' 8" INF.	14' 9" INF.	11' 6" INF.	8' 7" INF.

CIRCLE OF CONFUSION = .001" (1/1000")

F/5.6	F/8	F/11	F/16	F/22
7′ 5″	5′ 2″	3′ 9″	2′ 7″	1′10″
Near Far	Near Far	Near Far	Near Far	Near Far
1′ 7″ 2′ 8″	1′ 5″ 3′ 2″	1′ 3″ 4′ 0″	1′ 1″ 7′ 9″	0′11″ INF.
2′ 1″ 4′11″	1′11″ 6′10″	1′ 8″ 13′ 2″	1′ 4″ INF.	1′ 2″ INF.
2′ 7″ 8′ 5″	2′ 3″ 16′ 2″	1′11″ INF.	1′ 7″ INF.	1′ 3″ INF.
3′ 0″ 14′ 9″	2′ 6″ 90′ 1″	2′ 2″ INF.	1′ 8″ INF.	1′ 4″ INF.
3′ 4″ 29′ 3″	2′ 9″ INF.	2′ 4″ INF.	1′10″ INF.	1′ 5″ INF.
3′10″ INF.	3′ 2″ INF.	2′ 7″ INF.	1′11″ INF.	1′ 6″ INF.
4′ 3″ INF.	3′ 5″ INF.	2′ 9″ INF.	2′ 0″ INF.	1′ 7″ INF.
5′ 0″ INF.	3′10″ INF.	3′ 0″ INF.	2′ 2″ INF.	1′ 8″ INF.
5′ 9″ INF.	4′ 4″ INF.	3′ 3″ INF.	2′ 4″ INF.	1′ 9″ INF.
6′ 6″ INF.	4′ 8″ INF.	3′ 6″ INF.	2′ 5″ INF.	1′10″ INF.

LENS FOCAL LENGTH = 20 MM

Lens Aperture	F/1.4	F/2	F/2.8	F/4
Hyperfocal Dist.	36'10"	25' 9"	18' 5"	12'10"
Lens Focus (Feet)	Near Far	Near Far	Near Far	Near Far
2	1'10" 2' 1"	1'10" 2' 1"	1' 9" 2' 2"	1' 8" 2' 4"
3	2' 9" 3' 3"	2' 8" 3' 4"	2' 7" 3' 6"	2' 5" 3'10"
4	3' 7" 4' 5"	3' 5" 4' 8"	3' 3" 5' 1"	3' 0" 5' 9"
5	4' 4" 5' 9"	4' 2" 6' 2"	3'11" 6' 9"	3' 7" 8' 1"
6	5' 2" 7' 1"	4'10" 7' 9"	4' 6" 8'10"	4' 1" 11' 1"
8	6' 7" 10' 2"	6' 1" 11' 6"	5' 7" 14' 0"	4'11" 20' 8"
10	7'10" 13' 8"	7' 2" 16' 2"	6' 6" 21' 7"	5' 7" 43' 3"
15	10' 8" 25' 2"	9' 6" 35' 6"	8' 3" 78' 8"	6'11" INF.
25	14'11" 77' 0"	12' 8" 718' 5"	10' 7" INF.	8' 6" INF.
50	21' 2" INF.	17' 0" INF.	13' 5" INF.	10' 3" INF.

CIRCLE OF CONFUSION = .001″ (1/1000″)

F/5.6	F/8	F/11	F/16	F/22
9′ 2″	6′ 5″	4′ 8″	3′ 2″	2′ 4″
Near	Near	Near	Near	Near
Far	Far	Far	Far	Far
1′ 7″	1′ 6″	1′ 4″	1′ 3″	1′ 1″
2′ 6″	2′10″	3′ 4″	4′11″	11′ 4″
2′ 3″	2′ 0″	1′10″	1′ 6″	1′ 4″
4′ 4″	5′ 5″	7′11″	32′10″	INF.
2′ 9″	2′ 5″	2′ 2″	1′ 9″	1′ 5″
6′11″	10′ 2″	24′ 7″	INF.	INF.
3′ 3″	2′10″	2′ 5″	1′11″	1′ 7″
10′ 8″	21′ 2″	INF.	INF.	INF.
3′ 7″	3′ 1″	2′ 7″	2′ 1″	1′ 8″
16′ 9″	73′11″	INF.	INF.	INF.
4′ 3″	3′ 7″	2′11″	2′ 3″	1′ 9″
57′ 1″	INF.	INF.	INF.	INF.
4′ 9″	3′11″	3′ 2″	2′ 5″	1′10″
INF.	INF.	INF.	INF.	INF.
5′ 8″	4′ 6″	3′ 7″	2′ 8″	2′ 0″
INF.	INF.	INF.	INF.	INF.
6′ 9″	5′ 1″	3′11″	2′10″	2′ 1″
INF.	INF.	INF.	INF.	INF.
7′ 9″	5′ 8″	4′ 3″	3′ 0″	2′ 2″
INF.	INF.	INF.	INF.	INF.

LENS FOCAL LENGTH = 25 MM

Lens Aperture	F/1.4	F/2	F/2.8	F/4
Hyperfocal Dist.	57' 7"	40' 4"	28' 9"	20' 2"
Lens Focus (Feet)	Near Far	Near Far	Near Far	Near Far
2	1'11" 2' 0"	1'10" 2' 1"	1'10" 2' 1"	1' 9" 2' 2"
3	2'10" 3' 1"	2' 9" 3' 2"	2' 8" 3' 4"	2' 7" 3' 6"
4	3' 8" 4' 3"	3' 7" 4' 5"	3' 6" 4' 7"	3' 4" 4'11"
5	4' 7" 5' 5"	4' 5" 5' 8"	4' 3" 6' 0"	4' 0" 6' 7"
6	5' 5" 6' 8"	5' 2" 7' 0"	4'11" 7' 6"	4' 7" 8' 5"
8	7' 0" 9' 3"	6' 8" 9'11"	6' 3" 11' 0"	5' 8" 13' 1"
10	8' 6" 12' 0"	8' 0" 13' 3"	7' 5" 15' 2"	6' 8" 19' 7"
15	11'11" 20' 2"	10'11" 23' 9"	9'10" 31' 0"	8' 7" 57' 6"
25	17' 5" 44' 0"	15' 5" 65' 3"	13' 4" 184' 2"	11' 2" INF.
50	26' 9" 372' 2"	22' 4" INF.	18' 3" INF.	14' 4" INF.

CIRCLE OF CONFUSION = .001" (1/1000")

F/5.6	F/8	F/11	F/16	F/22
14' 4"	10' 1"	7' 4"	5' 0"	3' 8"
Near	Near	Near	Near	Near
Far	Far	Far	Far	Far
1' 9"	1' 8"	1' 7"	1' 5"	1' 3"
2' 3"	2' 5"	2' 8"	3' 2"	4' 2"
2' 5"	2' 3"	2' 1"	1'10"	1' 8"
3' 9"	4' 2"	4'11"	7' 1"	14' 7"
3' 1"	2'10"	2' 7"	2' 3"	1'11"
5' 5"	6' 6"	8' 6"	17'10"	INF.
3' 8"	3' 4"	2'11"	2' 6"	2' 1"
7' 7"	9' 9"	15' 1"	197' 8"	INF.
4' 3"	3' 9"	3' 3"	2' 9"	2' 3"
10' 2"	14' 6"	30'11"	INF.	INF.
5' 1"	4' 5"	3'10"	3' 1"	2' 6"
17' 8"	37' 1"	INF.	INF.	INF.
5'11"	5' 0"	4' 3"	3' 4"	2' 8"
32' 0"	582' 9"	INF.	INF.	INF.
7' 4"	6' 0"	4'11"	3' 9"	2'11"
INF.	INF.	INF.	INF.	INF.
9' 1"	7' 2"	5' 8"	4' 2"	3' 2"
INF.	INF.	INF.	INF.	INF.
11' 2"	8' 4"	6' 4"	4' 7"	3' 5"
INF.	INF.	INF.	INF.	INF.

LENS FOCAL LENGTH = 35 MM

Lens Aperture	F/1.4	F/2	F/2.8	F/4
Hyperfocal Dist.	113' 0"	79' 1"	56' 6"	39' 6"
Lens Focus (Feet)	Near Far	Near Far	Near Far	Near Far
2	1'11" 2' 0"	1'11" 2' 0"	1'11" 2' 0"	1'10" 2' 1"
3	2'11" 3' 0"	2'10" 3' 1"	2'10" 3' 1"	2' 9" 3' 2"
4	3'10" 4' 1"	3' 9" 4' 2"	3' 8" 4' 3"	3' 7" 4' 5"
5	4' 9" 5' 2"	4' 8" 5' 3"	4' 7" 5' 5"	4' 5" 5' 8"
6	5' 8" 6' 3"	5' 7" 6' 5"	5' 5" 6' 8"	5' 2" 7' 0"
8	7' 5" 8' 7"	7' 3" 8'10"	7' 0" 9' 3"	6' 8" 9'11"
10	9' 2" 10'11"	8'10" 11' 5"	8' 6" 12' 1"	8' 0" 13' 3"
15	13' 3" 17' 3"	12' 7" 18' 5"	11'10" 20' 4"	10'10" 24' 0"
25	20' 5" 32' 0"	19' 0" 36' 5"	17' 4" 44' 8"	15' 4" 67' 4"
50	34' 8" 89' 6"	30' 7" 135' 4"	26' 6" 426' 5"	22'1" INF.

CIRCLE OF CONFUSION = .001″ (1/1000″)

F/5.6	F/8	F/11	F/16	F/22
28′ 3″	19′ 9″	14′ 4″	9′10″	7′ 2″
Near Far	Near Far	Near Far	Near Far	Near Far
1′10″ 2′ 1″	1′ 9″ 2′ 2″	1′ 9″ 2′ 3″	1′ 8″ 2′ 5″	1′ 7″ 2′ 8″
2′ 8″ 3′ 4″	2′ 7″ 3′ 6″	2′ 5″ 3′ 9″	2′ 3″ 4′ 2″	2′ 1″ 5′ 0″
3′ 6″ 4′ 7″	3′ 4″ 4′11″	3′ 1″ 5′ 5″	2′10″ 6′ 7″	2′ 7″ 8′ 8″
4′ 3″ 6′ 0″	4′ 0″ 6′ 7″	3′ 8″ 7′ 6″	3′ 4″ 9′10″	2′11″ 15′ 7″
4′11″ 7′ 6″	4′ 7″ 8′ 6″	4′ 3″ 10′ 1″	3′ 9″ 14′ 9″	3′ 3″ 33′ 0″
6′ 3″ 11′ 1″	5′ 8″ 13′ 3″	5′ 2″ 17′ 8″	4′ 5″ 39′ 5″	3′ 9″ INF.
7′ 4″ 15′ 4″	6′ 8″ 19′11″	5′11″ 31′11″	5′ 0″ INF.	4′ 2″ INF.
9′ 9″ 31′ 8″	8′ 6″ 60′ 7″	7′ 4″ INF.	5′11″ INF.	4′10″ INF.
13′ 3″ 209′ 7″	11′ 0″ INF.	9′ 1″ INF.	7′ 1″ INF.	5′ 7″ INF.
18′ 0″ INF.	14′ 2″ INF.	11′ 2″ INF.	8′ 3″ INF.	6′ 3″ INF.

LENS FOCAL LENGTH = 40 MM

Lens Aperture	F/1.4	F/2	F/2.8	F/4
Hyperfocal Dist.	147' 7"	103' 3"	73' 9"	51' 7"
Lens Focus (Feet)	Near Far	Near Far	Near Far	Near Far
2	1'11" 2' 0"	1'11" 2' 0"	1'11" 2' 0"	1'11" 2' 0"
3	2'11" 3' 0"	2'11" 3' 1"	2'10" 3' 1"	2'10" 3' 2"
4	3'10" 4' 1"	3'10" 4' 1"	3' 9" 4' 2"	3' 8" 4' 3"
5	4'10" 5' 2"	4' 9" 5' 2"	4' 8" 5' 4"	4' 6" 5' 6"
6	5' 9" 6' 2"	5' 8" 6' 4"	5' 6" 6' 6"	5' 4" 6' 9"
8	7' 7" 8' 5"	7' 5" 8' 7"	7' 2" 8'11"	6'11" 9' 5"
10	9' 4" 10' 8"	9' 1" 11' 0"	8' 9" 11' 6"	8' 4" 12' 4"
15	13' 7" 16' 8"	13' 1" 17' 6"	12' 5" 18' 9"	11' 7" 21' 0"
25	21' 4" 30' 0"	20' 1" 32'11"	18' 8" 37' 8"	16'10" 48' 2"
50	37' 4" 75' 6"	33' 8" 96' 7"	29'10" 154' 1"	25' 5" INF.

CIRCLE OF CONFUSION = .001″ (1/1000″)

F/5.6	F/8	F/11	F/16	F/22
36′10″	25′ 9″	18′ 9″	12′10″	9′ 4″
Near Far	Near Far	Near Far	Near Far	Near Far
1′10″ 2′ 1″	1′10″ 2′ 1″	1′ 9″ 2′ 2″	1′ 8″ 2′ 4″	1′ 8″ 2′ 5″
2′ 9″ 3′ 3″	2′ 8″ 3′ 4″	2′ 7″ 3′ 6″	2′ 5″ 3′10″	2′ 3″ 4′ 3″
3′ 7″ 4′ 5″	3′ 5″ 4′ 8″	3′ 3″ 5′ 0″	3′ 0″ 5′ 8″	2′ 9″ 6′ 9″
4′ 5″ 5′ 9″	4′ 2″ 6′ 1″	3′11″ 6′ 8″	3′ 7″ 8′ 0″	3′ 3″ 10′ 4″
5′ 2″ 7′ 1″	4′10″ 7′ 9″	4′ 6″ 8′ 8″	4′ 1″ 10′11″	3′ 8″ 15′11″
6′ 7″ 10′ 2″	6′ 1″ 11′ 6″	5′ 7″ 13′ 9″	4′11″ 20′ 5″	4′ 4″ 49′ 3″
7′10″ 13′ 7″	7′ 2″ 16′ 2″	6′ 6″ 21′ 0″	5′ 8″ 42′ 4″	4′10″ INF.
10′ 8″ 25′ 1″	9′ 6″ 35′ 4″	8′ 4″ 71′10″	6′11″ INF.	5′ 9″ INF.
14′11″ 76′ 7″	12′ 8″ 669′7″	10′ 9″ INF.	8′ 6″ INF.	6′10″ INF.
21′ 3″ INF.	17′ 0″ INF.	13′ 8″ INF.	10′ 3″ INF.	7′11″ INF.

LENS FOCAL LENGTH = 50 MM

Lens Aperture	F/1.4	F/2	F/2.8	F/4
Hyperfocal Dist.	230′ 7″	161′ 5″	115′ 3″	80′ 8″
Lens Focus (Feet)	Near Far	Near Far	Near Far	Near Far
2	1′11″ 2′ 0″	1′11″ 2′ 0″	1′11″ 2′ 0″	1′11″ 2′ 0″
3	2′11″ 3′ 0″	2′11″ 3′ 0″	2′11″ 3′ 0″	2′10″ 3′ 1″
4	3′11″ 4′ 0″	3′10″ 4′ 1″	3′10″ 4′ 1″	3′ 9″ 4′ 2″
5	4′10″ 5′ 1″	4′10″ 5′ 1″	4′ 9″ 5′ 2″	4′ 8″ 5′ 3″
6	5′10″ 6′ 1″	5′ 9″ 6′ 2″	5′ 8″ 6′ 3″	5′ 7″ 6′ 5″
8	7′ 8″ 8′ 3″	7′ 7″ 8′ 4″	7′ 5″ 8′ 6″	7′ 3″ 8′10″
10	9′ 7″ 10′ 5″	9′ 5″ 10′ 7″	9′ 2″ 10′11″	8′10″ 11′ 4″
15	14′ 1″ 16′ 0″	13′ 8″ 16′ 6″	13′ 3″ 17′ 2″	12′ 8″ 18′ 4″
25	22′ 6″ 28′ 0″	21′ 8″ 29′ 6″	20′ 6″ 31′10″	19′ 1″ 36′ 1″
50	41′ 1″ 63′ 9″	38′ 2″ 72′ 3″	34′10″ 88′ 0″	30′10″ 130′ 7″

CIRCLE OF CONFUSION = .001″ (1/1000″)

F/5.6	F/8	F/11	F/16	F/22
57′ 7″	40′ 4″	29′ 4″	20′ 2″	14′ 8″
Near	Near	Near	Near	Near
Far	Far	Far	Far	Far
1′11″	1′10″	1′10″	1′ 9″	1′ 9″
2′ 0″	2′ 1″	2′ 1″	2′ 2″	2′ 3″
2′10″	2′ 9″	2′ 8″	2′ 7″	2′ 6″
3′ 1″	3′ 2″	3′ 3″	3′ 5″	3′ 8″
3′ 9″	3′ 7″	3′ 6″	3′ 4″	3′ 2″
4′ 3″	4′ 5″	4′ 7″	4′11″	5′ 4″
4′ 7″	4′ 5″	4′ 3″	4′ 0″	3′ 9″
5′ 5″	5′ 8″	5′11″	6′ 6″	7′ 5″
5′ 5″	5′ 2″	5′ 0″	4′ 7″	4′ 3″
6′ 8″	7′ 0″	7′ 5″	8′ 5″	9′11″
7′ 0″	6′ 8″	6′ 3″	5′ 9″	5′ 2″
9′ 3″	9′11″	10′10″	13′ 0″	17′ 1″
8′ 6″	8′ 0″	7′ 5″	6′ 8″	5′11″
12′ 0″	13′ 2″	15′ 0″	19′ 6″	30′ 3″
11′11″	10′11″	9′11″	8′ 7″	7′ 5″
20′ 2″	23′ 8″	30′ 3″	56′ 7″	INF.
17′ 5″	15′ 5″	13′ 6″	11′ 2″	9′ 3″
43′10″	64′11″	162′ 4″	INF.	INF.
26′ 9″	22′ 4″	18′ 6″	14′ 4″	11′ 4″
368′ 4″	INF.	INF.	INF.	INF.

LENS FOCAL LENGTH = 68 MM

Lens Aperture	F/2	F/2.8	F/4	F/5.6
Hyperfocal Dist.	298′ 7″	213′ 3″	149′ 3″	106′ 7″
Lens Focus (Feet)	Near Far	Near Far	Near Far	Near Far
4	3′11″ 4′ 0″	3′11″ 4′ 0″	3′10″ 4′ 1″	3′10″ 4′ 1″
5	4′11″ 5′ 0″	4′10″ 5′ 1″	4′10″ 5′ 1″	4′ 9″ 5′ 2″
6	5′10″ 6′ 1″	5′10″ 6′ 2″	5′ 9″ 6′ 2″	5′ 8″ 6′ 4″
7	6′10″ 7′ 1″	6′ 9″ 7′ 2″	6′ 8″ 7′ 3″	6′ 6″ 7′ 5″
8	7′ 9″ 8′ 2″	7′ 8″ 8′ 3″	7′ 7″ 8′ 5″	7′ 5″ 8′ 7″
10	9′ 8″ 10′ 4″	9′ 6″ 10′ 5″	9′ 4″ 10′ 8″	9′ 1″ 11′ 0″
15	14′ 3″ 15′ 9″	14′ 0″ 16′ 1″	13′ 7″ 16′ 7″	13′ 2″ 17′ 4″
25	23′ 1″ 27′ 3″	22′ 4″ 28′ 3″	21′ 5″ 29′11″	20′ 3″ 32′ 6″
50	42′10″ 60′ 0″	40′ 6″ 65′ 2″	37′ 5″ 75′ 0″	34′ 1″ 93′ 9″
100	74′11″ 150′ 2″	68′ 1″ 187′10″	59′11″ 301′ 4″	51′ 7″ INF.

CIRCLE OF CONFUSION = .001″ (1/1000″)

F/8	F/11	F/16	F/22	F/32
74′ 7″	54′ 3″	37′ 3″	27′ 1″	18′ 7″
Near	Near	Near	Near	Near
Far	Far	Far	Far	Far
3′ 9″	3′ 8″	3′ 7″	3′ 6″	3′ 3″
4′ 2″	4′ 3″	4′ 5″	4′ 7″	5′ 0″
4′ 8″	4′ 7″	4′ 5″	4′ 3″	3′11″
5′ 4″	5′ 5″	5′ 8″	6′ 0″	6′ 8″
5′ 6″	5′ 5″	5′ 2″	4′11″	4′ 6″
6′ 6″	6′ 8″	7′ 1″	7′ 7″	8′ 8″
6′ 5″	6′ 2″	5′11″	5′ 7″	5′ 1″
7′ 8″	7′11″	8′ 6″	9′ 3″	10′11″
7′ 2″	6′11″	6′ 7″	6′ 2″	5′ 7″
8′11″	9′ 4″	10′ 1″	11′ 2″	13′ 8″
8′10″	8′ 5″	7′11″	7′ 4″	6′ 6″
11′ 6″	12′ 2″	13′ 6″	15′ 7″	21′ 0″
12′ 6″	11′ 9″	10′ 8″	9′ 8″	8′ 4″
18′ 8″	20′ 7″	24′ 9″	32′10″	72′ 0″
18′ 9″	17′ 1″	15′ 0″	13′ 0″	10′ 8″
37′ 5″	45′11″	74′ 4″	286′ 2″	INF.
29′11″	26′ 1″	21′ 5″	17′ 7″	13′ 7″
150′ 0″	600′ 7″	INF.	INF.	INF.
42′ 9″	35′ 2″	27′ 2″	21′ 4″	15′ 9″
INF.	INF.	INF.	INF.	INF.

LENS FOCAL LENGTH = 75 MM

Lens Aperture	F/2	F/2.8	F/4	F/5.6
Hyperfocal Dist.	363' 3"	259' 5"	181' 7"	129' 8"
Lens Focus (Feet)	Near Far	Near Far	Near Far	Near Far
4	3'11" 4' 0"	3'11" 4' 0"	3'11" 4' 1"	3'10" 4' 1"
5	4'11" 5' 0"	4'10" 5' 1"	4'10" 5' 1"	4' 9" 5' 2"
6	5'10" 6' 1"	5'10" 6' 1"	5' 9" 6' 2"	5' 8" 6' 3"
7	6'10" 7' 1"	6' 9" 7' 2"	6' 8" 7' 3"	6' 7" 7' 4"
8	7' 9" 8' 2"	7' 9" 8' 2"	7' 8" 8' 4"	7' 6" 8' 6"
10	9' 8" 10' 3"	9' 7" 10' 4"	9' 5" 10' 6"	9' 3" 10' 9"
15	14' 4" 15' 7"	14' 2" 15'10"	13'10" 16' 3"	13' 5" 16'11"
25	23' 4" 26' 9"	22' 9" 27' 7"	22' 0" 28'11"	20'11" 30'10"
50	43'11" 57'11"	41'11" 61'10"	39' 2" 68'10"	36' 1" 81' 1"
100	78' 5" 137'10"	72' 2" 162' 5"	64' 6" 221' 9"	56' 6" 432' 7"

CIRCLE OF CONFUSION = .001″ (1/1000″)

F/8	F/11	F/16	F/22	F/32
90′ 9″	66′ 0″	45′ 4″	33′ 0″	22′ 8″
Near	Near	Near	Near	Near
Far	Far	Far	Far	Far
3′10″	3′ 9″	3′ 8″	3′ 7″	3′ 5″
4′ 2″	4′ 2″	4′ 4″	4′ 6″	4′ 9″
4′ 9″	4′ 7″	4′ 6″	4′ 4″	4′ 1″
5′ 3″	5′ 4″	5′ 7″	5′10″	6′ 3″
5′ 7″	5′ 6″	5′ 3″	5′ 1″	4′ 9″
6′ 4″	6′ 6″	6′10″	7′ 3″	8′ 0″
6′ 6″	6′ 4″	6′ 1″	5′ 9″	5′ 4″
7′ 6″	7′ 9″	8′ 2″	8′ 9″	9′11″
7′ 4″	7′ 1″	6′ 9″	6′ 5″	5′11″
8′ 8″	9′ 0″	9′ 7″	10′ 5″	12′ 1″
9′ 0″	8′ 8″	8′ 2″	7′ 8″	6′11″
11′ 2″	11′ 8″	12′ 8″	14′ 2″	17′ 6″
12′10″	12′ 3″	11′ 3″	10′ 4″	9′ 1″
17′10″	19′ 3″	22′ 2″	27′ 1″	42′10″
19′ 7″	18′ 2″	16′ 2″	14′ 3″	11′11″
34′ 4″	39′11″	54′11″	99′ 9″	INF.
32′ 3″	28′ 6″	23′10″	19′11″	15′ 8″
110′ 6″	202′ 7″	INF.	INF.	INF.
47′ 7″	39′10″	31′ 3″	24′10″	18′ 6″
INF.	INF.	INF.	INF.	INF.

LENS FOCAL LENGTH = 85 MM

Lens Aperture	F/2	F/2.8	F/4	F/5.6
Hyperfocal Dist.	466' 7"	333' 3"	233' 3"	166' 7"
Lens Focus (Feet)	Near Far	Near Far	Near Far	Near Far
4	3'11" 4' 0"	3'11" 4' 0"	3'11" 4' 0"	3'10" 4' 1"
5	4'11" 5' 0"	4'11" 5' 0"	4'10" 5' 1"	4'10" 5' 1"
6	5'11" 6' 0"	5'10" 6' 1"	5'10" 6' 1"	5' 9" 6' 2"
7	6'10" 7' 1"	6'10" 7' 1"	6' 9" 7' 2"	6' 8" 7' 3"
8	7'10" 8' 1"	7' 9" 8' 2"	7' 8" 8' 3"	7' 7" 8' 4"
10	9' 9" 10' 2"	9' 8" 10' 3"	9' 7" 10' 5"	9' 5" 10' 7"
15	14' 6" 15' 5"	14' 4" 15' 8"	14' 1" 16' 0"	13' 9" 16' 5"
25	23' 8" 26' 4"	23' 3" 27' 0"	22' 7" 27'11"	21' 9" 29' 4"
50	45' 2" 55'11"	43' 6" 58' 9"	41' 2" 63' 6"	38' 6" 71' 3"
100	82' 4" 127' 2"	76'11" 142' 8"	70' 0" 174' 7"	62' 6" 249' 0"

CIRCLE OF CONFUSION = .001″ (1/1000″)

F/8	F/11	F/16	F/22	F/32
116′ 7″	84′10″	58′ 3″	42′ 5″	29′ 1″
Near Far	Near Far	Near Far	Near Far	Near Far
3′10″ 4′ 1″	3′ 9″ 4′ 2″	3′ 9″ 4′ 3″	3′ 8″ 4′ 4″	3′ 6″ 4′ 7″
4′ 9″ 5′ 2″	4′ 8″ 5′ 3″	4′ 7″ 5′ 5″	4′ 5″ 5′ 7″	4′ 3″ 5′11″
5′ 8″ 6′ 3″	5′ 7″ 6′ 5″	5′ 5″ 6′ 7″	5′ 3″ 6′11″	5′ 0″ 7′ 5″
6′ 7″ 7′ 5″	6′ 5″ 7′ 7″	6′ 3″ 7′10″	6′ 0″ 8′ 3″	5′ 8″ 9′ 1″
7′ 6″ 8′ 6″	7′ 3″ 8′ 9″	7′ 0″ 9′ 2″	6′ 9″ 9′ 9″	6′ 3″ 10′10″
9′ 2″ 10′10″	8′11″ 11′ 3″	8′ 6″ 12′ 0″	8′ 1″ 12′11″	7′ 5″ 15′ 0″
13′ 3″ 17′ 1″	12′ 9″ 18′ 1″	11′11″ 20′ 0″	11′ 1″ 22′11″	9′11″ 30′ 3″
20′ 7″ 31′ 8″	19′ 4″ 35′ 3″	17′ 6″ 43′ 4″	15′ 9″ 59′11″	13′ 6″ 164′ 1″
35′ 0″ 87′ 1″	31′ 6″ 120′ 9″	26′11″ 338′10″	23′ 0″ INF.	18′ 5″ INF.
53′10″ 688′11″	45′11″ INF.	36′10″ INF.	29′10″ INF.	22′ 7″ INF.

LENS FOCAL LENGTH = 90 MM

Lens Aperture	F/2	F/2.8	F/4	F/5.6
Hyperfocal Dist.	523' 1"	373' 7"	261' 6"	186' 9"
Lens Focus (Feet)	Near Far	Near Far	Near Far	Near Far
4	3'11" 4' 0"	3'11" 4' 0"	3'11" 4' 0"	3'11" 4' 0"
5	4'11" 5' 0"	4'11" 5' 0"	4'10" 5' 1"	4'10" 5' 1"
6	5'11" 6' 0"	5'10" 6' 1"	5'10" 6' 1"	5' 9" 6' 2"
7	6'10" 7' 1"	6'10" 7' 1"	6' 9" 7' 2"	6' 9" 7' 3"
8	7'10" 8' 1"	7'10" 8' 2"	7' 9" 8' 2"	7' 8" 8' 4"
10	9' 9" 10' 2"	9' 8" 10' 3"	9' 7" 10' 4"	9' 6" 10' 6"
15	14' 7" 15' 5"	14' 5" 15' 7"	14' 2" 15'10"	13'10" 16' 3"
25	23'10" 26' 2"	23' 5" 26' 9"	22'10" 27' 7"	22' 0" 28' 9"
50	45' 7" 55' 2"	44' 1" 57' 8"	42' 0" 61' 8"	39' 5" 68' 1"
100	83'11" 123' 6"	78'11" 136' 4"	72' 4" 161' 7"	65' 2" 214' 5"

CIRCLE OF CONFUSION = .001" (1/1000")

F/8	F/11	F/16	F/22	F/32
130′ 9″	95′ 1″	65′ 4″	47′ 6″	32′ 8″
Near Far	Near Far	Near Far	Near Far	Near Far
3′10″ 4′ 1″	3′10″ 4′ 1″	3′ 9″ 4′ 2″	3′ 8″ 4′ 4″	3′ 7″ 4′ 6″
4′ 9″ 5′ 2″	4′ 9″ 5′ 3″	4′ 7″ 5′ 4″	4′ 6″ 5′ 6″	4′ 4″ 5′10″
5′ 8″ 6′ 3″	5′ 7″ 6′ 4″	5′ 6″ 6′ 6″	5′ 4″ 6′ 9″	5′ 1″ 7′ 3″
6′ 7″ 7′ 4″	6′ 6″ 7′ 6″	6′ 4″ 7′ 9″	6′ 1″ 8′ 1″	5′ 9″ 8′ 9″
7′ 6″ 8′ 6″	7′ 4″ 8′ 8″	7′ 1″ 9′ 0″	6′10″ 9′ 6″	6′ 5″ 10′ 5″
9′ 3″ 10′ 9″	9′ 0″ 11′ 1″	8′ 8″ 11′ 8″	8′ 3″ 12′ 6″	7′ 8″ 14′ 2″
13′ 5″ 16′10″	12′11″ 17′ 8″	12′ 2″ 19′ 4″	11′ 5″ 21′ 8″	10′ 4″ 27′ 3″
21′ 0″ 30′ 9″	19′10″ 33′ 9″	18′ 1″ 40′ 2″	16′ 5″ 52′ 0″	14′ 2″ 102′ 3″
36′ 2″ 80′ 7″	32′10″ 104′ 8″	28′ 4″ 208′ 5″	24′ 5″ INF.	19′10″ INF.
56′ 8″ 420′10″	48′ 9″ INF.	39′ 7″ INF.	32′ 3″ INF.	24′ 8″ INF.

LENS FOCAL LENGTH = 95 MM

Lens Aperture	F/2	F/2.8	F/4	F/5.6
Hyperfocal Dist.	582'10"	416' 3"	291' 5"	208' 1"
Lens Focus (Feet)	Near Far	Near Far	Near Far	Near Far
2	1'11" 2' 0"	1'11" 2' 0"	1'11" 2' 0"	1'11" 2' 0"
3	2'11" 3' 0"	2'11" 3' 0"	2'11" 3' 0"	2'11" 3' 0"
4	3'11" 4' 0"	3'11" 4' 0"	3'11" 4' 0"	3'11" 4' 0"
5	4'11" 5' 0"	4'11" 5' 0"	4'11" 5' 0"	4'10" 5' 1"
6	5'11" 6' 0"	5'11" 6' 0"	5'10" 6' 1"	5'10" 6' 2"
8	7'10" 8' 1"	7'10" 8' 1"	7' 9" 8' 2"	7' 8" 8' 3"
10	9'10" 10' 2"	9' 9" 10' 2"	9' 8" 10' 4"	9' 6" 10' 5"
15	14' 7" 15' 4"	14' 5" 15' 6"	14' 3" 15' 9"	14' 0" 16' 1"
25	23'11" 26' 1"	23' 7" 26' 6"	23' 0" 27' 3"	22' 4" 28' 4"
50	46' 0" 54' 7"	44' 8" 56' 9"	42' 8" 60' 3"	40' 4" 65' 8"

CIRCLE OF CONFUSION = .001″ (1/1000″)

F/8	F/11	F/16	F/22	F/32
145′ 8″	105′ 11″	72′10″	52′11″	36′ 5″
Near Far	Near Far	Near Far	Near Far	Near Far
1′11″ 2′ 0″	1′11″ 2′ 0″	1′11″ 2′ 0″	1′11″ 2′ 0″	1′10″ 2′ 1″
2′11″ 3′ 0″	2′11″ 3′ 0″	2′10″ 3′ 1″	2′10″ 3′ 1″	2′ 9″ 3′ 2″
3′10″ 4′ 1″	3′10″ 4′ 1″	3′ 9″ 4′ 2″	3′ 8″ 4′ 3″	3′ 7″ 4′ 5″
4′10″ 5′ 1″	4′ 9″ 5′ 2″	4′ 8″ 5′ 4″	4′ 7″ 5′ 5″	4′ 5″ 5′ 8″
5′ 9″ 6′ 2″	5′ 8″ 6′ 4″	5′ 6″ 6′ 6″	5′ 5″ 6′ 8″	5′ 2″ 7′ 1″
7′ 7″ 8′ 5″	7′ 5″ 8′ 7″	7′ 2″ 8′11″	6′11″ 9′ 4″	6′ 7″ 10′ 1″
9′ 4″ 10′ 8″	9′ 1″ 11′ 0″	8′ 9″ 11′ 6″	8′ 5″ 12′ 2″	7′10″ 13′ 7″
13′ 7″ 16′ 8″	13′ 2″ 17′ 4″	12′ 5″ 18′ 9″	11′ 8″ 20′ 9″	10′ 8″ 25′ 1″
21′ 4″ 30′ 1″	20′ 3″ 32′ 7″	18′ 8″ 37′ 9″	17′ 0″ 46′ 9″	14′10″ 77′ 6″
37′ 3″ 75′10″	34′ 0″ 94′ 1″	29′ 8″ 157′ 2″	25′ 9″ 803′ 0″	21′ 1″ INF.

LENS FOCAL LENGTH = 100 MM

Lens Aperture	F/2	F/2.8	F/4	F/5.6
Hyperfocal Dist.	645' 9"	461' 3"	322'10"	230' 7"
Lens Focus (Feet)	Near Far	Near Far	Near Far	Near Far
4	3'11" 4' 0"	3'11" 4' 0"	3'11" 4' 0"	3'11" 4' 0"
5	4'11" 5' 0"	4'11" 5' 0"	4'11" 5' 0"	4'10" 5' 1"
6	5'11" 6' 0"	5'11" 6' 0"	5'10" 6' 1"	5'10" 6' 1"
7	6'11" 7' 0"	6'10" 7' 1"	6'10" 7' 1"	6' 9" 7' 2"
8	7'10" 8' 1"	7'10" 8' 1"	7' 9" 8' 2"	7' 8" 8' 3"
10	9'10" 10' 1"	9' 9" 10' 2"	9' 8" 10' 3"	9' 7" 10' 5"
15	14' 8" 15' 4"	14' 6" 15' 5"	14' 4" 15' 8"	14' 1" 16' 0"
25	24' 0" 25'11"	23' 8" 26' 4"	23' 2" 27' 0"	22' 7" 27'11"
50	46' 5" 54' 1"	45' 1" 56' 0"	43' 4" 59' 1"	41' 1" 63' 8"
100	86' 7" 118' 2"	82' 2" 127' 6"	76' 4" 144' 7"	69' 9" 176' 1"

CIRCLE OF CONFUSION = .001" (1/1000")

F/8	F/11	F/16	F/22	F/32
161' 5"	117' 5"	80' 8"	58' 8"	40' 4"
Near	Near	Near	Near	Near
Far	Far	Far	Far	Far
3'10"	3'10"	3' 9"	3' 9"	3' 7"
4' 1"	4' 1"	4' 2"	4' 3"	4' 4"
4'10"	4' 9"	4' 8"	4' 7"	4' 5"
5' 1"	5' 2"	5' 3"	5' 5"	5' 7"
5' 9"	5' 8"	5' 7"	5' 5"	5' 3"
6' 2"	6' 3"	6' 5"	6' 7"	6'11"
6' 8"	6' 7"	6' 5"	6' 3"	6' 0"
7' 3"	7' 5"	7' 7"	7'10"	8' 4"
7' 7"	7' 6"	7' 3"	7' 0"	6' 8"
8' 4"	8' 6"	8'10"	9' 2"	9'10"
9' 5"	9' 2"	8'11"	8' 7"	8' 0"
10' 7"	10'10"	11' 4"	11'11"	13' 1"
13' 9"	13' 4"	12' 8"	12' 0"	11' 0"
16' 5"	17' 1"	18' 3"	19'11"	23' 6"
21' 8"	20' 7"	19' 1"	17' 7"	15' 6"
29' 6"	31' 7"	36' 0"	43' 1"	64' 3"
38' 2"	35' 1"	30'11"	27' 1"	22' 4"
72' 2"	86' 7"	129'11"	324' 8"	INF.
61' 9"	54' 1"	44' 8"	37' 0"	28' 9"
261' 3"	661' 5"	INF.	INF.	INF.

LENS FOCAL LENGTH = 120 MM

Lens Aperture	F/2	F/2.8	F/4	F/5.6
Hyperfocal Dist.	929'11"	664' 3"	464'11"	332' 1"
Lens Focus (Feet)	Near Far	Near Far	Near Far	Near Far
4	3'11" 4' 0"	3'11" 4' 0"	3'11" 4' 0"	3'11" 4' 0"
5	4'11" 5' 0"	4'11" 5' 0"	4'11" 5' 0"	4'11" 5' 0"
6	5'11" 6' 0"	5'11" 6' 0"	5'11" 6' 0"	5'10" 6' 1"
7	6'11" 7' 0"	6'11" 7' 0"	6'10" 7' 1"	6'10" 7' 1"
8	7'11" 8' 0"	7'10" 8' 1"	7'10" 8' 1"	7' 9" 8' 2"
10	9'10" 10' 1"	9'10" 10' 1"	9' 9" 10' 2"	9' 8" 10' 3"
15	14' 9" 15' 2"	14' 8" 15' 4"	14' 6" 15' 5"	14' 4" 15' 8"
25	24' 4" 25' 8"	24' 1" 25'11"	23' 8" 26' 4"	23' 3" 27' 0"
50	47' 5" 52' 9"	46' 6" 54' 0"	45' 2" 55'11"	43' 6" 58' 9"
100	90' 3" 111'11"	86'11" 117' 7"	82' 4" 127' 3"	76'11" 142'10"

CIRCLE OF CONFUSION = .001" (1/1000")

F/8	F/11	F/16	F/22	F/32
232' 5"	169' 1"	116' 2"	84' 6"	58' 1"
Near Far	Near Far	Near Far	Near Far	Near Far
3'11" 4' 0"	3'10" 4' 1"	3'10" 4' 1"	3'10" 4' 2"	3' 9" 4' 3"
4'10" 5' 1"	4'10" 5' 1"	4' 9" 5' 2"	4' 8" 5' 3"	4' 7" 5' 5"
5'10" 6' 1"	5' 9" 6' 2"	5' 8" 6' 3"	5' 7" 6' 5"	5' 5" 6' 7"
6' 9" 7' 2"	6' 8" 7' 3"	6' 7" 7' 5"	6' 5" 7' 7"	6' 3" 7'10"
7' 8" 8' 3"	7' 7" 8' 4"	7' 6" 8' 6"	7' 4" 8' 9"	7' 0" 9' 2"
9' 7" 10' 5"	9' 5" 10' 7"	9' 2" 10'10"	8'11" 11' 3"	8' 6" 11'11"
14' 1" 16' 0"	13' 9" 16' 5"	13' 3" 17' 1"	12' 9" 18' 1"	11'11" 20' 0"
22' 7" 27'11"	21' 9" 29' 3"	20' 7" 31' 8"	19' 4" 35' 3"	17' 6" 43' 4"
41' 2" 63' 6"	38' 7" 70' 9"	35' 0" 87' 2"	31' 6" 120'11"	26'11" 341' 1"
70' 0" 174'11"	62'11" 243' 4"	53'10" 698' 5"	45'10" INF.	36'10" INF.

LENS FOCAL LENGTH = 150 MM

Lens Aperture	F/2	F/2.8	F/4	F/5.6
Hyperfocal Dist.	1453'	1038'	726' 6"	518'11"
Lens Focus (Feet)	Near Far	Near Far	Near Far	Near Far
6	5'11" 6' 0"	5'11" 6' 0"	5'11" 6' 0"	5'11" 6' 0"
8	7'11" 8' 0"	7'11" 8' 0"	7'11" 8' 1"	7'10" 8' 1"
10	9'11" 10' 0"	9'10" 10' 1"	9'10" 10' 1"	9' 9" 10' 2"
12	11'10" 12' 1"	11'10" 12' 1"	11' 9" 12' 2"	11' 8" 12' 3"
15	14'10" 15' 1"	14' 9" 15' 2"	14' 8" 15' 3"	14' 7" 15' 5"
20	19' 8" 20' 3"	19' 7" 20' 4"	19' 5" 20' 6"	19' 3" 20' 9"
25	24' 7" 25' 5"	24' 5" 25' 7"	24' 2" 25'10"	23'10" 26' 2"
50	48' 4" 51' 9"	47' 8" 52' 6"	46' 9" 53' 7"	45' 7" 55' 3"
75	71' 4" 79' 0"	69'11" 80' 9"	68' 0" 83' 6"	65' 7" 87' 6"
100	93' 7" 107' 4"	91' 3" 110' 7"	87'11" 115'10"	83'10" 123' 8"

CIRCLE OF CONFUSION = .001″ (1/1000″)

F/8	F/11	F/16	F/22	F/32
363′ 3″	264′ 2″	181′ 7″	132′ 1″	90′ 9″
Near Far	Near Far	Near Far	Near Far	Near Far
5′10″ 6′ 1″	5′10″ 6′ 1″	5′ 9″ 6′ 2″	5′ 9″ 6′ 3″	5′ 7″ 6′ 4″
7′10″ 8′ 2″	7′ 9″ 8′ 2″	7′ 8″ 8′ 4″	7′ 6″ 8′ 5″	7′ 4″ 8′ 8″
9′ 8″ 10′ 3″	9′ 7″ 10′ 4″	9′ 6″ 10′ 6″	9′ 3″ 10′ 9″	9′ 0″ 11′ 2″
11′ 7″ 12′ 4″	11′ 5″ 12′ 6″	11′ 3″ 12′ 9″	11′ 0″ 13′ 1″	10′ 7″ 13′ 8″
14′ 5″ 15′ 7″	14′ 2″ 15′10″	13′10″ 16′ 3″	13′ 6″ 16′10″	12′11″ 17′10″
18′11″ 21′ 1″	18′ 7″ 21′ 7″	18′ 0″ 22′ 4″	17′ 5″ 23′ 5″	16′ 5″ 25′ 5″
23′ 5″ 26′ 9″	22′10″ 27′ 6″	22′ 0″ 28′10″	21′ 1″ 30′ 8″	19′ 8″ 34′ 2″
44′ 0″ 57′10″	42′ 1″ 61′ 6″	39′ 3″ 68′ 8″	36′ 4″ 79′11″	32′ 4″ 109′11″
62′ 2″ 94′ 4″	58′ 6″ 104′ 5″	53′ 2″ 127′ 1″	47′11″ 172′ 0″	41′ 2″ 417′ 6″
78′ 5″ 137′ 8″	72′ 7″ 160′ 5″	64′ 7″ 221′ 1″	57′ 0″ 405′ 3″	47′ 8″ INF.

LENS FOCAL LENGTH = 200 MM

Lens Aperture	F/2.8	F/4	F/5.6
Hyperfocal Dist.	1845'	1292'	922' 7"
Lens Focus (Feet)	Near Far	Near Far	Near Far
6	5'11" 6' 0"	5'11" 6' 0"	5'11" 6' 0"
8	7'11" 8' 0"	7'11" 8' 0"	7'11" 8' 0"
10	9'11" 10' 0"	9'11" 10' 0"	9'10" 10' 1"
12	11'11" 12' 0"	11'10" 12' 1"	11'10" 12' 1"
15	14'10" 15' 1"	14'10" 15' 2"	14' 9" 15' 2"
20	19' 9" 20' 2"	19' 8" 20' 3"	19' 7" 20' 5"
25	24' 8" 25' 4"	24' 6" 25' 5"	24' 4" 25' 8"
50	48' 8" 51' 4"	48' 1" 51'11"	47' 5" 52' 9"
75	72' 1" 78' 1"	70'11" 79' 6"	69' 4" 81' 6"
100	94'10" 105' 8"	92'10" 108' 3"	90' 3" 112' 0"

CIRCLE OF CONFUSION = .001″ (1/1000″)

F/8	F/11	F/16	F/22	F/32
645′ 9″	469′ 8″	322′10″	234′10″	161′ 5″
Near Far	Near Far	Near Far	Near Far	Near Far
5′11″ 6′ 0″	5′11″ 6′ 0″	5′10″ 6′ 1″	5′10″ 6′ 1″	5′ 9″ 6′ 2″
7′10″ 8′ 1″	7′10″ 8′ 1″	7′ 9″ 8′ 2″	7′ 9″ 8′ 3″	7′ 7″ 8′ 4″
9′10″ 10′ 1″	9′ 9″ 10′ 2″	9′ 8″ 10′ 3″	9′ 7″ 10′ 4″	9′ 5″ 10′ 7″
11′ 9″ 12′ 2″	11′ 8″ 12′ 3″	11′ 7″ 12′ 5″	11′ 5″ 12′ 7″	11′ 2″ 12′10″
14′ 8″ 15′ 4″	14′ 6″ 15′ 5″	14′ 4″ 15′ 8″	14′ 1″ 15′11″	13′ 9″ 16′ 5″
19′ 5″ 20′ 7″	19′ 2″ 20′10″	18′10″ 21′ 3″	18′ 5″ 21′ 9″	17′10″ 22′ 8″
24′ 1″ 25′11″	23′ 9″ 26′ 4″	23′ 2″ 27′ 0″	22′ 7″ 27′10″	21′ 8″ 29′ 5″
46′ 5″ 54′ 1″	45′ 2″ 55′10″	43′ 4″ 59′ 0″	41′ 3″ 63′ 3″	38′ 3″ 72′ 0″
67′ 3″ 84′ 9″	64′ 9″ 89′ 1″	60′11″ 97′ 5″	56′11″ 109′ 8″	51′ 4″ 139′ 0″
86′ 8″ 118′ 2″	82′ 6″ 126′ 9″	76′ 5″ 144′ 5″	70′ 3″ 173′ 3″	61′10″ 259′11″

LENS FOCAL LENGTH = 240 MM

Lens Aperture	F/2.8	F/4	F/5.6
Hyperfocal Dist.	2657′	1850′	1328′
Lens Focus (Feet)	Near Far	Near Far	Near Far
6	5′11″ 6′ 0″	5′11″ 6′ 0″	5′11″ 6′ 0″
8	7′11″ 8′ 0″	7′11″ 8′ 0″	7′11″ 8′ 0″
10	9′11″ 10′ 0″	9′11″ 10′ 0″	9′11″ 10′ 0″
12	11′11″ 12′ 0″	11′11″ 12′ 0″	11′10″ 12′ 1″
15	14′11″ 15′ 0″	14′10″ 15′ 1″	14′10″ 15′ 1″
20	19′10″ 20′ 1″	19′ 9″ 20′ 2″	19′ 8″ 20′ 3″
25	24′ 9″ 25′ 2″	24′ 8″ 25′ 3″	24′ 6″ 25′ 5″
50	49′ 1″ 50′11″	48′ 8″ 51′ 4″	48′ 2″ 51′11″
75	72′11″ 77′ 1″	72′ 1″ 78′ 1″	71′ 0″ 79′ 5″
100	96′ 4″ 103′10″	94′11″ 105′ 7″	93′ 0″ 108′ 0″

CIRCLE OF CONFUSION = .001″ (1/1000″)

F/8	F/11	F/16	F/22	F/32
929′11″	676′ 4″	464′11″	338′ 2″	232′ 5″
Near Far	Near Far	Near Far	Near Far	Near Far
5′11″ 6′ 0″	5′11″ 6′ 0″	5′11″ 6′ 0″	5′10″ 6′ 1″	5′10″ 6′ 1″
7′11″ 8′ 0″	7′10″ 8′ 1″	7′10″ 8′ 1″	7′ 9″ 8′ 2″	7′ 9″ 8′ 3″
9′10″ 10′ 1″	9′10″ 10′ 1″	9′ 9″ 10′ 2″	9′ 8″ 10′ 3″	9′ 7″ 10′ 4″
11′10″ 12′ 1″	11′ 9″ 12′ 2″	11′ 8″ 12′ 3″	11′ 7″ 12′ 4″	11′ 5″ 12′ 7″
14′ 9″ 15′ 2″	14′ 8″ 15′ 3″	14′ 6″ 15′ 5″	14′ 4″ 15′ 7″	14′ 1″ 15′11″
19′ 7″ 20′ 5″	19′ 5″ 20′ 7″	19′ 2″ 20′10″	18′11″ 21′ 2″	18′ 5″ 21′ 9″
24′ 4″ 25′ 8″	24′ 1″ 25′11″	23′ 9″ 26′ 4″	23′ 3″ 26′11″	22′ 7″ 27′10″
47′ 5″ 52′ 9″	46′ 7″ 53′11″	45′ 2″ 55′11″	43′ 7″ 58′ 6″	41′ 3″ 63′ 5″
69′ 5″ 81′ 6″	67′ 7″ 84′ 2″	64′ 8″ 89′ 2″	61′ 6″ 96′ 1″	56′10″ 110′ 1″
90′ 4″ 111′11″	87′ 2″ 117′ 2″	82′ 4″ 127′ 1″	77′ 3″ 141′ 6″	70′ 1″ 174′ 5″

LENS FOCAL LENGTH = 300 MM

Lens Aperture	F/4	F/5.6	F/8
Hyperfocal Dist.	2906′	2076′	1453′
Lens Focus (Feet)	Near Far	Near Far	Near Far
6	5′11″ 6′ 0″	5′11″ 6′ 0″	5′11″ 6′ 0″
8	7′11″ 8′ 0″	7′11″ 8′ 0″	7′11″ 8′ 0″
10	9′11″ 10′ 0″	9′11″ 10′ 0″	9′11″ 10′ 0″
12	11′11″ 12′ 0″	11′11″ 12′ 0″	11′10″ 12′ 1″
15	14′11″ 15′ 0″	14′10″ 15′ 1″	14′10″ 15′ 1″
20	19′10″ 20′ 1″	19′ 9″ 20′ 2″	19′ 8″ 20′ 3″
25	24′ 9″ 25′ 2″	24′ 8″ 25′ 3″	24′ 7″ 25′ 5″
50	49′ 2″ 50′10″	48′10″ 51′ 2″	48′ 4″ 51′ 8″
75	73′ 1″ 76′11″	72′ 5″ 77′ 9″	71′ 4″ 79′ 0″
100	96′ 8″ 103′ 6″	95′ 5″ 105′ 0″	93′ 7″ 107′ 3″

CIRCLE OF CONFUSION = .001″ (1/1000″)

F/11	F/16	F/22	F/32
1057′	726′ 6″	528′ 4″	363′ 3″
Near Far	Near Far	Near Far	Near Far
5′11″ 6′ 0″	5′11″ 6′ 0″	5′11″ 6′ 0″	5′11″ 6′ 1″
7′11″ 8′ 0″	7′11″ 8′ 0″	7′10″ 8′ 1″	7′10″ 8′ 1″
9′10″ 10′ 1″	9′10″ 10′ 1″	9′ 9″ 10′ 2″	9′ 9″ 10′ 3″
11′10″ 12′ 1″	11′ 9″ 12′ 2″	11′ 9″ 12′ 3″	11′ 7″ 12′ 4″
14′ 9″ 15′ 2″	14′ 8″ 15′ 3″	14′ 7″ 15′ 4″	14′ 5″ 15′ 7″
19′ 7″ 20′ 4″	19′ 5″ 20′ 6″	19′ 3″ 20′ 8″	19′ 0″ 21′ 1″
24′ 5″ 25′ 6″	24′ 2″ 25′10″	23′10″ 26′ 2″	23′ 5″ 26′ 9″
47′ 9″ 52′ 5″	46′10″ 53′ 7″	45′ 9″ 55′ 1″	44′ 0″ 57′ 9″
70′ 1″ 80′ 7″	68′ 0″ 83′ 6″	65′ 9″ 87′ 2″	62′ 3″ 94′ 2″
91′ 5″ 110′ 4″	88′ 0″ 115′ 9″	84′ 2″ 123′ 0″	78′ 6″ 137′ 5″

LENS FOCAL LENGTH = 500 MM

Lens Aperture	F/4	F/5.6	F/8
Hyperfocal Dist.	8073'	5766'	4036'
Lens Focus (Feet)	Near Far	Near Far	Near Far
6	5'11" 6' 0"	5'11" 6' 0"	5'11" 6' 0"
8	7'11" 8' 0"	7'11" 8' 0"	7'11" 8' 0"
10	9'11" 10' 0"	9'11" 10' 0"	9'11" 10' 0"
12	11'11" 12' 0"	11'11" 12' 0"	11'11" 12' 0"
15	14'11" 15' 0"	14'11" 15' 0"	14'11" 15' 0"
20	19'11" 20' 0"	19'11" 20' 0"	19'10" 20' 1"
25	24'11" 25' 0"	24'10" 25' 1"	24'10" 25' 1"
50	49' 8" 50' 3"	49' 7" 50' 5"	49' 4" 50' 7"
75	74' 3" 75' 8"	74' 0" 75'11"	73' 7" 76' 4"
100	98' 9" 101' 2"	98' 3" 101' 8"	97' 7" 102' 5"

CIRCLE OF CONFUSION = .001″ (1/1000″)

F/11	F/16	F/22	F/32
2936′	2018′	1468′	1009′
Near	Near	Near	Near
Far	Far	Far	Far
5′11″	5′11″	5′11″	5′11″
6′ 0″	6′ 0″	6′ 0″	6′ 0″
7′11″	7′11″	7′11″	7′11″
8′ 0″	8′ 0″	8′ 0″	8′ 0″
9′11″	9′11″	9′11″	9′11″
10′ 0″	10′ 0″	10′ 0″	10′ 1″
11′11″	11′11″	11′10″	11′10″
12′ 0″	12′ 0″	12′ 1″	12′ 1″
14′11″	14′10″	14′10″	14′ 9″
15′ 0″	15′ 1″	15′ 1″	15′ 2″
19′10″	19′ 9″	19′ 9″	19′ 7″
20′ 1″	20′ 2″	20′ 3″	20′ 4″
24′ 9″	24′ 8″	24′ 7″	24′ 5″
25′ 2″	25′ 3″	25′ 4″	25′ 7″
49′ 2″	48′ 9″	48′ 4″	47′ 8″
50′10″	51′ 2″	51′ 8″	52′ 6″
73′ 2″	72′ 4″	71′ 5″	69′11″
76′11″	77′ 9″	78′11″	80′10″
96′ 9″	95′ 4″	93′ 8″	91′ 1″
103′ 5″	105′ 1″	107′ 2″	110′ 9″

APPENDIX D

CONFORMING THE ORIGINAL

When the workprint has been put into a fine cut and there is to be no more cutting of the picture, and all the effects have been marked (see Chapter XII), then you are ready to conform your camera original with your workprint.

Before you begin to splice the original, you should find a place to work which is as free of dust and dirt as possible. When handling original you should wear clean white editing gloves, which can be purchased by the dozen at most labs. The cement splicer should be properly aligned and the splicing cement should be fresh. The cans in which the original is stored should be marked with the latent edge-numbers so that any shot can be easily located by edge-number. It is extremely helpful to have two pairs of rewinds. One pair can be used for searching shots, while the other pair is used for splicing and, with the aid of a synchronizer, for matching workprint with original. Make sure the workprint is properly marked, as explained in Chapter XII.

Place the edited workprint in the front gang of the synchronizer and run down the first shot until you find the first latent edge-number. Since most 16mm films have edge-numbers every half foot, you should come to the first edge-number within the first foot. Lock the shot in place by turning down the lever on front of the synchronizer. Locate the corresponding shot in the original by latent edge-number and place it in the second gang of the synchronizer, opposite the corresponding shot on the workprint so the edge-numbers correspond frame by frame. Unlock the synchronizer, run the two shots back to the head of the workprint shot, and then cut the original with a scissors, at least one half frame longer (to the right) than the workprint. It is easiest to line up the head of the shot, mark the original, and cut it on the right side of the synchronizer. Now wind down the workprint and original to the tail of the first workprint shot, and again cut the original at least one half frame longer (to the left now) than the workprint shot. It is easiest to do this operation on the left side of the synchronizer. The additional half frames are needed for scraping when cement splicing. Roll up the first shot of original. Continue in the same manner with the second shot, attaching the second cut shot of original to the first with a small piece of ¼" or ⅜" masking tape. If any shots are to be used in a dissolve (only possible with A & B rolls), do not forget to cut the shot at the end of the dissolve mark on the workprint— that is, the shot should be cut one half the length of the dissolve longer than where the physical splice occurs in the middle of the dissolve on the workprint.

When all the shots of the original are cut, they are spliced together in order, using the workprint as a guide, if the printing is to be single strand. If you are preparing A & B rolls for checkerboard printing (see p. 106), then you must prepare the rolls differently. The operation of cutting and splicing could have been done together, avoiding having to put masking tape on the original.

To prepare A & B rolls it is advisable to have a synchronizer with at least three gangs. The first shot of cut original is placed on the "A" roll in the synchronizer. In the next gang is placed a length of black leader which matches the first shot in length. This is the "B" roll. The second shot of cut original is spliced to the tail of the black leader on the "B" roll. Opposite, on the "A" roll, black leader the length of the second shot is spliced to the tail of the first shot. *It is imperative that the emulsion of the black leader never be scraped during splicing* as this will defeat the purpose of checkerboard printing— invisible splices. The overlap to be scraped for cement splices should always be in the picture area and never on the black leader. Splicing continues with odd number shots on the "A" roll and even number shots on the "B" roll, always splicing an equal length of black leader on the opposite roll. When superimposition or double-exposure is desired, the two shots (rather than a shot and black leader) are spliced opposite one another. When a dissolve is marked on the workprint, the two shots must overlap the length of the dissolve. When a fade is to be made with negative film, *clear* leader must be spliced opposite from where the fade is to occur. If a fade-out fade-in is to be made on negative, the two shots should be spliced together on the *same* roll and clear leader placed opposite for the length of the effect. The workprint should be run through in the third gang of the synchronizer to insure proper cutting of shots and effects on the A & B rolls. When the rolls are assembled they should again be checked against the workprint for possible errors. A list of effects and where they occur, marked by footage and frame count should be included with the original when it is sent off to the lab for final printing. Some labs prefer to have you send your marked workprint with the original, while others prefer to have you mark effects on the rolls of cut original in prescribed ways. Check with your lab. The lab will also supply you with standard leader and a chart for the preparation of head and tail leaders for your cut original and for your optical sound track. The lab can also tell you what length effects its printer is capable of doing and how much space it needs between effects.

Black leader for A & B rolls must be of high quality. If it is not dense enough, contrast will be lowered on your release print. There will be an overall graying of the picture. Any pinholes in the black leader will appear as dust on your release print. Most labs will prepare black leader for you.

APPENDIX E

SUGGESTED READING

An Alphabetical Guide to Motion Picture, Television, and Videotape Production. Eli Levitan. McGraw-Hill Co., 1221 Avenue of the Americas, New York, N.Y. 10020, 1970, 797 pp.

A guide to equipment and techniques. Well-illustrated. The best and most complete book of its kind. Expensive.

The American Cinematographer. ASC Agency, Inc., 1782 North Orange Drive, Hollywood, California 90028. (Subscription rate is $7/yr. for U.S.)

A monthly magazine devoted to articles about equipment and technique for professional filmmakers. The emphasis is on feature films. The advertisements are particularly helpful.

American Cinematographer Manual. Third Edition. Joseph V. Mascelli, Editor. American Society of Cinematographers, 1782 North Orange Drive, Hollywood, Calif. 90028, 1969.

A pocket-size reference book, often considered to be the cameraman's bible. Lots of technical information and charts. Expensive.

Creative Film-Making. Kirk Smallman. Collier Books, 866 Third Avenue, New York, N.Y. 10022. 1969, 245 pp.

Meant to be a practical guide. Offers many useful hints. Has suggestions for directing nonactors and actors, creating motion and filmic expression.

Elements of Color in Professional Motion Pictures. Society of Motion Picture and Television Engineers, 9 East 41st Street, New York, N.Y. 10017.

Elements of Sound Recording. John G. Frayne and Halley Wolfe. John Wiley & Sons, Inc., 605 Third Avenue, New York, N.Y. 10016, 1949, 580 pp.

The classic book on sound recording.

Film and Its Techniques. Raymond Spottiswoode. University of California Press, Berkeley, Calif. 94704, 1951, 516 pp.

The classic text on the technical side of documentary film production. Seriously out of date, but is to be revised soon.

Filmmakers' Newsletter. Filmmakers' Newsletter Co., 80 Wooster St., New York, N.Y. 10012. (Subscription rate is $5/yr. for U.S.)

> Many useful articles on technique, with lots of information that would concern the serious filmmaker not necessarily connected with the motion picture industry. Festivals and distribution information. Eleven issues a year.

The Five C's of Cinematography. Joseph V. Mascelli. Cine/Grafic Publications, P.O. Box 430, Hollywood, Calif. 90028, 1965, 250 pp.

> Deals with camera angle, continuity, cutting, close-ups, composition. Tends to be old-fashioned.

Handbook of Basic Motion Picture Techniques. Emil E. Brodbeck. Amphoto, 915 Broadway, New York, N.Y. 10010, 1966. Illustrated, 224 pp.

An Introduction to Cinematography. John Mercer. Stipes Publishing Company, 10 Chester Street, Champaign, Ill. 61823, 1967, 199 pp.

> A manual of film production. Contains a lot of practical information and avoids theory. Probably more useful to makers of low-budget films than any other book in the Bibliography.

Journal of the Society of Motion Picture and Television Engineers. SMPTE, 9 East 41st St., New York, N.Y. 10017. (Subscription rate is $26/yr. for nonmembers. Members receive the journal free. Student membership per year is $5.)

> Highly technical monthly publication. The most recent research is reported here. Some articles are useful to the filmmaker.

Painting with Light. John Alton. Macmillan Company, 866 Third Avenue, New York, N.Y. 10022, 1949. Illustrated, 295 pp.

> A Hollywood cameraman discusses his craft.

Principles of Cinematography. Leslie J. Wheeler. The Macmillan Company, 866 Third Avenue, New York, N.Y. 10022, 1959, 472 pp.

> Processes and equipment used in motion picture production.

INDEX

(Numbers in boldface refer to Plate numbers)

More MENTOR and SIGNET Books You'll Enjoy

☐ **AN INTRODUCTION TO AMERICAN MOVIES by Steven C. Earley.** The most comprehensive history of the movie industry, this excellent guide analyzes every major film genre for plot, acting, directing, and cinematic techniques. "Immensely readable, handsomely illustrated and excellently written, it's an important addition to the film library. . . ."—*Variety* Glossary, Index, and eight pages of photos.
(#ME1638—$2.25)

☐ **SINATRA: An Unauthorized Biography by Earl Wilson.** Sinatra the swinger . . . the singer . . . the legend . . . the man. The nationally syndicated columnist and bestselling author reveals all in this sensational biography. With 8 pages of candid photos. (#E7487—$2.25)

☐ **MARILYN: An Untold Story by Norman Rosten.** A flesh-and-blood memoir of the real Marilyn Monroe, this is the intimate truth about America's most enchanting sex legend. Everything that is human, Marilyn was. Her story is unending, but what is told here has never been told before! Includes 8 pages of rare and revealing photos. (#W8880—$1.50)

☐ **BOGIE: The Biography of Humphrey Bogart by Joe Hyams; with an Introduction by Lauren Bacall.** The brawls, the sprees, the razor-edged wisecracks: Hyams describes them all. He recaptures the deep friendships—with Spencer Tracy, Judy Garland, Katharine Hepburn. He probes Bogart's stormy youth; his stubborn climb to stardom; his three rocky marital adventures and his last happy marriage to Lauren Bacall.
(#E9189—$1.75)